Men in Early Years Settings

of related interest

Promoting Emotional Wellbeing in Early Years Staff
A Practical Guide for Looking after Yourself and Your Colleagues
Sonia Mainstone-Cotton
ISBN 978 1 78592 335 7
eISBN 978 1 78450 656 8

Performance Management in Early Years Settings
A Practical Guide for Leaders and Managers
Debbie Garvey
ISBN 978 1 78592 222 0
eISBN 978 1 78450 507 3

How to Transform Your School into an LGBT+ Friendly Place
A Practical Guide for Nursery, Primary and Secondary Teachers
Dr Elly Barnes MBE and Dr Anna Carlile
ISBN 978 1 78592 335 7
eISBN 978 1 78450 656 8

Building Your Early Years Business
Planning and Strategies for Growth and Success
Jacqui Burke
ISBN 978 1 78592 059 2
ISBN 978 1 78450 319 2

British Values and the Prevent Duty in the Early Years
A Practitioner's Guide
Kerry Maddock
ISBN 978 1 78592 048 6
ISBN 978 1 78450 307 9

MEN IN EARLY YEARS SETTINGS

BUILDING A MIXED GENDER WORKFORCE

David Wright and Simon Brownhill

Jessica Kingsley *Publishers*
London and Philadelphia

First published in 2019
by Jessica Kingsley Publishers
73 Collier Street
London N1 9BE, UK
and
400 Market Street, Suite 400
Philadelphia, PA 19106, USA

www.jkp.com

Library of Congress Cataloging in Publication Data
A CIP catalog record for this book is available from the Library of Congress

British Library Cataloguing in Publication Data
A CIP catalogue record for this book is available from the British Library

ISBN 978 1 78592 221 3
eISBN 978 1 78450 506 6

Printed and bound in Great Britain

To Anna, without whom I would never have known the joy and fulfilment of helping so many young children develop

DW

To darling Poppet

SPB

Acknowledgements

It is with the most heartfelt thanks that the following people are recognised:

- All of the participants who took part in our research – thank you for the time you gave to share your interesting thoughts and opinions with us.

- Our critical friends – thank you for reading and passing comment on the numerous chapter drafts we produced.

- Our amazing families and friends – thank you for your continued love and support.

- All at Jessica Kingsley Publishers for their diligent efforts in putting us in print.

Thank you all very much indeed.

DW and SPB

Contents

Glossary/Abbreviations

The following terms/abbreviations are used consistently throughout this book:

ARRD Attract, recruit, retain and develop
BaME Black, Asian, and minority ethnic
BBC British Broadcasting Corporation
BEd Bachelor of Education
BMIEY Bristol Men in Early Years (network)
CCTV Closed-circuit television
CEO Chief Executive Officer
CPD Continuing Professional Development
CWDC Children's Workforce Development Council
CYPW Children's and Young People's Workforce
DBS Disclosure and Barring Service
DfE Department for Education
DfEE Department for Education and Employment
DfES Department for Education and Skills
DoH Department of Health
DSS Department of Social Security
DUGS Dads, Uncles and Grandads
Early Years Educator Early Years practitioner holding a Level 3 Vocational Diploma for the Early Years workforce
Early Years Teacher Graduate specialist in early childhood development, holding an Early Years Teacher Status qualification
ECC Early Childhood and Care
ECCE Early Childhood Care and Education
ECE Early Childhood Education
ECEC Early Childhood Education and Care
EC-MENz The New Zealand based national network for men in early childhood education
EU European Union
EY Early Years
EYFS Early Years Foundation Stage (0–5 years old). The mandatory curriculum for all registered Early Years providers in England
EYPS Early Years Professional Status

FEI Further Education Institution, e.g. a college

FGP Focus Group Participant

HEFCE Higher Education Funding Council for England

HEI Higher Education Institution, e.g. a university

II Individual interviewee

IPD Initial Professional Development

ISA Independent Safeguarding Authority

ISC Independent Schools Council

ITE Initial Teacher Education

ITT Initial Teacher Training

LA Local Authority

LEYF London Early Years Foundation

LSA Learning Support Assistant

MiC Men in Childcare

MPG Major Provider Group

n.d. No date of publication indicated

NDNA National Day Nurseries Association

NVQ National Vocational Qualifications

OECD Organisation for Economic Co-operation and Development

OFSTED Office for Standards in Education, Children's Services and Skills

PDF Portable Document Format

PHSCE Personal, Health, Social and Citizenship Education

PLEYS Professional Love in Early Years Settings

PPA Planning, Preparation and Assessment

PR Public relations

Practitioner Anyone who supports children/young people in their learning, be they a volunteer, training (student) or qualified (nursery nurse, teaching assistant, teacher)

Primary school Educational setting for children aged 5–11

Principals Synonym for head teachers/managers

PSED Personal, Social and Emotional Development

PVI Private, Voluntary and Independent (sector)

QA Quality Assure

Q&A Questions and answers

SAMEY Southampton Area Men in Early Years (network)

Secondary school Educational setting for young people aged 11–16

SEF Setting Evaluation Form (also see SIP)

SEND Special Education Needs and Disability

SIP Setting Improvement Plan (also see SEF)

SMARTC Specific, Measurable, Achievable, Realistic, Time-related, Challenging

SMS Short Message Service

SMT Senior management team

TA Teaching Assistant

UK United Kingdom

UKS2 Upper Key Stage Two (9–11 years old)

USA United States of America

Introduction

DAVID WRIGHT AND SIMON BROWNHILL

Why we have written this book

As two men who have actively worked in various capacities in the Early Years sector in England over the last 14 plus years, we are conscious that we are, and continue to be, in the minority with less than 2 per cent of the workforce being male (DfE 2014), a statistic that has persisted for many decades, right up to the present day. Whilst there are a limited number of professional and academic publications exploring the numbers and profiling male practitioners in the Early Years, we know of no book that that has been written for professionals, head teachers/managers, and policy makers in the Early Years sector which critically explores new and established research findings and provides practical guidance to support those who want to not only attract men to their team but also retain and develop them.

This book explores and challenges many of the reasons attributed to the present 'men crisis' (situation). We critically examine the evidence of media reportage, men's stories and, by conducting our own research, we gauge current public opinion. We consider the *so what?* of the status quo – is there a case for change? If so, why? How can it be changed? Does a balanced gender workforce make a difference for children/men/families/society as a whole or should we just leave things as they are?

It is recognised and widely accepted in both public and professional discourse that the role of the adult is key to the provision of high quality Early Years care and child development (DfE 2017, p.10). It is our assertion that outcomes for children have a greater chance of being improved when they are exposed to the widest spectrum of character types across a mixed gender workforce, an area of the diversity agenda which we feel has long been untargeted in terms of policy making and implementation. If we need the nation's best Early Years practitioners to nurture our youngest children during their formative years, then we should not discount potential candidates in the 50 per cent of the population that are represented by men.

In this book we explore what children need and want in terms of gender representation from their carers/educators; similarly, we critique the views of parents/carers and practitioners. Barriers to men entering and successfully working in the Early Years profession are richly illustrated by the inclusion of examples from relevant organisations and testimonials from men, women and families. We reflect on ways in which these barriers can be broken down, investigating the perceived and actual benefits of having men working with young children.

Our book asserts that nothing will change without positive action. We want to make it clear to all readers that we are not advocating discrimination – we need the best people for the job regardless of gender – but an honest evaluation of the facts, along with a determination to address the gender imbalance in the Early Years workforce, must be accompanied by a range of initiatives, practical strategies, approaches, tips, ideas and suggestions to encourage and support job and course applications from men, coupled with an evaluation of working practices and environments for their appropriateness for both sexes. Through this we ask and answer the following questions:

- How do we create a culture in our organisation, team and in society where it is normal for children to be cared for by men and women?

- In organisations where this is already the case, what are the characteristics of their culture? What has changed and what are the benefits? What actions have been taken? In other words, what does success 'look like' and how do we replicate it or adapt it for different contexts?

- How should we review our marketing, recruitment, public relations, our perceptions, expectations and beliefs about our roles and the roles of men as Early Years practitioners?

We invite readers to consider their responses to these questions, being mindful of them as they engage with the rest of this book.

Any recommendations we offer in this book for making positive change are equally applicable to all sectors, be they private, voluntary or state. The discussion in this book largely focuses on contexts in England with some consideration given to other countries at both a national and international level. We also consider issues of policy making at the individual setting level and offer a 'call for action' to support change at the macro level, asking questions such as:

- What should the role of local and national government be?

- What part do Ofsted, training providers, schools, careers advisors and local authorities have in effecting change?

Again, we invite readers to consider their responses to these questions, being mindful of them as they engage with the rest of this book.

Why now?

The idea for this book was born out of the energy and momentum generated from the first UK National Men in Early Years conference that was held in Southampton in February 2016. Over 100 people attended this event and it was clear that there was, and continues to be, an appetite for change. In the following chapters, we explore some of the many initiatives that have resulted from this passionate gathering. Alongside this, we believe it is helpful to document our own perspectives of the current situation, the issues underpinning it, and to provide practical suggestions and proposals for positive action. Now is the time for change.

Who is this book for?

Our aim is to invite reflection, discussion, collaboration and action. If we are to effect change – to see more men working with our youngest children in Early Years settings – then such change must start with those of us who bear responsibility for recruiting and maintaining our workforce. Whilst our book is aimed primarily at a professional Early Years readership, the themes explored are relevant to anyone who has an interest in society, gender roles, and the experiences of and interactions between children, men and women; in other words, everyone! We hope that Early Years head teachers/managers, practitioners, administrators, trainers and students/trainees, class teachers and senior management teams including governors will find this book a useful resource. We also believe that parents and carers will find much to interest them so please raise their awareness to this book if they like it! As the cultural themes are universally applicable, they also have international interest. The issues raised and the proposed actions are not specific to the UK but we largely situate ideas in English settings and contexts, as this is where our experience lies

How were men 'researched'?

When considering the content of this book, we were keen to include some 'new voices' to enrich the discussion we offered and to reflect on current experiences and opinions. By this we mean that we wanted to find out what men who actively work in the Early Years sector thought about some of the issues we intended to explore in various chapters. We also wanted to present the attitudes of parents and of Early Years providers – different perspectives are important! To achieve this, we sought to capture the opinions and views of various stakeholders through conducting primary research on both a small and large scale. We offer brief details to the reader below in an effort to highlight:

- what kind of research we undertook

- who was involved in our research

- when the research was collected

- where the research was undertaken, and

- how the research was collected and analysed.

For the most part, contributions were anonymous. Some data, however, identify the individuals concerned and the settings where they work. All research participants were asked if they wished to remain anonymous or whether they were happy to be named. Those who agreed to be identified felt that doing so provided context and a real-life example. We have thus respected their decision by using their real identity.

We were both in agreement that our research was interested in people (especially men), what they thought and what their understandings were. As opposed to carrying research out *on* people, e.g. using tests or carrying out observations, we were keen to conduct research *with* people (Sharp 2009). As such, we embraced a mixed-methods approach to data collection (Tashakkori and Teddlie 2003), combining the use of different types of questionnaires and interviews to yield interesting 'numbers and narrative' (Plowright 2011).

In Chapter 2, our review of reasons for the paucity of male practitioners in the Early Years workforce in England is grounded in research from a wider perspective that examines culture through various lenses including evidence from media reports, commentaries and public policy documents. The two case studies presented – one anonymous, the other named with permission – were generated from individual telephone interviews lasting between 20 to 30 minutes. Each interview was digitally recorded and added to a protected resource bank. Quotations were selected from the resulting data and presented to exemplify some of the points raised and to act as reflection points for readers in considering the implications for effecting change in their own context.

For Chapter 3, research data was generated using two data collecting tools. The first was a 'split questionnaire' which consisted of seven main questions that were separated onto individual sheets of paper, an example of which is included below:

What is it like for men working/training in the Early Years?

Questions:
- What made you decide to work in the Early Years sector?
- When did you make this decision?
- Who helped you to make the decision and why?
- How did you 'get into' the Early Years, i.e. what route did you take (e.g. college, volunteer, Foundation Degree, apprenticeship, other)?
- Why did you take this route?
- What do you think is the 'best way' to get into the Early Years, and why?

Please offer your answers below, with as much detail as possible/appropriate. Please do not worry about your spelling, grammar, punctuation or handwriting if this is of concern to you – it is your message that Simon is interested in! If you need more space then please use the back of the sheet.

The 'split questionnaire' was offered in paper-based form to all members of the Bristol Men in Early Years Network as part of a meeting that Simon had been invited to attend and present at in April 2017. In total, 14 written responses were made to the open questions that respondents could freely choose from, five of which were completed by pairs of male practitioners. Conventional content analysis (Hsieh and Shannon 2005, p.1286) was subsequently used to analyse the data generated. A one-hour semi-structured focus group discussion was also conducted. This involved seven randomly selected members of the Bristol Network, including two of the Network leads. The focus group discussion centred on four key questions, these being:

- Why do you think there are so few men training/working in the Early Years sector?

- What is it like for men who actually train/work in the Early Years sector?

- Do we need a balanced mixed gender Early Years workforce? Why/why not?

- How can we get more men training/working in the Early Years sector?

The focus group discussion was digitally voice recorded and directed content analysis (Hsieh and Shannon 2005, p.1286) was used to code the data once it had been transcribed.

The primary research conducted to inform the content of Chapter 4 was generated by an online survey promoted by Early Years providers across England through social media to the parents of children registered to their settings. These settings comprised private day nurseries, pre-schools and childminders. The survey was anonymous and consisted of nine short questions. It was completed between November and December 2017. A total of 440 responses were received, of which 402 respondents (91%) were female and 38 (9%) male.

Of those respondents who provided pertinent details, the age distribution of their children is shown in the figure overleaf. The majority of respondents' children were aged between two and three years. It is worth considering whether or how much responses are influenced by the respondents answering with respect to their own child's age and whether there would have been different results if, for example, all of the children had been aged two years or under.

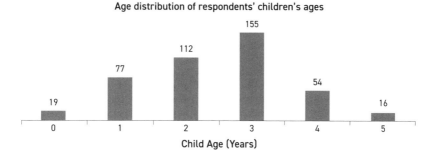

The survey questions are presented below:

1. I am Male / Female

2. What is the age of your child? (in years) _____

3. I believe it is beneficial for children aged 0–5 years to be cared for by men as well as women in Early Years settings (nursery, pre-school, childminder). Yes / No

4. What are the benefits, if any, of having a mixed gender Early Years workforce? _____

5. I am happy for a male Early Years worker to care for my child. Yes / No

6. I have concerns about men working in Early Years. Yes / No

7. If you answered Yes to Question 6, please could you give your reasons? _____

8. What does the term 'male role-model' mean to you? _____
   _____

9. Any other comments about men working in Early Years settings? _____

The two case studies also presented in this fourth chapter are based on 30-minute interviews, the first conducted face-to-face with a male manager of a private day nursery in South London, the other held over a video conference with the female owner of another day nursery in Manchester. In both cases, with the permission of the interviewees, the interviews were digitally recorded to enable transcription and analysis of the data gathered.

For Chapter 5 we continue to draw on interesting findings generated from the 'split questionnaire' and the focus group completed by involving male members of the Bristol Men in Early Years Network (see Chapter 3). Data were also drawn from members of an online special interest Facebook group in July 2017. With the permission of the group administrator, the following post was made:

> *Been pondering? What do you think are the*
> *benefits of a mixed gender EY workforce?*

In total, nine posted responses were made. Of the data collected, select findings were anonymised for inclusion in the chapter, especially those views proffered by female members of the group. Data have also been taken from Simon's doctoral study (Brownhill 2015) which critically examined the ambiguities of the 'male role model' in the Early Years (defined as 0–8). Select extracts from the Stage Two focus group interview transcript involving men who worked in the Early Years at an operational level are included in the latter part of the chapter to stimulate the discussion.

Chapter 6 addresses the character and lived experiences of mixed gender Early Years teams. To investigate the characterisation of their culture and practice, telephone/video conference interviews lasting between 20 and 30 minutes were conducted with three Early Years providers operating in different contexts. The first of these was with the female owner of a group of Forest Day Nurseries in South London established in 2014. The second interview was conducted with the male leader of several kindergartens based in the Asker community in southern Norway, a post he has held for 29 years. Finally, we conducted a telephone interview with a male childminder located in Hampshire who works alongside his wife as a childminding team. All three interviews were digitally recorded and the transcriptions are reproduced in full in the chapter. Analysis of the data uses illustrative quotes from each respondent to support each emerging theme.

For Chapter 7 four individual semi-structured telephone interviews (each lasting about 35 minutes each) were conducted with men who worked in the Early Years sector in August 2017. Two of these were core team members of the Bristol Men in Early Years Network, one interviewee was an active Early Years professional in East Anglia, and one was the lead author of this book! A combination of handwritten notes and voice recordings of the interviews were subsequently analysed using key point coding (Glaser 1992), with key phrases, ideas and substantial interview extracts being selected and included to enhance the chapter content.

What needs to be considered when reading this book?

Throughout this book, we refer to the aspiration of a mixed gender Early Years workforce in preference to one that is gender-balanced. We feel this is a preferable term for several reasons. Gender-balanced infers the identical number of individuals of the same gender in the workforce. We question whether this is achievable or even desirable. Equal opportunities is not the same as equal outcomes. Changes in attitudes and working practices can lead to an increase in awareness, encouragement and support for more men to apply to join the Early Years workforce but the job vacancies may not exist and no one knows if there are sufficient men available, willing or able to apply for jobs. And, as we are at great pains to emphasise throughout this book, it is the best, most suitable individuals – regardless of their gender – that are needed to care for and educate our nation's children during their formative years.

As authors, we freely acknowledge slight variations in writing style between different chapters in the book. In some respects, this is an inevitable outcome of having two contributors, but it is also a deliberate decision to match the chapter format to the content, e.g. in Chapter 6 we have reproduced the transcripts of interviews in full for readers to explore and reflect on. We believe that this provides a unique insight and context to the evidence presented that would be otherwise lacking. We have included case studies, quotations and interviews with practitioners to ensure our findings and proposals are grounded in real-life experience, and to enable readers to relate to the various points we are making. We believe that this variation in approach adds interest for the reader. Consistency between the chapters, however, is evident in our use of overviews at the start of the chapter and the use of Activity and Reflection boxes for readers to engage with on their own and with their colleagues.

Overall, as authors, we have set out to challenge the status quo and to invite individuals and organisations to effect change in their sphere of influence. Our book contains regular opportunities for questioning, discussion and action planning. It is a 'doing' book, one that we hope will support the continuing momentum towards a more tolerant and inclusive society. We look forward to a time when there is no longer a need for a campaign to build a mixed gender Early Years workforce because it has become the norm. How long it takes to achieve this is dependent on the actions of all readers and all those who are passionate about men in the Early Years.

References

Brownhill, S. (2015) The *'Brave' Man in the Early Years (0–8): The Ambiguities of Being a Role Model*. Saarbrücken, Germany: LAMBERT Academic Publishing.

DfE (Department for Education) (2014) National Statistics, School Workforce in England: November. Accessed 13 June 2016 at www.gov.uk/government/statistics/school-workforce-in-england-november-2014

DfE (2017) Statutory framework for the early years foundation stage: Setting the standards for learning, development and care for children from birth to five. Accessed 25 June 2017 at www.foundationyears.org.uk/files/2017/03/EYFS_STATUTORY_FRAMEWORK_2017.pdf

Glaser, B. (1992) *Emergence vs. Forcing: Basics of Grounded Theory*. Mill Valley, CA: Sociology Press.

Hsieh, H-F. and Shannon, S. E. (2005) 'Three approaches to qualitative content analysis.' *Qualitative Health Research*, 15(9), 1277–1288.

Plowright, D. (2011) *Using Mixed Methods*. London: Sage Publications.

Sharp, J. (2009*) Success With Your Education Research Project*. Exeter: Learning Matters.

Tashakkori, A. and Teddlie, C. (2003) *Handbook of Mixed Methods in Social and Behavioral Research*. Thousand Oaks, CA: Sage.

CHAPTER 1

Men in the Early Years – Where Are We At?

SIMON BROWNHILL WITH DAVID WRIGHT

Overview

In this initial chapter we explore the 'men climate' in the Early Years. We define this as the current situation that the Early Years sector finds itself in with regard to the proportion of men who work with young children aged 0–5. By drawing on a wealth of literature and established research findings, we offer an adapted potted history that reflects the story of men in the Early Years, along with a critical evaluation of *where we are at* in the present-day. Whilst the conversation centres on the English context, efforts are made to highlight international perspectives to enrich the discussion and illustrate similarities and differences that either previously existed or remain prevalent on the global platform. The chapter opens with a succinct summary of the current Early Years 'men climate' in the form of a tweet!

'In a nutshell': the current situation

M.E.N. @MenintheEarlyYears

@jeremydavies (2017, p.2) says that 'The proportion of male staff in the ECE workforce remains at 2 per cent in England.' We'd say it's been stubbornly like this for years!

07:36 AM – 20 Sept 2018

'Out of the nutshell': exploring the current situation

Simon, Owen and Hollingworth (2016, p.13) assert that 'the overall childcare workforce is overwhelmingly female (98%) compared with other occupations (46%), and hasn't changed at all between 2005–14'. To suggest that the Early Years is 'an almost entirely gendered career' (Penn and McQuail, 1997: iv) would be a bit of an understatement; to say that a man in the Early Years is 'gold dust'[1] is far from an exaggeration. Bartlett (2015, p.3) offers an interesting breakdown of the percentages of male childcare workers in England in the diverse provision for children aged 0–5 years which we offer below:

- 'Full day care – 2%

- Sessional day care – 1%

- Childminders – 2%

- Nursery schools – 2%

- Primary schools – 1%

- After school clubs – 7%

- Holiday clubs – 14%.'

REFLECTION

Take a moment to consider the figures above. What is your response to these different statistics? Does it concern you that the percentage of men in the Early Years is so low – why/not? Share your personal/professional thoughts with colleagues/peers – how do their views compare with yours?

The current percentage of men who work in the Early Years sector raises several important questions in our minds, these being:

1. How does the percentage of men who work in the Early Years compare with those of men who are employed in the primary school (5–11) and secondary school (11–16) sectors in England?

---

1   A noun once used to verbally describe Simon as a Reception class teacher by a former Mayor of the City of Derby.

2. How does the percentage of men who work in the Early Years sector in England compare to the rest of the United Kingdom (UK)?

3. Is the absence of men who work with young children (0–5) of national and international concern?

4. Why is the percentage of men who work in the Early Years so low? Has it always been like this?

It is our intention to address each of these four questions through a **Simon says / David says** set of responses to 'open the nutshell' a little more. We begin by examining some interesting numerical data.

1. How does the percentage of men who work in the Early Years compare with those of men who are employed in the primary school (5–11) and secondary school (11–16) sectors in England?

Simon says: The Department for Education (DfE) (2017, p.7) states that '84.6 per cent of FTE nursery/primary school teachers are female [as are] 62.5 per cent of secondary school teachers'. This means that just 15.4 per cent of the teachers in state-funded nursery/primary schools in England are male; in secondary schools men represent 37.5 per cent of the teaching workforce. But how does this compare with other important professionals who work in schools? The DfE (2017, p.7) asserts that '91.4 per cent of teaching assistants and 82.2 per cent of school support staff are female' (this covers the nursery, primary and secondary school sectors combined). This means that just 8.6 per cent of teaching assistants are male, with men representing 17.8 per cent of the school support staff workforce in England. In total, men serve as less than 20 per cent of the school workforce (19.8%).

David says: Some readers may wonder why we asked this first question given that the focus of this professional book is on men who work in the Early Years! First of all, the statistics we presented earlier by Bartlett (2015, p.3) clearly show men to be 'few and far between' in the 0–5 sector. Second, whilst I was quoted a few years ago as saying that it would be great to 'see the United Kingdom lead the world in the gender-balance of our Early Years workforce' (Wright in Bernard 2015), we can actually see, right across the full 0–16 age range, that we have quite a long way to go to achieve a gender-balance, especially in the Early Years!

Simon says: Having reflected on the state sector, it is of value to compare the percentages of men in maintained primary and secondary schools in England with those who work in the independent school sector. Of interest are two key statistics reported by the Independent Schools Council (as cited in Ward 2014):

- 'According to a 2014 census by the Independent Schools Council (ISC), which represents more than 1,200 independent schools in the UK and overseas, almost 40 per cent of full-time equivalent teachers in its member schools are men.'

- 'Another ISC report in 2009 found 29 per cent of all teaching hours in independent prep schools [for children age 8–13] are worked by men.'

These statistics support Ward's (2014) assertion that '[w]hile women dominate both sectors, significantly more men enter – and stay in – private education' than in the public sector. But what about men who work in private, voluntary and independent (PVI) nurseries and pre-schools? Ceeda (2017, p.4) suggests that the percentage of men who work in these settings collectively stands at 5 per cent, more than double the 2 per cent put forward by Davies (2017) in relation to state Early Years provision. It is worthy of note that this difference in 'men numbers' between the private and public sector is not limited to the English context: in Israel, for example, Gravé-Lazi (2016) cites the following statistics from the work of researcher David Brody: 'there are about 40 male teachers in early education in the public sector, among 17,000 women. In the private sector, Brody estimated that there are an additional 300 to 400 men, though this number seems to be declining'.

I intend to return to these statistics later on in this chapter in an effort to highlight some of the reasons why the proportion of men teaching/practising in the private sector is significantly higher than in their state counterparts. However, more pressing questions need to be answered, such as question 2!

2. How does the percentage of men who work in the 0–5 sector in England compare to the rest of the UK?

David says: Table 1.1 helps to quickly summarise the percentage of men who currently work in the Early Years across the UK:

Table 1.1: Percentage of men working in the Early Years sector in the UK

Island	Country	Percentage of men who work in the Early Years sector	Source
Great Britain	England	2%	Learner (2017)
	Wales	3%	Skills for Care and Development (2017)
	Scotland	3%	Skills Development Scotland (2017)
Ireland	Northern Ireland	2%	Garbutt (2017)

Slight variations between the percentages do little to detract from the clear picture which shows men to be a 'significant minority' in a profession characterised by an overwhelming female presence (Lindon, Lindon and Beckley 2016).

Simon says: The statistics in the table David has just presented supports what has long been known in the Early Years sector:

- The absence of men who work in the Early Years is common right across the UK.

- The proportion of male Early Years practitioners in each country in the UK is approximately the same – between 2–3%.

- The percentage of men working in the Early Years in the UK has scarcely changed over recent decades (see Haywood 2011).

These UK-based points of knowledge and associated figures are useful as they help to highlight the troubling dearth of men that are present (or are not present as is unfortunately the case!) in the Early Years sector. But should we really be worried about this? Is this of concern at a national level? Does this mirror any attention given to this issue at an international level? Responding to question 3 will help us to answer these different questions!

3. Is the absence of men who work with young children (0–5) of national and international concern?

Simon says: Given the publication of various strategies, frameworks, proposals and manifestos across the UK in recent years (see Chapter 7), the absence of men who work in the Early Years is certainly of national concern (Mistry and Sood 2015). This is coupled with an abundance of sensational headlines, bold titles and forthright statements found in newspapers, professional publications, blogs and books which all serve to fuel increased levels of discussion and debate about men in the Early Years sector. Examples include:

- We need more men in childcare (Tanuku 2014)

- Meet the male teachers changing the perception of nursery school education (Kemp 2016)

- The importance of male role models in childcare (Adams 2016)

- 'Men's involvement in early childhood is something we need to continue to encourage and value if we have any chance of nurturing all aspects of PSED [Personal, Social and Emotional Development] in early childhood' (Garvey 2018, p.80).

Further afield, there are numerous countries across the world where there are 'a few good men' [my words] working in Early Years sector equivalents, examples of which are offered in the table below:

Table 1.2: Percentage of men who work in the Early Years sector (equivalent)

Country	Percentage of men who work in the Early Years sector (equivalent)	Source
Poland	'almost no male workers'	Johnson (2010, p.105)
Greece	<1%	Pan-Hellenic Union of Day Care Workers (2009, cited in Sakellariou and Rentzou 2010, p.2)
Ireland	<1%	Conroy (in ChildLinks 2012)
Taiwan	1.1%	Fu and Li (2010)
Canada	2%	Yousefi (2016)
China	2%	Ministry of Education of the People's Republic of China (2014, cited in Xu and Waniganayake 2017, p.1)
New Zealand	2.2%	Koch and Farquhar (2015)
USA	3.2%	MenTeach (2015)
Indonesia	3.34%	Central Education Statistic (2009/2010)
Sweden	4%	Heikkilä and Hellman (2017)
Finland	4%	Oberhuemer (2012)
Sub-Saharan Africa	<5%	Mukuna and Mutsotso (2011)

Japan	Approximately 6%	Ministry of Internal Affairs and Communications (2008, cited in Marshall 2014)
Turkey	7%	Ministry of National Education Statistics (2011, cited in Sak, Sahin and Sahin 2012, p.586)
Norway	9%	Statistics Norway (2017)

Whilst Brody (2015) points out that the general pattern in the world as a whole is that less than 3 per cent of pre-school educators are male, there are a number of countries in Europe that seem to buck the trend. Indeed, recent statistics suggest that 'as a whole, men accounted for…4.6 per cent of all pre-primary school teachers in the EU' (eurostat 2017). However, the figures in the table above collectively reinforce the low percentage of men that work in the Early Years sector (equivalent) and continue to highlight the apparent shortage of men in the early childhood profession (Joseph and Wright 2016).

David says: I came across a really interesting graph in a recent OECD publication that Simon sent me. It focuses on early childhood education and care staff recruitment and retention in relation to the percentage of women among teaching staff in public and private institutions at pre-primary level (2013):

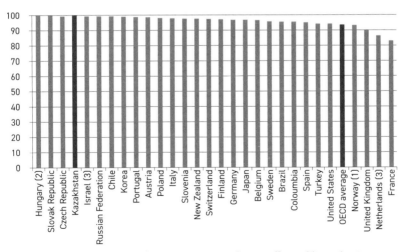

Figure 1.1: Percentage of women among teaching staff in public and private institutions at pre-primary level (2013) (Litjens and Taguma 2017, p.49)

ACTIVITY

Take a few moments to study the graph above. What information particularly interests you? Is there anything that surprises or shocks you? Share your responses with your colleagues/peers – how do their responses compare to yours?

There are several things that are of interest to me in relation to this graph:

- Only four of the 29 identified countries are *below* the OECD average, all of these being located in Europe (at least at the time of writing). This can, in part, be attributed to the investment in 'long-term projects set up to increase the participation of men in ECEC settings' in countries such as Norway (see Peeters, Rohrmann and Emilsen 2015, p.304).

- A good number of countries that have very few/virtually no men working in the Early Years sector equivalents are geographically located in the East, e.g. Eastern Europe and Asia. I believe that it is likely that one or more of the following factors influences why this is the case:

Figure 1.2: The absence of men working in the Early Years in Eastern Countries: influencing factors

Let me take tradition as an example. In most countries, women have long been charged with caring for young children. Wardle (2016, p.598) supports this, arguing that '[e]arly childhood development theorists such as … Pestalozzi and … Froebel recognised the important role of mothers in helping nurture and educate young children'. Those countries that continue to subscribe to this practice/thinking are unlikely to see men as being a natural adult influence on young children's learning and development – their role is to be the bread winner, not the bread maker. As such, it is doubtful that the notion of men working with young children is actively promoted or performed in these countries. There may, of course, be other factors at play, and it is the collaborative intention of Simon and I to explore these throughout this book, comparing these to the English context.

I recently learned that in Turkey 'there were only 166 (1.39%) male ECE teachers in 2000 and this number had increased to 3387 (5.34%) by 2014. Interestingly, this was not the result of intervention by the government or any other institution, but rather a "natural" increase in the number of male ECE teachers' (Sak, Sak and Yerlikaya 2015, pp.329–330). I believe that this '"natural" increase' is unlikely to have occurred in many of the countries presented in Figure 1.1 due to the small suite of factors I have identified in Figure 1.2. Other factors are highlighted in our responses to question 4 which asks why the percentage of men who work in the Early Years is so low and whether this figure has always been like this.

4.   Why is the percentage of men who work in the Early Years so low? Has it always been like this?

ACTIVITY

Make a list of between five and ten possible reasons why you think the percentage of men who work in the Early Years in England is so low. As you read our responses, see how your list compares with ours. How/is our thinking similar or different to yours?

Simon says: Men are typically recognised as 'a bit of a rarity' in the Early Years sector, especially when one reflects on the statistics presented earlier. There are many reasons proffered to explain why this is the case, key examples of which include:

•   poor pay

- the low status of the job, and

- the fear of false allegations of child abuse.

It is difficult to avoid these three reasons, largely because they reflect the hard reality of working in the 0–5 sector:

- Those who work in the Early Years are far from well paid for the tremendous work they do (see Hawthorne and Brown 2016).

- An and Bonetti (2017) argue that '[t]he epidemic of low teacher recruitment and high dropout that our Early Years face is only symptomatic of a much larger problem: the low status of and insufficient regard for our Early Years practitioners'.

- Russell (2013) asserts that in New Zealand '[t]here is also the stigma surrounding child abuse when it comes to men teaching in ECE, which came about after the Civic Crèche incident in 1992, when a male ECE teacher was charged with sexually abusing children in his care. Even though there are huge misperceptions about this case, the result of all the media attention and gossip that followed would put many men off the idea of becoming an ECE teacher'.

Interestingly, Williams (in Tcaffell 2013) challenges all three of the 'key example' reasons offered above. I present Williams' assertions in the table below, each with a reflective response from David and I:

Reason	Williams' claim	A reflective response
a) Poor pay	'Early childhood education isn't that badly paid anymore'	David and I strongly challenge this – please see Crown (2017)!
b) The low status of the job	'[T]here are many examples where men are quite happy to do low-status work, although it is important that their sense of masculinity remains intact'	Miller (2017) argues that more men are indeed taking lower-status jobs traditionally held by women, particularly those who are already disadvantaged in the labour market ('black, Hispanic, less educated, poor and immigrant men'). However, David and I believe that many men are not happy to engage in 'low-status' Early Years work because it can challenge their masculinity.

c) The fear of false allegations of child abuse	'Statistically, child abuse doesn't happen in early childhood centres, it happens in the home, by people children know and trust'	David and I agree with this unfortunate fact. Radford *et al.* (2011) support this, highlighting that 'over 90% of sexually abused children were abused by someone they knew'.

So why does Williams think there is a lack of men in Early Years? *I'll let him speak for himself!*

> Ultimately it's an issue about gender stereotyping and traditional gender roles. When we look more deeply at the way society has framed up and perpetuated gender stereotypes around what men and women do, we start to get at the heart of the problem. Society just doesn't see working with young children as something that men do. It's been framed up as a woman's activity, an extension of mothering, a nurturing and caring role and that's something we don't see as synonymous with what men do. This needs to change. (Williams in Tcaffell 2013)

David says: Whilst I am in support of Williams' thinking, I believe that cultural ideologies have some part to play in this issue of gender stereotyping and time-honoured gender roles. Yousefi (2016) argues that '[c]ertain countries...like Pakistan or Kuwait, tend to devalue women and have very specific roles dedicated to women, which don't allow much freedom when it comes to choosing a career. In the same way, men in countries like this can't do certain jobs for fear of judgment or ridicule'. Whilst I would argue that this is less applicable to England, due to it being a more progressive country, I agree with Yousefi (2016) who recognises that '[s]tereotypes against men are also quite prevalent here [in England], and they often lead to mental health problems or prevent men from pursuing careers they're passionate about', e.g. working in the Early Years sector.

I also support Simon's assertion that there are many reasons why the percentage of men who work in the Early Years is so low. Research by Cronin (2014), for example, suggests that being 'the subject of scrutiny from either family/friends or service users' and having 'their masculinity com[e] into question' (p.12) serve as real barriers to male participation in the sector. It frustrates me that the motives of men who enter the Early Years sector are questioned by some parents/carers and members of their immediate circle – surely men want to do the job because they relish the opportunity of working with young children? I also think there is something to be said about the attitudes of colleagues – I am not convinced that their views are always positively responsive to the idea of having men work in the 0–5 sector. Might their views (verbalised or otherwise) serve as a deterrent for some men who feel that they are being viewed with suspicion or disapproval?

Simon says: Building on David's comments, I believe that there are many more reasons that can be attributed to the low number of men who work in the Early Years workforce. These help us to understand why we are at where we are at! I offer a selection of these reasons in bullet point form below with examples of the kinds of things that I believe men might say or think about working in the sector:

- *A perceived lack of intellectual challenge*: 'It's just playing, counting to five and helping them to hold a pencil, isn't it?!'

- *Working in the Early Years is really hard work*: 'Young children are full on and can be annoying at times. I should know: I've got little ones of my own!'

- *Not wanting to feel isolated*: Kokoros (2012) asserts that 'to be a man in ECE is to be a man in the land of women'.

- *Limited career progression opportunities in the sector*: 'Where do you go next after being the manager of an Early Years setting?'

- *The fear of being discriminated against*: 'Because I'm the only bloke I'm likely to be the one who's always confined to the cold in the outdoor play area!'

- *Not knowing that the Early Years is an employment choice*: Lang (2013) argues that young people 'need time to learn about and consider all the options' rather than making 'hurried, expedient decisions, which may not be for the best in the long-term'.

- *The challenges to one's sexuality*: 'Most people think you must be gay if you work with young kids. Does it matter if I'm gay or not? Of course not!'

- *The appeal of other forms of employment*: Research suggests that men are more interested in business and financial operations and computers and mathematics than in the traditional 'caring professions' (Indeed 2016).

- *Workplace politics*: 'If I'm the only man in the nursery I might struggle to make friends at work.'

Conversely, there are numerous reasons proposed to explain why the proportion of men teaching in the private sector is significantly higher than in state provision. Examples, drawn from the work of Ward (2014), include:

- *After-school attraction*: 'The huge emphasis on extra-curricular activities' that is found in the private sector (e.g. sports teams, overseas trips, and cub packs) is seen as being rather appealing to many men.

- *Specialist versus Generalist*: Teachers in the private sector tend to teach specialist subjects rather than teach a single class; men prefer this as many of them are secondary trained.

- *Image*: It is argued that there is a 'more positive media image' of men in independent schools than in state schools.

- *Men equals more men*: There exists '[t]he cyclical effect of men joining schools that already employ male teachers'. Therefore, if you already have men working in private schools you are likely to get more wanting to join these schools.

- *Priorities*: Men prefer the academic focus of private schools which seemingly draws them to the sector.

- *Prospects*: 'Men, it appears, are getting promotions in the independent sector ahead of women with similar amounts of experience'.

David says: It is not just an examination of reasons from the present-day that tells us why the percentage of men who work in the Early Years is so low. Looking back to the past also helps us to understand why so few men worked with young children. I have put together some interesting points in the form of a 'potted history' that I have adapted and summarised from the work of Burn and Pratt-Adams (2015, pp.15–32):

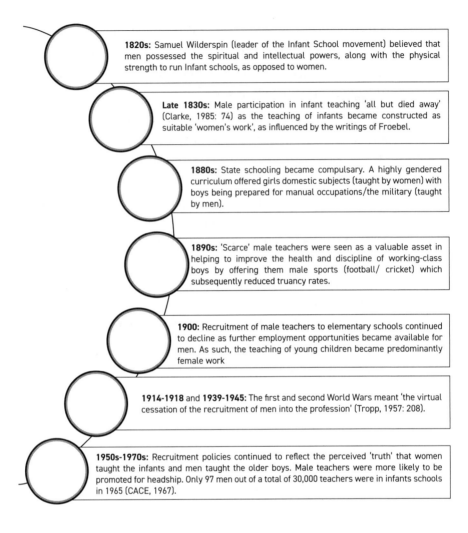

With such a varied suite of reasons (as highlighted above), some readers may think that it is just too difficult to increase the percentage of men who work in the Early Years sector. Numerous initiatives have, however, been implemented in an effort to improve the number of men working with young children. It is to several of these that this chapter now turns.

Initiatives

In the 2000s there was a noticeable surge of initiatives, largely driven by a number of western governments (for example the UK, Canada, the USA and New Zealand) to increase the number of male primary school teachers (Skelton 2009). Practical strategies included:

- aggressive targeting
- setting male quotas for ITE providers
- offering 'taster courses', and
- providing financial incentives.

Unfortunately, all of these strategies failed to sufficiently improve male recruitment.

But this is about male primary school teachers. Why are you telling me this? I want to know about men who work in the Early Years!

We are making you, the reader, aware of this because many of the strategies identified above have been used/adapted/are currently being used to try and increase the number of men who work in the Early Years sector!

Before we continue we would like to make it clear that we are by no means being deliberately critical of any initiatives that have been/are currently being implemented to increase the presence of men in the Early Years – *far from it!* Instead, we feel it is important to offer readers an open and honest assessment of what we like to call 'men efforts' to ascertain the effects (if any) on the number of men that are working in the Early Years sector.

Let us initially turn to Germany. The government there, with the Ministry of Family Affairs and the European Social Fund, demonstrated a commitment to increasing the proportion of male educators in the sector by spending a combined total of €13m on the More Men in Early Childhood Education and Care programme (Friedmann 2012). It set out to pilot a wide range of different projects and measures such as information buses, internships for school children, 'discovery days' to encounter new career options, volunteer placements and mentor programmes. The programme also sought to actively engage fathers and to foster the gender debate among young male job-seekers and in the day-to-day activities of ECEC centres. Roundtables and networks of male educators were also seen as being a helpful way of recruiting more men into the profession and to maintain their enthusiasm in the long term. Completed in 2013, Zhang (2017, p.22) asserts that '[a]lthough the results have had limited success, there has been progress to establish a less gendered ECE workforce' across the country.

READING TASK

Visit mika.koordination-maennerinkitas.de (you may need to click on the 'Translate' option when prompted). Navigate your way around this interesting website, paying particular attention to the publications available under the 'About Us' tab. Reflect on your learning from engaging with a selection of these different materials, considering how they support, challenge or extend your thinking and understanding.

Staying in Germany, Hamann (2013) describes an advertising campaign that was rolled out a few years ago in Hamburg:

Countless posters are dotted around the northern German city. In subways and elsewhere the posters try to persuade young men to become kindergarten teachers. 'Diversity man' is romanticized on the posters: 'Musician, magician, mediator, philosopher, goalkeeper, baker – be all, become a kindergarten teacher!' is the advertising slogan'.

This pictorial approach is validated by Davies (2017, p.5) who argues that if we want to draw men into the 0–5 sector in England we need to carefully think about how we 'visually market' the Early Years profession:

Despite a dearth of stock images of men working with children (particularly BaME [Black, Asian, and minority ethnic] men), striking male-focused materials can be produced easily, and prove popular and impactful. There is a need to develop a library of images of a range of men engaging with children of all ages, and with fathers and mothers, in a professional capacity.

Interestingly, having graphical representation of men 'doing the job' serves as just one part of some of the recruitment initiatives conducted by various agencies, campaign bodies and special interest groups in England. Cook (2012, p.122) highlights how 'organising recruitment fairs, placing advertisements in the local press and on local radio, producing leaflets and information packs and publishing articles in specific magazines and newspapers' were some of the many ways that the North East Lincolnshire Council's Children's Information Service attempted to increase the percentage of unrepresented groups of people (including men) in the Early Years sector. However, as is so often the case, 'although these marketing activities did increase interest from [men], this interest was short-lived…and despite [our] efforts the numbers of men have not significantly increased' (p.122). Cook concludes that 'clearly, advertising campaigns targeted at men have little impact on increasing their representation within the Foundation Stage and pre-school childcare workforce' (p.122). So what does seem to work then? 'Word-of-mouth' appears to have been rather effective when reflecting on the headway made by Gingerbread Nursery in Oatby in Leicester in recruiting male Early Years practitioners, at least on a very small scale.

ACTIVITY

Visit tinyurl.com/yc8xte8x, reflecting on the verbalised views of Mr Karl, Ms Cluley and Ms Garrett from Gingerbread Nursery, as reported by Albert (2016). Consider how 'word-of-mouth' has helped/ could help you/your setting/institution to recruit more men in the Early Years sector, either as volunteers, trainees or employees.

Other strategies to entice men into the profession include the use of positive discrimination and working in collaboration with agencies, two ways which Silva (2017) is using to 'make change happen' in Hackney:

I'm opening a new Second Home workspace in London Fields this autumn – which is going to include an OFSTED-accredited crèche with as close to a 50:50 male-female staff ratio as possible. We've partnered with an organisation called Manny and Me to make it happen, who are doing a brilliant job of getting more guys into childcare.

It is our intention to highlight other initiatives throughout this book. Our purpose for briefly discussing the initiatives presented above is intentional for it helps us to recognise that there are numerous 'players' who have influenced and who can influence policy, attitudes and practice in relation to men in the Early Years at different levels. Many of these are presented in the table below for your reflection:

Table 1.3: Various 'players' and their influence on policy, attitudes and practice in the Early Years at different levels

Level	'Player'	Influence
Local	Men who work/ train to work with young children in the Early Years sector, e.g. practitioners and class teachers	• Help students/trainees/parents/carers/ colleagues see that it is 'okay' for men to work in the Early Years • Serve as a role model for young boys in Early Years settings who come from single-parent families, are poorly behaved or are reluctant learners
	Male family members, e.g. brothers, (step) fathers, grandfathers and uncles	• Support the idea that men can be caring, enjoy being with young children and have no hidden motives for doing so • Enrich local Early Years provision by volunteering some of their time to work directly with young children
	Senior management teams members, e.g. setting managers, head teachers and governing bodies	• Demonstrate a commitment to establishing a mixed gender Early Years workforce by actively seeking applications from and employing men as Early Years practitioners (if suitable) • Support existing male practitioners so that they feel valued members of the workforce and that their equal opportunities are defended when parents object to men changing nappies, for example

Regional	Educational institutions, e.g. colleges and universities	• Put strategies in place to specifically target the recruitment and retention of male applicants/ students to their Early Years courses • Promote the idea of men working in the Early Years sector by employing male students as Student Ambassadors, using their image in printed/online marketing materials, and presenting them to others as 'Success case studies' • Work with local Early Years provider networks and local authorities to assure successful and supported placements for male students and job applications from men
	Men in Early Years networks	• Serve as a support group for men who either feel isolated or who want to make professional connections with other men in the Early Years sector • Offer a 'safe space' for men to exchange ideas and openly discuss any difficulties they experience being 'the only man' in the Early Years • Provide support for local outreach work/ promotions, e.g. work in secondary schools and careers fairs
National	Government departments, e.g. the Department for Education (DfE)	• Support the national strategic commitment to diversity in the workplace in terms of advocating a mixed gender workforce in the Early Years • Promote the idea of the Early Years being a rewarding career choice for both men and women
	Men in Early Years advocates, e.g. David Wright	• Ensure that men have a strong and committed voice that represents them and their thinking on the national platform, e.g. 'I think it's [a] child's right to be educated by men and women, and I think men have the right to work with young children' (Wright 2017)

Another influence in relation to men in the Early Years that can greatly impact on local, national and international policies, attitudes and practices is research. But this raises an important question, one which drives the direction of the next section in this chapter.

What does the research say about men in the Early Years?

> We find that children who get their first offer of child care enrollment in a child care center with a higher share of male staff perform better on tests in language and mathematics in the Early Years of school. (Drange and Rønning 2017, p.1)

The conclusion above is taken from a piece of Norwegian research that not only recognises the benefits of gender-mixed ECEC teams for children's development but also contributes to a growing body of international research about men in the Early Years. It is our intention to drip-feed this 'men research' through this book to fuel our discussion. We also feel that it is important to ask critical questions about the research that is presented, e.g. *why* do these Norwegian children perform better on these tests if there are more men in the Early Years setting?[2] To facilitate some reader engagement with the research that is available, we offer four research summaries below, one of which draws on findings from England and three which report on research conducted in locations further afield. We encourage readers to have a look at each of these, engaging in the Activity at the end of the chapter.

Table 1.4: Research summary 1: 'Men in Early Years: a personal reflection and study by music practitioner John Webb' (Webb 2017)

Research summary 1	'Men in Early Years: a personal reflection and study by music practitioner John Webb' (Webb 2017)
The research	The research sought to explore the perceptions of 26 men with regard to whether they saw their gender making a difference to their practice with young children.
What the research found	Most respondents felt that they 'might provide a different kind of role model for the children' (p.5) through the behaviours they exhibited, e.g. 'being silly, displaying emotions, engaging imaginatively and playfully, [and] laughing'. (p.6)
Conclusions of the research	'[M]en possibly do act differently with young children compared to women… Sometimes this difference might be more obvious, such as using more physical play, and sometimes it might be much more subtle and nuanced: focusing on the "what of doing rather than the how of doing."' (p.8)

2   The researchers are unable to explicitly say why this is the case, offering a number of '*maybes*' linked to their explanations.

Recommendations of the research	Webb argues that '[o]ur awareness and understanding of the benefits of these tendencies might be greater if there was a better gender balance and openness to discuss these factors'. (p.8)

Table 1.5: Research summary 2: 'Men in childcare services: From enrolment in training programs to job retention' (Pirard, Schoenmaeckers and Camus 2015)

Research summary 2	'Men in childcare services: From enrolment in training programs to job retention' (Pirard, Schoenmaeckers and Camus 2015)
The research	This research, in part, reflected on the experiences of seven men during their internship placements as part of their initial childcare training programme. The pertinent data were collected from individual 'comprehensive interviews'.
What the research found	'During the actual training programme, informants were generally supported: teachers encouraged them…, sometimes made changes to the programme (generally in regards to physical education), and adapted the premises (locker rooms, toilets) or clothing. However, the training programmes were simply responding to the demands of male students rather than taking a proactive approach to include men.' (p.365)
Conclusions/ recommendations of the research	'[W]e propose that the sector's training providers be encouraged to change the current curricula, so that trainees can choose training that places gender-neutral competences at the core of the discussion.' (p.368)

Table 1.6: Research summary 3: 'Men and women in childcare: a study of caregiver-child interactions' (van Polanen *et al.* 2017)

Research summary 3	'Men and women in childcare: a study of caregiver-child interactions' (van Polanen *et al.* 2017)
The research	'In this observational study, male and female professional caregivers' (42 in total) levels of sensitivity and stimulation toward three-year-old children (42 in total) were observed in a semi-structured play situation.' (p.412)
What the research found	'Male and female caregivers showed the same levels of attention, sensitivity, and stimulation toward boys and girls. Furthermore, all caregivers were classified as feminine or androgynous, but not masculine.' (p.421)
Conclusions of the research	'These findings provide evidence that male and female staff in childcare share similar interaction styles and sex roles' (p.412). Arguments that the 'proportion of men in childcare should be increased in order to have role models of both sexes and, hence, to break gender-stereotyped perceptions, the impact of caregivers' role models in this occupation may be questioned.' (p.421)

Table 1.7: Research summary 4: 'Pedagogical differences and similarities between male and female educators, and their impact on boys' and girls' behaviour in early childhood education and care institutions in Austria' (Huber and Traxl 2017)

Research summary 4	'Pedagogical differences and similarities between male and female educators, and their impact on boys' and girls' behaviour in early childhood education and care institutions in Austria' (Huber and Traxl 2017)
The research	A pilot study, carried out between 2010 and 2012, used a cross-sectional mixed-methods design (video-based observation and questionnaires) to research, amongst other things, the impact of male and female educators on boys' and girls' behaviour (4–6 years) in early childhood education institutions (adapted from p.1).
What the research found	When '[a]nalysing children's behaviour towards educators, clear gender specific effects can be found across various levels of inquiry: girls react less obviously to an educator's gender; boys, especially, are drawn significantly more frequently to a man in the ECEC team'. (p.1)
Conclusions of the research	While '[t]his study cannot yet conclusively clarify why exactly this 'man-boy effect' occurs, boys more frequently seek and maintain contact to male educators' (p.14). As such, '[b]oys have a fundamental need for same-gender exchange and identification'. (p.15)

ACTIVITY

Read all of the four research summaries. How are they similar or different in terms of their findings? Reflect on the conclusions/recommendations offered – do you agree or disagree with these? What impact do you think this research could/will have on your thinking/practice/the thinking and practice of those that you work with?

We bring this initial chapter to a close by briefly considering some of the main ideas which have been discussed in it. We have explored *where we are at* regarding the current 'men climate' in the Early Years sector in England. We have highlighted how the low percentage of men in the 0–5 sector reflects the low percentage of men working across the 5–16 state sectors. We have shown that there is a level of consistency across the UK in terms of the percentage of men who work with young children (2–3%). This consistency, however, is not reflected in the proportion of men who work in Early Year sector equivalents across the world; despite these being low, they vary between 'almost no male workers' (Poland) and 9 per cent (Norway). In an effort to understand why we are at where we are at, we have raised awareness of a range of factors and reasons (both historical and present-day) that give some explanation to the dearth of men in the Early Years sector. Consideration has been given to a select number of initiatives which have been deployed, with limited success, in the active pursuit of recruiting men in the Early Years sector. We have also drawn attention to a suite of 'players' who can help to promote the 'more men in the Early Years' agenda', recognising the importance of recent research in informing our professional understanding and future actions.

So…let us return to the question that opened this initial chapter: Men in the Early Years – where are we at? As has been shown, this is a big question to answer! We suggest that you re-read this chapter and draw your own informed conclusions!

References

Adams, J. (2016) 'The importance of male role models in childcare.' Accessed 9 December at https://dadbloguk.com/importance-male-role-models-childcare

Albert, A. (2016) 'Why so few men in childcare and who are the Gingerbread men?' Accessed 15 November 2017 at www.daynurseries.co.uk/news/article.cfm/id/1579855/Men-in-childcare-in-search-of-the-gingerbread-men

An, R. and Bonetti, S. (2017) 'Analysis – Developing the Early Years Workforce: what does the evidence tell us?' Education Policy Institute. Accessed 10 December 2017 at https://epi.org.uk/analysis/early-years-workforce

Bartlett, D. (2015) 'Men in childcare: How can we achieve a more gender-balanced Early Years and childcare workforce?' Marlborough: Fatherhood Institute. Accessed 5 August 2017 at www.fatherhoodinstitute.org/wp-content/uploads/2015/04/Men-into-Childcare-PDF.pdf

Bernard, R. (2015) 'First national men in Early Years conference launches in 2016.' Nursery World. Accessed 5 August 2017 at www.nurseryworld.co.uk/nursery-world/news/1154056/first-national-men-in-early-years-conference-launches-in-2016

Brody, D. L. (2015) 'The construction of masculine identity among men who work with young children: An international perspective.' *European Early Childhood Education Research Journal*, 23(3), 351–361.

Burn, E. and Pratt-Adams, S. (2015) *Men Teaching Children 3–11: Dismantling Gender Barriers*. London: Bloomsbury.

Ceeda (2017) 'About Early Years: Summer snapshot.' Accessed 9 December 2017 at www.aboutearlyyears.co.uk/media/1091/ceeda-aey-summer-2017-snapshot_issue-1.pdf

Central Advisory Council for Education (CACE) (1967) *Children and their Primary Schools*. London: HMSO.

Central Education Statistic (2009/2010) *List of Tables of School Statistic Summary Education Data Year 2009/2010*. Edited by Kementerian Pendidikan dan Kebudayaan Kemdikbud. Jakarta.

Clarke, K. (1985) 'Public and private children: infant education in the 1820s and 1830s.' In Steedman, C., Urwin, C. and Walkerdine, V. (Eds) *Language, Gender and Childhood*. London: Routledge & Kegan Paul, pp. 74–87.

Conroy, A. (2012) 'ChildLinks: Men in Early Years Care and Education. Issue 1' Barnardos. Accessed 10 December 2017 at www.ncn.ie/images/Play-Tab/childlinks_body28meninchildcareireland.pdf

Cook, C. (2012) 'It's Not What Men Do': Investigating the Reasons for the Low Number of Men in the Early Childhood Workforce.' In: Clough, P. and Nutbrown, C. *A Student's Guide to Methodology*. 3rd edn. London: Sage.

Cronin, M. (2014) 'Men in Early Childhood: A Moral Panic? A research report from a UK University.' *Social Change Review*, 12(1), 3–24. Accessed 13 September 2017 at www.degruyter.com/downloadpdf/j/scr.2014.12.issue-1/scr-2014-0001/scr-2014-0001.pdf

Crown, H. (2017) 'New research finds childcare has poor record on minimum wage.' *Nursery World*, 3 August. Accessed 3 February 2018 at www.nurseryworld.co.uk/nursery-world/news/1161878/new-research-finds-childcare-has-poor-record-on-minimum-wage

Davies, J. (2017) 'How can we attract more men into London's Early Years workforce?' The Father Institute. Accessed 14 November 2017 at www.fatherhoodinstitute.org/wp-content/uploads/2017/05/MITEY-2017-London-report.pdf

DfE (2017) School Workforce in England: November 2016. SFR 25/2017, 22 June. Accessed 5 August 2017 at www.gov.uk/government/uploads/system/uploads/attachment_data/file/620825/SFR25_2017_MainText.pdf

Drange, N. and Rønning, M. (2017) 'Child care center staff composition and early child development.' Discussion Papers No. 870. Oslo: Statistics Norway. Accessed 13 January 2018 at www.ssb.no/en/forskning/discussion-papers/_attachment/332823?_ts=1604982ebc8

eurostat (2017) Early childhood and primary education statistics. Accessed 9 September 2017 at https://ec.europa.eu/eurostat/statistics-explained/index.php/Early_childhood_and_primary_education_statistics

Friedmann, J. (2012) 'Desperately seeking male child care workers.' *Spiegel Online*, 7 September. Accessed 14 November 2017 at www.spiegel.de/international/germany/germany-efforts-to-recruit-men-in-child-care-fall-short-a-854311.html

Fu, C-S. and Li, K-C. (2010) 'Learning experiences of male pre-service preschool teachers in Taiwan.' *New Horizons in Education*, 58(2), 34–42. Accessed 10 December 2017 www.hkta1934.org.hk/NewHorizon/abstract/2010Oct/3.pdf

Garbutt, N. (2017) Redressing the balance: Early Years and the absence of men. *ScopeNI*, 9 June. Accessed 5 August 2017 at http://scopeni.nicva.org/article/redressing-the-balance-early-years-and-the-absence-of-men

Garvey, D. (2018) *Nurturing Personal, Social and Emotional Development in Early Childhood: A Practical Guide to Understanding Brain Development and Young Children's Behaviour*. London: Jessica Kingsley Publishers.

Gravé-Lazi, L. (2016) 'Where are the men in Israel's Early Childhood Education?' *The Jerusalem Post*, 11 January. Accessed 9 December 2017 at www.jpost.com/Israel-News/Where-are-the-men-in-Israels-early-childhood-education-441061

Hamann, G. (2013) 'German government campaigns for more male kindergarten teachers.' *Deutsche Welle*, 8 October. Accessed 14 November 2017 at www.dw.com/en/german-government-campaigns-for-more-male-kindergarten-teachers/a-17143449

Hawthorne, S. and Brown, M. (2016) 'Early Years Pay and Conditions Survey 2016.' *Nursery World*, 16 October. Accessed 13 September 2017 at www.nurseryworld.co.uk/nursery-world/news/1159248/early-years-pay-and-conditions-survey-2016

Haywood, J. (2011) 'Early Years development: why it is a job for the boys.' *The Guardian*, 9 February. Accessed 10 September 2017 at www.theguardian.com/local-government-network/2011/feb/09/early-years-teaching-job-boys

Heikkilä, M. and Hellman, A. (2017) 'Male preschool teacher students negotiating masculinities: a qualitative study with men who are studying to become preschool teachers.' *Early Child Development and Care*, 187(7), 1208–1220.

Huber, J. and Traxl, B. (2017) 'Pedagogical differences and similarities between male and female educators, and their impact on boys' and girls' behaviour in early childhood education and care institutions in Austria.' *Research Papers in Education*. Accessed 9 January 2018 at www.tandfonline.com/doi/pdf/10.1080/02671522.2017.1353674

Indeed (2016). 'Do Millennial Men and Women Want the Same Things in a Job?' Accessed: 20 September 2018 at http://blog.indeed.com/2016/07/18/do-millennial-men-women-want-same-things-job

Johnson, P. (2010) 'Current debates in Early Years education and provision'. In Farrelly, P. (Ed.) *Early Years Work-Based Learning*. Exeter: Learning Matters, pp. 85–107.

Joseph, S. and Wright, Z. (2016) 'Men as early childhood educators: Experiences and perspectives of two male prospective teachers.' *Journal of Education and Human Development*, 5(1), 213–219. Accessed 9 September 2017 at http://jehdnet.com/journals/jehd/Vol_5_No_1_March_2016/22.pdf

Kemp, R. (2016) 'Meet the male teachers changing the perception of nursery school education.' *The Telegraph*, 3 June. Accessed 10 December 2017 at www.telegraph.co.uk/men/thinking-man/meet-the-male-teachers-standing-front-and-centre-of-nursery-scho

Koch, B. and Farquhar, S. (2015) 'Breaking through the glass doors: men working in early childhood education and care with particular reference to research and experience in Austria and New Zealand.' *European Early Childhood Education Research Journal*, 23(3), 380–391.

Kokoros, T. (2012) 'In the land of women: Being a man in early childhood education.' *The Wheelock Blog*, Wheelock College, 19 December. Accessed 13 September 2017 at https://blog.wheelock.edu/in-the-land-of-women-being-a-man-in-early-childhood-education

Lang, A. (2013) 'Young people are having to take career decisions too early.' *The Guardian*, 26 July. Accessed 19 September 2017 at www.theguardian.com/careers/young-people-take-career-decisions-too-early

Learner, S. (2017) 'Redressing the balance: How to get more men working in your nursery.' *Nursery World*, 27 April. Accessed 6 August 2017 at www.daynurseries.co.uk/news/article.cfm/id/1583980/redressing-balance-how-more-men-working-nursery

Lindon, J., Lindon, L. and Beckley, P. (2016) *Leadership in Early Years*. 2nd edn. London: Hodder Education.

Litjens, I. and Taguma, M. (2017) *Early Childhood Education and Care Staff Recruitment and Retention: A Review for Kazakhstan*. OECD. Accessed 9 September 2017 at www.oecd.org/edu/school/Early-Childhood-Education-and-Care-Staff-Recruitement-Retention-Kazakhstan.pdf

Marshall, J. (2014) *Introduction to Comparative and International Education*. London: Sage.

MenTeach (2017) 'Data About Men Teachers: The percentage of men teachers – 2015.' US Bureau of Labor Statistics. Accessed 21 August 2017 at www.menteach.org/resources/data_about_men_teachers

Miller, C. C. (2017) 'More men taking lower-status jobs traditionally held by women.' *The Seattle Times*, 11 March. Accessed 3 February 2018 at www.seattletimes.com/business/more-men-taking-lower-status-jobs-traditionally-held-by-women

Mistry, M. and Sood, K. (2015) 'Why are there still so few men within Early Years in primary schools: views from male trainee teachers and male leaders?' *Education 3–13*, 43(2), 115–127.

Mukuna, T. E. and Mutsotso, S. N. (2011) 'Gender inequalities in early childhood development education teaching profession in Kenya.' *Educational Research*, 2(13), 1876–1885. Accessed 9 December 2017 at www.earlychildhoodworkforce.org/sites/default/files/resources/gender-inequalities-in-early-childhood-development-education-teaching-profession-in-kenya.pdf

Oberhuemer, P. (2012) 'Radical Reconstructions? Early Childhood Workforce Profiles in Changing European Early Childhood Education and Care Systems.' In Miller, L., Dalli, C. & Urban, M. (Eds) *Early Childhood Grows Up. Towards a Critical Ecology of the Profession. International Perspectives on Early Childhood Education and Development*, 6 (pp. 119–130). London: Springer.

Peeters, J., Rohrmann T. and Emilsen K. (2015) 'Gender balance in ECEC: Why is there so little progress?' *European Early Childhood Education Research Journal*, 23(3), 302–314.

Penn, H. and McQuail, S. (1997) *Childcare as a Gendered Occupation*. DfEE Research Report RR23. London: HMSO. Accessed 5 August 2017 at http://webarchive.nationalarchives.gov.uk/20130402111310/www.education.gov.uk/publications/eOrderingDownload/RR23.pdf

Pirard, F., Schoenmaeckers, P. and Camus, P. (2015) 'Men in childcare services: From enrolment in training programs to job retention.' *European Early Childhood Education Research Journal*, 23(3), 362–369.

Radford, L. *et al*. (2011) *Child abuse and neglect in the UK today*. London: NSPCC. Accessed 3 February 2018 at www.nspcc.org.uk/services-and-resources/research-and-resources/pre-2013/child-abuse-and-neglect-in-the-uk-today

Russell, K. (2013) 'The gender divide: Men in ECE.' *Education Review*, January. Accessed 10 December 2017 at http://educationreview.co.nz/the-gender-divide-men-in-ece

Sak, R., Sahin, I. T. and Sahin, B. K. (2012) 'Views of female preschool pre-service teachers about male teaching colleagues.' *Procedia – Social and Behavioral Sciences*, 47, 586–593. Accessed 9 September 2017 at ac.els-cdn.com/S1877042812024366/1-s2.0-S1877042812024366-main.pdf?_tid=63446508-9580-11e7-a02b-00000aacb3 61&acdnat=1504976611_079200489cddb05e5fd1a55ed8573080

Sak, R., Sak, I. T. S. and Yerlikaya, İ. (2015) 'Behavior management strategies: Beliefs and practices of male and female early childhood teachers.' *European Early Childhood Education Research Journal*, 23(3), 328–339.

Sakellariou, M. and Rentzou, K. (2010) 'Greek Female Early Childhood Educators' Perceptions Towards Their Male Co-workers.' Accessed 9 September 2017 at www.ucy.ac.cy/unesco/documents/unesco/Articles_2010-2010_conference/Sakellariou_paper.pdf

Silva, R. (2017) 'Rohan Silva: Childcare needs more male workers for an equal balance of role models.' *Evening Standard*, 19 July. Accessed 9 January 2018 at www.standard.co.uk/comment/comment/rohan-silva-childcare-needs-more-male-workers-for-an-equal-balance-of-role-models-a3591416.html

Simon, A., Owen, C. and Hollingworth, K. (2016) 'Is the 'quality' of preschool childcare, measured by the qualifications and pay of the Childcare workforce, improving in Britain?' *American Journal of Educational Research*, 4(1), 11–17. Accessed 5 August 2017 at htpp://pubs.sciepub.com/education/4/1/4

Skelton, C. (2009) 'Failing to get men into primary teaching: A feminist critique.' *Journal of Education Policy*, 24(1), 39–54.

Skills Development Scotland (2017) *Skills Investment Plan: Prospectus. For Scotland's early learning and childcare sector*. Glasgow: Skills Development Scotland. Accessed 5 August 2017 at www.skillsdevelopmentscotland.co.uk/media/43127/early-learning-and-childcare-sip-digital.pdf

Skills for Care and Development (2017) 'Professional Framework in Children's Care, Learning and Development (Wales).' Skills for Care & Development. Accessed 5 August 2017 at www.afo.sscalliance.org/frameworkslibrary/index.cfm?id=FR04089&back

Statistics Norway (2017) 'Facts about education in Norway 2017 – key figures 2015.' Accessed 21 August 2017 at www.ssb.no/en/utdanning/artikler-og-publikasjoner/_attachment/287176?_ts=158d834b638

Tanuku, P. (2014) 'We need more men in childcare.' *Early Years Educator*, 3 April. Accessed 9 December 2017 at www.magonlinelibrary.com/doi/abs/10.12968/eyed.2014.16.1.8?journalCode=eyed

Tropp, A. (1957) *The School Teachers: The Growth of the Teaching Profession in England and Wales from 1800 to the Present Day*. London: Heinemann.

van Polanen, M. *et al.* (2017) 'Men and women in childcare: A study of caregiver–child interactions.' *European Early Childhood Education Research Journal*, 25(3), 412–424.

Ward, L. (2014) 'Spot the difference: Why do more men teach in independent schools?' *The Guardian*, 21 October. Accessed 9 December 2017 at www.theguardian.com/teacher-network/teacher-blog/2014/oct/21/independent-schools-men-women-teachers-career-options

Wardle, F. (2016) 'Fathers.' In Couchenour, D, and Chrisman, J. K. (Eds) *The SAGE Encyclopaedia of Contemporary Early Childhood Education* (pp. 598–601) Thousand Oaks, California: Sage.

Webb, J. (2017) *Men in Early Years: A personal reflection and study by music practitioner John Webb*. London: Sound Connections. Accessed 8 December 2017 at www.sound-connections.org.uk/wp-content/uploads/Men-in-Early-Years-.pdf

Williams, A. (2013) In Tcaffel. 'Where Are All The Men?' *Advance*, Unitec, 19 December. Accessed 13 September 2017 at www.unitec.ac.nz/advance/index.php/men-in-early-childhood-education

Wright, D. (2017) In Spreeuwenberg, R. 'Men in childcare as a right for children.' *Hi Mima*, 14 March. Accessed 8 December 2017 at www.himama.com/men-in-childcare-as-a-right-for-children

Xu, Y. and Waniganayake, M. (2017) 'An exploratory study of gender and male teachers in early childhood education and care centres in China.' *Compare: A Journal of Comparative and International Education*, DOI: 10.1080/03057925.2017.1318355

Yousefi, S. (2016) 'Lack of Men in Early Childhood Education.' *Novak Djokovic Foundation*, 16 October. Accessed 7 August 2017 at https://novakdjokovicfoundation.org/lack-men-early-childhood-education

Zhang, W. (2017) 'Male teachers in early childhood education: Why more men? A review of the literature.' *Culminating Projects in Child and Family Studies, 18*. Accessed 14 November 2017 at htpp://repository.stcloudstate.edu/cgi/viewcontent.cgi?article=1022&context=cfs_etds

CHAPTER 2

Reasons for the 2%ers

DAVID WRIGHT

Overview

There is a complex interplay of factors affecting the gender make-up of the UK Early Years workforce. In the previous chapter, we catalogued some of the reasons why there are so few men. In this chapter we now examine what we consider to be some of the main factors influencing the sustained gender imbalance, in more detail. We offer points for reflection and actions to consider in reviewing your own situation and practice.

We start by considering the relationship between the set of factors that influence and are in turn influenced by culture. The following diagram illustrates some of the key factors we have identified as elements influencing the culture in the Early Years sector.

Culture

Each of us exists in a context which frames our attitudes and practices. Our ideas, values, beliefs and implicit and explicit behaviours are largely shaped by the collective expectations of our society. Culture is a powerful determinant of lifestyle, programming compliance with group rules, expectations and behaviours. This culture of the group distinguishes its members from those belonging to other groups, for example, the perception of the roles of men and women. Generally, identities are formed from a prescribed set of characteristics according to the predominant rules (norms) of compliance. According to Marshall, 'Norms in every culture create conformity that allows for people to become socialized to the culture in which they live' (Marshall 2009). Culture affects both the composition and the characteristics of the Early Years workforce. The notion of belonging is a powerful force for attracting and keeping members within the confines of the group ('us') or for possibly excluding or discriminating against the other ('them') (Terry and Hogg 2001) – anyone deemed not to fit the expectations of a group member, such as a male potential childcare practitioner.

How culture develops, how it is sustained and how it evolves are profound sociological questions which can be applied at different levels. Once a group culture is established, it becomes difficult to change. Its values and perspectives persist even as membership changes. Research into the practice of Early Years education may address culture across different countries, such as the work of Brody (2014, p.29–143) in his book *Men Who Teach Young Children, an International Perspective*. It may consider the relative value placed on the Early Years education sector in a particular country along with attitudes and practices that pertain to that workforce. What our society believes about Early Years education and those tasked with delivering it can be deduced from our observations of policy and public opinion. An analysis of reportage reveals how beliefs are reinforced and shaped by our media and how, in turn, these create and sustain a national culture. Our beliefs about ourselves and our roles as Early Years practitioners is evident in who we are (mainly female) and what we say about ourselves. The look and feel of culture in the setting or context we currently work in is something we can reflect on individually using behavioural and environmental cues such as who we interact with day-to-day. Apart from the children, how many of these people are male?

Public opinion may be considered as the representation of macro culture – what constitutes our national attitudes. The Encyclopedia Britannica (1998) defines it as 'an aggregate of the individual views, attitudes and beliefs about a particular topic expressed by a significant proportion of the community'. Is public opinion singular? Does it depend on who and the circumstances in which we are asking about attitudes and beliefs? As an example, according to our own research described in Chapter 4, 95 per cent of parents surveyed were happy for their child to be cared for by a male Early Years worker, indicating that public opinion is strongly in favour of men working in Early Years. At the same time, 14 per cent of the same respondents indicated that they have concerns about men working in Early Years. It seems that the same people are giving conflicting responses.

When it comes to discernment, we are not sure we can always trust public opinion to speak on behalf of culture and less sure that we can trust the media to represent public opinion. Selection and framing are important media tools in agenda-setting (McCombs and Shaw 1972). The media decides what information to publish and how to present it. We are influenced by the views of others, those around us – our parents/carers, our peers, our teachers, the images we see on screens. These opinions influence our attitudes towards gender roles. It becomes expedient to categorise individuals according to assumed stereotypes. These assumptions are often inherited, powerful and persuasive – (Nickerson and Femiano 1989). They are difficult to change. To do so involves challenging our culture and that can be a daunting prospect requiring self-assuredness, courage and sometimes self-sacrifice.

REFLECTION

Ask yourself the following:

- Who or what do I consider to be the main influences on my personal beliefs and values?

- Am I conscious of the predominant culture and the effect it has on my beliefs and values:

  1. In my place of work?

  2. In my society/community?

3.   In my nation? If so, why? If not, why not?

–   How would I describe my response to culture – am I accepting of it or am I willing to challenge it? Why/not?

–   Am I accepting, tolerant and welcoming of ideas and practices from other cultures? If so, why? If not, why not?

–   What, if anything, would cause me to challenge social mores?

An important consideration is not just culture in the wider sense but also gender expectations/perceptions and how these are influenced by culture.

Gender expectations/perceptions

The World Health Organization (1998) has defined gender as the 'characteristics, roles and responsibilities of women and men, boys and girls, which are socially constructed'. According to this definition, gender is related to how we are perceived and expected to think and act as men and women, not because of biological difference but the way that society is organised. The common perceptions and expectations that we hold form our culture and this has a direct influence on gender roles. In the 21st century, is our notion of the family unit still exclusively the traditional nuclear family comprising a married man and woman with their own biological children; a unit in which the man is the 'hunter-gatherer' bringing the spoils back home to the female carer and mistress of the domestic realm, each with their respective roles, responsibilities and division of labour? In 2012, a Netmums survey identified 35 different family types in the UK. Whilst a significant majority of these (over 80%) are characterised by cohabiting heterosexual couples, 10 per cent of families consist of a lone parent with their own children and one in 111 families is headed by gay, bisexual or transgender parents (Netmums 2012). This begs the question what to do with traditional ideas about parental roles based on gender in such families. As David's youngest daughter once asked when told that a female couple they knew were living together: 'Who puts the bins out?'

A figure of 98 per cent female practitioners (DfE 2014) in the Early Years workforce suggests that, despite the changes in family and parenting models, in our society the care and education of young children is not seen as an expected, appropriate or necessary role for men; that caring for and educating young children is 'women's work' and men should be pursuing other 'manly' pursuits. The beliefs we have about such roles are expressed and reinforced through the terminology that we use. The names we give for people who care for and help to develop young children and the facilities in which they operate have associations within our society – for example, think *child carer, nursery, childminder* and *nursery nurse*. On the spectrum of gender characteristics, we tend to relate these terms to notions of nurture, care and protection – what both men and women might refer to as 'maternal traits'. Whilst more gender-neutral terms exist, such as *Early Years centre, setting, practitioner, educator or teacher,* there is still a tendency for the traditional nomenclature to be employed.

ACTIVITY

During a staff/team meeting, facilitate some critical discussion by responding to these five questions:

- Do I have a mental association of job roles with specific genders? If so, what are they?

- Do I expect men to be 'child carers' in our society? If so, why? If not, why not?

- Do I perceive men as 'nursery nurses'? Why/not?

- Do I believe men have a role to play in the care of and development of young children? If so, why and how? If not, why not?

- What do I think influences my response to these questions?

Paid statutory paternity leave was introduced in the UK for the first time in 2003. In January 2010, fathers were given the right to take six months' statutory paternity leave. From 2015, couples can now claim up to 52 weeks shared parental leave. Whilst, in this way, the laws recognise the importance of fathers in their children's lives, particularly in light of the rebalancing of paternity and maternity leave allowance, in practice this provision has not been utilised much by new fathers. Research by law firm EMW indicates that only 8700 or 1 per cent of eligible couples took advantage of the scheme between April 2016 and March 2017 (Taylor 2018). Reasons given for this low take-up are thought to be partly because of cultural assumptions which perceive childcare as a woman's job and in part because many families consider it is better that the (usually) lower paid women take the leave rather than higher earning men.

In our culture the role of men in relation to their own and to other people's young children can be marginalised. He may be the only 'Dad' at the 'Mother and Toddler' group on a Tuesday morning, a man attempting to change a child's nappy in the gents' toilets, or one who is pushing a double buggy around a shopping centre on his own. Stay-at-home dads may be admired but there may also be suspicion that they are shirking the responsibilities of providing for their family. Extend this to the minding of other people's children and we have someone who is rather unusual: an individual who has crossed established gender domains.

CASE STUDY

John Adams gave up a well-paid job in communications and PR to become his children's main carer in 2011. He has two daughters – Helen, aged nine, and Izzy, aged five. John's wife, Gill, works full-time and provides materially for the family. The family lives in the South East of England in Surrey. John's blog – dadbloguk – is a 'Best UK Dad Blog' award winner.

John received mixed reactions to his decision to become his children's main carer. He says, 'It isn't really spoken about with my family. It's just not the done thing for a man to give up work in the way I did so best not acknowledged! I'd say that men are more open to the idea than you might imagine. It pains me to say it, but I've had more negative reactions from women. It's understandable, men and women are raised to think that caring is a woman's job. Very rarely do you see men in caring roles. When a man turns up on the scene with children and explains he is their father and main carer, well, it rocks the boat. Some women derive huge status from being mothers. A man such as myself threatens that status because we prove men can do the job just as well.'

John says that he found acceptance for himself as the main carer for his children from staff in both childcare facilities and later on from school staff. He contrasts this with the challenge of being 'the only man in the room' at a music group where 'the same group of mums have been socialising with each other since they were attending pre-natal classes'. He had avoided other groups because he 'didn't want to have to go into a room full of 20 women and explain my status to everyone'.

We asked John for his opinion about the term 'gender domains'. He says, 'I totally recognise the phrase "gender domains". It wasn't until I refocused my life to concentrate on family and home that I appreciated just how rigid these domains still are. For a man to look after kids in their Early Years, wow, that's mind blowing for most people. That is definitely a woman's domain!'

Fears – the role of the media

Over the last few years, the media has reported an almost continuous chronicle of both allegations and actual proven cases of abuse perpetrated against children by men from various walks of life including politics, entertainment, sports and education. Operation Hydrant is an investigation of allegations of 'non-recent' child sex abuse within UK institutions set up in 2014. Media reporting of it is an example of the use of ostensibly large numbers categorised by institution type, and phrases such as 'high profile' or people of 'public prominence' add weight to the story, e.g.:

> 'Extensive U.K. child abuse probe includes high-profile figures' (Newsweek headline 20/05/2015)

> 'Operation Hydrant: UK police identify 2,228 child abuse suspects' (BBC News online, 01/12/2015)

Such headlines are terrifying for parents, and there is doubtless a large-scale problem of male sexual violence against children in this country still. However, given the lack of reporting of the child abuse accusations that are disproven, it's reasonable to infer that it is in the tabloid media's interest to stoke parents' fears. No wonder then that people so often question the motives of any man who interacts with a person under the age of 16, known or unknown to him.

The effects of such fear can be clearly seen in the establishment of the Independent Safeguarding Authority (ISA) and the associated vetting and barring scheme by the Labour administration in 2006, as a reaction to a media campaign following the Bichard report (2004) into the Soham Murders. In 2009, *The Telegraph* reported its opinion on the ISA in an article entitled 'Vetting and barring: This culture of suspicion needs to change':

> ...its (the ISA's) foundation on a belief that every adult is a potential molester. This atmosphere of mutual suspicion and distrust is not healthy for any country and is more likely to be detrimental to our children than to improve their well-being. It is not so much the legislation that needs amending as a whole culture that requires a complete rethink.

In 2010, announcing a review of vetting and barring, Theresa May, new Home Secretary, said that

> You were assumed to be guilty, in a sense, until you were proven innocent and told you could work with children. By scaling it (the vetting and barring scheme) back we will be able to introduce a greater element of common sense. What we have got to do is actually trust people again. (Travis 2010)

Today, seven years on from this statement, it is evident that we still do not trust people. The media is still generating suspicion in its reporting of opinions on men working with young children. So how does our media report the subject of men and their motives? Let us examine a few examples.

CASE STUDY

Andrea Leadsom (2016), MP, reported in *The Sunday Times*:

> As an employer we're not, let's face it, most of us don't employ men as nannies, most of us don't. Now you can call that sexist, I call that cautious and very sensible when you look at the stats. Your odds are stacked against you if you employ a man. We know paedophiles are attracted to working with children. I'm sorry but they're the facts.

What 'stats' or 'odds' are being referred to here? Where is the justification for this pronouncement? We think we can agree that paedophiles are most likely to be attracted to working with children and also that the vast majority of them are men, but how is the leap made from this to conclude that no men should ever be employed to work with children? How is that 'cautious and very sensible'? At the time of this reported quote, Andrea Leadsom was a government minister and (briefly) a candidate for the leadership of her political party. She could have become the Prime Minister of the United Kingdom. Because of her position, her views, as reported by the media, have an impact on our collective consciousness. They could result in actual policy being enacted by our government. In support of Andrea Leadsom's reported views, here is an extract from an article by Ben Kelly in *The Telegraph* (18 July 2016):

> I have a three-year-old son and if I could afford to hire a nanny there is absolutely no way I would hire a man. Not a chance. It's a shame to feel like this but, quite frankly, there is clearly, demonstrably, more of a risk involved than in hiring a woman. That is not a risk I am willing to take with my child. When my wife and I were recently looking at pre-schools, we came across one with a male nanny, I felt that unpleasant involuntary twinge immediately. I could not help it, many can't. It is pure instinct to protect one's child and assess all risks and possible threats. Even I, as a man, trust other men less than women.

Kelly is, of course, entitled to hold and to express his opinion on this subject but to claim that there is 'clearly, demonstrably more of a risk involved (in hiring a man) than in hiring a woman', without giving any idea of the scale of this risk, is irresponsible.

We are very familiar with statistics, particularly ostensibly large numbers, being used to support a position. In the following example, it is the addition of the journalist's own judgement through his use of adjectives such as 'shocking' and 'horrifically' that appears to move the reportage away from contextual objectivity:

> Up to 750,000 men living in Britain may have an interest in having sex with children, the Government has been warned. A shocking analysis by the National Crime Agency reveals that about one in 35 adult males poses a potential risk of being a child abuser or of seeking out child sex images online. Horrifically, as many as 250,000 men may be sexually attracted to pre-pubescent children – defined as those under 12. (Birrell 2015)

It is the use of the word 'may' above that causes us to question these findings. How were these figures arrived at? Surely 750,000 men were not asked whether they might have an interest in having sex with children? What do we imagine the answer to such a question would be? It is very hard to believe that as many as 3 per cent of men pose a potential threat to children. Unproven figures like this add to the tabloid media's fear-generation, and do nothing to help protect children from a very real, but thankfully rare, threat. Is this justification for excluding all men from the Early Years workforce, just in case? We would suggest that it is not.

The cumulative effect of unbalanced reporting is to affect opinions. The examples given above present individual feelings as fact. The conclusions that individuals have come to, also based on unrepresentative examples, are extrapolated and publicised to infer a general crisis, in this case with respect to any man having interaction with a child. Cast in such bald terms, this sounds absurd but that is what is being said. As an example, a male Educational Psychology MSc student recently tweeted: '*The habit of the male of the species is oft to murder the kids of others*'.

Such attitudes are now pervasive and there are many examples of fear and prejudice operative within the English Early Years sector:

- Parents choosing not to send their child to a nursery because the manager is male.

- Carers insisting that their child receives personal care only from women.

- Early Years settings where men are forbidden from toileting or changing children.

- A social media posting of a nursery receiving a complaint from a passing member of the public that there was a 'pervert' in the nursery garden – a male member of staff in uniform, making an observation of a child's development using a nursery-owned tablet as part of his professional duties.

- An Early Years setting reported to Ofsted for having a man working in it.

- A male Early Years practitioner in uniform eating his lunch on a park bench, being questioned and moved along by the police simply for being seated adjacent to a children's play area.

- A disproportionate (compared to women) catalogue of unsubstantiated allegations of abuse against children by male Early Years practitioners (as previously discussed).

REFLECTION

With reference to the discussion above, reflect on the following questions:

–   Do I believe that men represent a threat to children? If so, why? If not, why not?

–   What do I currently do to publicise good practice and positive images of both men and women working in the Early Years sector?

–   What can I do to counter negative stories in the press with testimonials of trustworthy and competent male practitioners?

All men are liable to come under suspicion because of heightened awareness of cases where men have perpetrated abuse. Men often feel they have to prove their innocence to justify their presence in what has traditionally been seen as a female domain. Electing to work in the Early Years sector is not an obvious choice for men who hold highly traditional gender attitudes. It could therefore be argued that, proportionately, male Early Years practitioners are less likely to sexually abuse children than the male population as a whole. Whilst safeguarding children has to be our highest priority, it is never pleasant to be judged by the assumptions of others and such prejudice serves as a significant cultural barrier to men entering and remaining in the workforce. According to research conducted by the London Early Years Foundation in 2012, 51 per cent of nursery workers thought the main reason for the low numbers of men in the Early Years sector was because of society's attitude to men in childcare.

So how can we reduce the suspicion that surrounds the motivation of men who want to work as practitioners in the Early Years? 'Professional Love in the Early Years Settings' (PLEYS), a research project set up by Dr Jools Page of Sheffield University, examines how those who work in Early Years settings can safely express the affectionate and caring behaviours which their role requires. The main outcome is an Attachment Toolkit available to practitioners to reflect on their interactions with the children they care for in terms of building authentic, reciprocal relationships with children and parents. Through its explicit focus on this area of practice, it is a helpful framework in both making professionals self-aware and providing reassurance to parents of the children being cared for by them.

ACTIVITY

Consider looking at the Attachment Toolkit available on the Professional Love in Early Years Settings (PLEYS) website – see professionallove.group.shef.ac.uk

Once reviewed, reflect on the following questions:

- How does my safeguarding policy and practice protect the team from allegations?

- What are my beliefs about the appropriateness of men working with young children?

- Do I believe men are inherently more of a threat to children's safety than women?

- How do I respond to the concerns of carers about a male practitioner caring for and expressing affection towards their child in an Early Years setting?

Job status

As we have seen, culture, gender role expectations and our media all combine to produce a context for society's notion of Early Years care and education as an occupation. This includes perceptions of who should be working in the sector, who should not and the duties the role encompasses. We now examine the status of the Early Years profession.

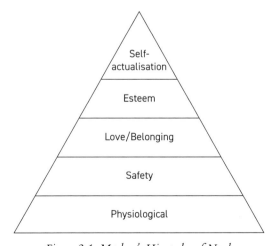

Figure 2.1: Maslow's Hierarchy of Needs

The provision of care, love and nurture meets fundamental human needs. Love occupies the third tier of Maslow's Hierarchy of Needs (Maslow 1954), above physiological and safety and below any notion of education – *Am I breathing, warm, fed and not in imminent danger of attack? I need love.* Why, therefore, do we attribute caring as low status and in the case of the male worker, as suspicious? Maybe we believe that men are more suited to be 'educators' or 'teachers' who are concerned with the development of infants' brains and their cognitive capabilities. In the UK, the introduction of the Early Years Educator and Early Years Teacher roles in 2013 sent a clear message in its nomenclature that the government considers the education sector to encompass the Early Years, arguably with a shift away from the focus on care. A review of the qualifications criteria for these roles (National College for Leadership 2013a, 2013b) confirms the emphasis on teaching and child development. By focusing on the education sector as a whole, it is conceivable that we might extend the role of the teacher into the birth to five age range so that we can construct a professional un-gendered status for the Early Years Teacher. This begs the question as to what stage 'teaching' replaces care for infants? Are we in danger of endorsing a formalised curriculum at the cost of children's need for play-based, experiential learning, and for nurture and love? If love matters, as Gerhardt (2014) states, then we need men and women who are not just teachers but who are able to love children. Does this fit, however, with the expectations of a teacher? On the one hand, the Early Years sector is presented as an opportunity to promote professional teaching careers, but if this is the case it is important that men and women who apply for such roles fully understand and are comfortable and supported in providing for the holistic needs of our youngest children, including care, nurture and physical touch, as appropriate. It is also important to create places where it is safe for children to be cared for by men and women and where it is safe and acceptable for them to provide this care in an environment of trust, free from continual suspicion. Our safeguarding challenge then is to get the good guys (men and women) in, and keep the bad guys out.

Childcare has acquired a pejorative reputation as a low status, unskilled profession requiring an ability to provide physical care and to 'play'. Our cultural challenge is to establish a professional status for men and women to practise in Early Years that values, validates, supports and recognises the importance of this role.

ACTIVITY

Write your answers to the following questions using your own initial response to each one. Reflect on what you have written.

- What term do I use to refer to my Early Years setting?

- What status do I ascribe to Early Years practice? Why?

- What job roles are defined in my organisation?

- What do I believe about the need for female and male Early Years practitioners to provide love to children? Why?

- What practices and policies effectively manage physical touch and care and nurture routines in my setting?

- Do these policies note any differences between men and women in these practices e.g. only women are allowed to toilet or change children?

Pay

The level of pay for an occupation carries with it the notion of relative value of the work performed. When comparing professions, sectors and differentials within particular pay scales, there can be moral discussions about who earns what and whether they deserve to do so. As we know, levels of pay do not always equate to our innate sense of worth. Our notion of fairness can be offended by the idea of a well-rewarded elite with bonuses and fringe benefits, particularly in the financial industries. We also question the large salaries and rewards accruing to celebrities. Status, it seems, is very much tied up with pay. The higher the salary, the greater the status and the perceived value or importance of the work performed by an individual. We also hold the converse to be true with relatively poorly paid work explicitly labelled low status.

The Equal Pay Act (1970) prohibited any less favourable treatment between men and women in terms of pay and conditions of employment, yet despite decades of campaigning, industrial action, education and changes in the law since, it is still the case that women earn less than men in Britain today – the gap is reported to be around 14 per cent (Fawcett Society 2016). So-called feminised sectors such as the Early Years tend to be less valued and therefore less well paid. Traditionally, Early Years education has come under the label of care work. Caring is considered a predominantly female characteristic. The perception has been that not only is this an exclusively female domain, it is also a default job for those who are less academic. As Professor Cathy Nutbrown observed in her review of Early Years qualifications:

> ...the Early Years workforce does not hold the status in society that it deserves. It is still the case that working in the Early Years is too often seen as a low level job which involves, as some have expressed, 'wiping noses' and 'playing with kids'. It is not always regarded as a professional occupation that demands good qualifications, strong communication skills, and expertise in child development and early learning. We need to raise our expectations, and make early education and childcare a more attractive sector to work in. (Nutbrown 2012, p.35)

The perception of Early Years practice as low status is not an exclusively English one. How hard can it be to change nappies, to play and to serve meals or 'wiping noses and stopping the kids from killing each other?', as Australian Senator David Leyonhjelm remarked in January 2017, in an interview on Australian TV's Channel Ten, when explaining why he would not support his government's $3 billion childcare reform package 'without amendment'.

There is tacit agreement on the relatively low status of the Early Years job role. Those successfully completing an Early Years Teacher qualification, having undergone identical training to their peers studying to become 'mainstream' teachers, end up being less qualified. They are not awarded Qualified Teacher Status. This limits their options for employment and their earning potential. Our society values those who it believes are responsible for delivering 'proper' education above those it deems to be 'child carers'.

This is a problem for our sector. In terms of household needs, pay is not a gender issue. Traditionally the 'breadwinner' may have been male but there are many families or households in our society where a woman is the sole earner. The proportion of maternal breadwinners rose from 23 per cent in 1996 to 33 per cent in 2013 according to the Institute for Public Policy Research (2015). The main wage earner can be a man or a woman and pay levels need to be sufficient to sustain a family's needs. To infer that more men would join our sector if they could afford to highlights the disservice being enacted towards the predominant female workforce both in terms of status and remuneration. These need addressing regardless of the gender composition of the Early Years workforce.

There is a compelling body of evidence from the fields of neuroscience, psychology, human biology and social science to show the foundational nature of quality Early Years provision.

Arguably, we are engaged in the most important of job roles – helping to shape the character and inherent qualities of each unique individual child during his or her formative years. According to the Too Much Too Soon campaign (2016), 'early childhood should be treated as a vital developmental stage in its own right – not merely as a preparation for school, but uniquely as a preparation for life'. We need to attract and retain the best people for this job. Pay needs to reflect this.

The UK childcare sector predominantly and increasingly comprises private, voluntary and independent providers (PVI). Publicly funded provision in the form of state nursery schools represents a very small proportion of the total. Such 'maintained' settings are under pressure from local authority budget cuts, and changes to the national funding formula have forced many nursery schools to close in recent years with the rest facing an uncertain future at the end of transitional funding in 2019. In February 2017, MP Helen Smith stated in a House of Commons debate that, 'one in ten nursery schools still think they will have to close by July and 67 per cent believe they will have to close by the end of the transitional funding' (Jones 2017).

With an increasing number of funded childcare hours paid for through government grants at a set rate, and with PVI providers continuing to face an upward challenge on operating costs, it is difficult to see any resolution to the low pay level in the sector relative to other professions, albeit increases in statutory national rates that compel employers to raise minimum wage rates. Providers are caught between the constraints of income and the pressure of operational costs. Apart from a change in government policy, regulation and increased levels of funding, there is no foreseeable way in which Early Years practitioners will receive greater remuneration and close the pay gap between themselves and their colleagues in other education sectors.

CASE STUDY

In Finland virtually all Early Years care and education is provided by the public sector. Almost all Early Years employees belong to trade unions. The national labour market organisations representing Early Years employees negotiate collective agreements on their behalf concerning their wages and other terms of employment. As a result, there are clearly defined pay scales which recognise and reward qualified kindergarten teachers at levels much closer to their colleagues teaching in schools.

Women as gatekeepers

As discussed above, our cultural tendency is both to comply with the group identity and behaviours and to feel more comfortable around those who we recognise as being 'like us'. Human nature tends to like the way things are and wants to preserve the status quo. If we need more group members, subconsciously we are looking to attract people like us in order to protect our culture. In a traditionally single-gender environment such as the Early Years workforce, the group may be very comfortable with the prevailing culture. It is natural to feel threatened by potential change and to take action to preserve it. In this context, a different gender represents a potential threat of disruption.

The male CV arriving in response to a job advert in a pre-school typically represents one of two things: either it is a novelty or an aberration. In the latter case, it is dismissed. This is not an individual who is like us; he has a different gender. In the case of the former, whilst there may be keen interest in acquiring 'a man', what values are used to assess him against, consciously or subconsciously, in terms of fitting within our organisation? Are we expecting new group members to adapt to our culture – the way we do things around here, or how far are we willing to change to accommodate somebody different? We could equally apply this challenge to those of other races, religions, beliefs, practices and culture. For some of us it is enriching and educational to absorb new ideas; for others it can be a challenge.

The welcome that awaits a new male practitioner could be reticent. Preconceived ideas about gender stereotypes can influence expectations of character and behaviours. *Will a new man be feckless? Will he get the children worked up? Maybe he will lack responsibility. Why does he want to work with children anyway? He will be good for physical outdoor activities. He will like football. He will be a role model, especially for the boys.* If an Early Years team comprises exclusively female staff, it is valid for them to ask themselves why this is the case, whether there is any conscious or subconscious gatekeeping, if there is any desire for a balanced gender team, what they are prepared to change, and what actions they might take to bring this about.

REFLECTION

- What expectations, if any, do I place on an individual joining our organisation?

- How would my colleagues feel about someone different from us joining our team in terms of their gender?

- What is my response to an application from a man for an Early Years practitioner position? Is it any different to an application from a woman?

- Do I take positive action to encourage job applications from men as well as women?

Gendered environments/practices

Given the low percentage of men working in the Early Years nationally, the chances are that your setting employs very few or no men working directly with the children. There are notable exceptions to this but these are rare. If your team is all-female, are you comfortable with the status quo? We have often heard the comment, 'We'd love to have male practitioners but we don't receive applications from them'. This is generally true. It is not the case that we are turning men away; they are simply not applying to work in Early Years settings. Seeing it from the man's perspective can be helpful in reflecting on what the barriers are to entry. Through auditing our own particular establishments, we can review various aspects of the environment, our practices, routines and culture by asking ourselves the following:

- Have we ever discussed the gender-balance of our team together? Are we actively looking to recruit both men and women?

- What positive action could we take to attract applications from men?

- If a man joined our team, would he feel comfortable and welcome here? Why/not?

- Does our environment have a gender bias? This might include colour schemes, decoration, furnishings, materials, pictures, ornaments and accessories. What could be done about this?

- What do we discuss in our staffroom? Would the content of our conversations be different if we had a mixed gender team?

- What is our dress code? Does this have a gender bias? If it does, how could it be developed to apply to men?

- How are the toilet facilities organised? (We know of one setting where the new male practitioner was informed that he was expected to share the caretaker's outside portaloo, the inside toilet being reserved for the exclusive use of female staff.)

In Chapter 6 we give examples of organisations that have successfully recruited and retained men. We consider what characterises their culture and practice and how lessons from these might be applied to different contexts. In Chapter 7 we consider what actions settings might take to attract and retain men. A good starting point is a gender audit.

ACTIVITY

Download our gender audit from here: www.samey.uk/audit

- Initiate a team discussion on their views on a mixed gender team.

- Conduct the audit with your team, discuss the results and plan any agreed actions.

The 'glass escalator'

Two per cent of the UK Early Years workforce and 14 per cent of primary school teachers are male. Thirty-two per cent of men working in primary and nursery schools are in senior leadership roles

(DfE 2014). This is a disproportionate level of male representation in management positions compared to the relative number of men in the workforce. The 'glass escalator' (Williams 1992) refers to the way in which men tend to be promoted above women in female-dominated industries. These figures suggest that this is true for practising in the Early Years and primary teaching sectors. Explanations for this include female careers suffering interruptions due to maternity leave and some women preferring day-to-day interactions and relationships with children over a management role. Another explanation, according to Goldberg (cited in Goudreau 2012), is that 'stereotypes about what a prototypical man is match with stereotypes about what a prototypical manager is'. As a rarity in female-dominated careers, men tend to get noticed and are considered by decision makers to be more suited to management roles. Not only are men a rarity in our workforce but they are also moving into management roles more quickly – typically, away from daily interaction with children. If this is the case, not only does it reinforce discrimination against women by unfairly promoting men based on gender rather than ability and sustaining the gender imbalance in management, but it also exacerbates the lack of opportunity for boys and girls to interact with men and women on an ongoing basis.

The few men we do have in the Early Years sector are sometimes fast-pathed up and away from day-to-day practice. The glass escalator theory suggests that such promotions are based purely on gender. *As traditionally the main bread winner in a family, could it be that men are in greater need of more money and therefore more likely to apply for these roles? Might men consider management as a route out of day-to-day hard work with the children into what might be perceived as a more office-based role?*

Scenarios

Connor, an experienced and qualified practitioner has recently joined your Early Years team, as the only male. You have noticed that he receives preferential treatment in terms of workload compared to his female colleagues; that your manager defers to him and avoids challenging him on his shortcomings such as incomplete development records.

- What are your feelings about this?

- What, if anything, do you feel you should do about it?

Following the promotion of Brian to the role of deputy manager, discussion in the staff room has expressed surprise and consternation that someone with so little experience gained promotion over a more experienced female colleague. There is a general feeling amongst the team that the decision was influenced by his gender.

- What evidence is there that Brian has benefited from a 'glass escalator' in this incidence?

- How could you challenge this decision?

Peer (and other) pressure/sense of identity

I am not aware of many seven-year-old boys who have an ambition to pursue a career as an Early Years practitioner. For the vast majority, not only is it nowhere near the top of their 'What I want to be when I grow up' list, it does not feature on the list at all. Notions of possible career options start to form at a very young age. As noted by Kandola and Kandola (2013, p.44), 'Children learn from a young age the gender of the person they expect to be carrying out certain roles. Since work is such an important part of our lives, these observations and decisions are critical for our subsequent life paths.' Established and accepted expectations of the gender of those eligible to work in Early Years results in a system that maintains the status quo. We are confident in asserting that 'childcare' is never offered as a career choice to teenage boys by advisors. It is simply not considered as a viable option for them.

Of the many men we have interviewed who do enter our sector, typically they relate an indirect route into their job role. In some cases, a family member – mother, sister or partner – was working in an Early Years setting and invited the male relative in, as a volunteer, for work experience or on a short-term basis. In other cases, the opportunity arose as a result of a voluntary or enforced career change. Having experienced the Early Years for himself, he discovered that not only is it a worthwhile endeavour but it is also a valid and fulfilling job. These men are often made aware of the potential for them to pursue a vocation in Early Years, almost by accident.

The challenge comes putting this idea into practice. Young men are at a stage in life when they are forging their identity in terms of personality, status, sexuality, beliefs and relationships. As we have previously discussed, there are tremendous social pressures affecting the decisions individuals make with respect to their plans for life. When it comes to a career, the reasons we have explored in this chapter have a significant influence on choices – culture, gender expectations, pay and status. As young adults, what others think of us can be hugely influential. For a young man to pronounce his intention to pursue a career in Early Years frankly takes courage. Parents/carers, teachers and peers may all hold a view that not only is this a strange thing to do but it also represents a rejection of the more normal career paths offering potentially more lucrative and higher-status possibilities. Let us consider the example of a hypothetical young man, Ben, who is interested in a career in Early Years. He may be seen as wasting his life and those around him may view it as their moral responsibility to dissuade him. To persist in the face of such discouragement takes a strong will and inner confidence. Ben can be assured that he will be in a minority in his workplace and on any training courses. Coupled with ongoing suspicion, this can be a precarious and socially isolating career choice. Without support and encouragement, it is unsurprising that a significant number of men are deterred. Perhaps initial expectations and promises of the role are not sustained. Disillusion can arise from any of the areas we have discussed above – low pay, status, suspicion, isolation, and fear. It is evident that induction, mentoring, networking, support, supervisions, anti-discriminatory practice, professional development and equal opportunities are all key elements in managing in a mixed gender staff team if we want to attract, retain and develop the best people.

CASE STUDY

Practitioner L had his first experience of working with children in an educational context, at age 15, when he undertook work experience at his local primary school. The opportunity to work with children aged four and five years, gave him a flavour of the possibilities of a career in Early Years. The class teacher recognised and documented his talent and suitability for this role, particularly how he managed to build supportive relationships with the children in such a short space of time. This encouragement helped him decide to pursue Early Years as a career. He says that without that initial support, he would not have had the confidence to apply for an apprenticeship and neither would he have had the backing of his parents who subsequently stood by his decision and helped him with the challenges he has faced as a man being a minority in the workforce.

As a target group for recruitment into the Early Years workforce, older men are potentially more confident in their identity, in some cases through the experience of being a father. They are at a later stage in life, possibly second career seekers, who are more likely to be comfortable in who they are and how they relate to others including children, female colleagues and the parents of children attending Early Years settings. This, by itself, does not mitigate all of the deterrents to men working in Early Years but it can provide a strong source of inner determination and greater social acceptance. Such men may have had more life experience and specific hands-on child care and development experience. If they have settled the issue of pay, status and identity in their own mind, they are arguably freer to pursue their vocation, relating to children and female colleagues from a position of security. *Men in Childcare, Scotland* (www.meninchildcare.co.uk) is an example of an organisation which continues to experience success in recruiting older men onto its all-male training programmes and placing them into jobs in Early Years.

ACTIVITY

Choose one of the following activities to undertake with the support of a colleague:

- Consider how to best support young men in your setting.

- Contact training providers and local colleges to ascertain their approach to and support for male students.

- Consider what actions to take to encourage second-career men to apply for job vacancies in your organisation.

- Produce literature explaining the importance of our role, career paths and the need for men and women in our sector that would support men in explaining their job to friends and relatives.

- Actively invite men into your setting for work experience or volunteering.

We bring this chapter to a close by briefly considering some of the main ideas which have been discussed in it. The historical and continuing gender imbalance in the Early Years workforce is sustained by a complex interplay of factors grounded in our cultural beliefs, perceptions and expectations about gender roles, promoted and reinforced by our media, and outworked in practice in the relative status and associated remuneration awarded to the job role. Any determination or initiative to effect change must acknowledge the current situation and the reasons for it. It is not possible to change the world overnight but we can all individually affect our sphere of influence and work together to enlarge it. It is for each of us to decide what our involvement will be in whatever capacity we perceive our role – as a colleague, employer, ambassador, advisor, blogger, policy maker, journalist, visitor into schools, careers advisor, training provider or network organiser. We all need one another to make a difference. We can each do our bit to inform, educate, counter prejudice, campaign, advocate, support and encourage. Reflecting on our own beliefs and practices is a good starting point for developing an action plan. It is our recommendation that you use the provocations and questions in this chapter to challenge the status quo in your organisation and explicitly formulate a plan for change. But what does success look like? Whilst an increase from 2 per cent to 3 per cent of men in the Early Years workforce is a small increment, this would be a 50 per cent increase on the current level. For a setting with no male workers, a single man joining the team represents a significant statement of diversity, equality and change of culture in our workforce. We can change the world – one man at a time!

References

Birrell, I. (2015) '750,000 UK men want child sex, say crime chiefs' *The Mail Online*, 21st June. Accessed 19 November 2016 at https://www.dailymail.co.uk/news/article-3132884/750-000-British-men-want-sex-children-Shock-new-abuse-statistics.html

BBC News (2015) 'Operation Hydrant.' Accessed 13 April 2017 at https://www.bbc.co.uk/news/uk-34977255

Bichard, M. (2004) *The Bichard Enquiry Report.* Accessed 13 April 2017 at http://dera.ioe.ac.uk/6394/1/report.pdf

Brody, D. (2014) *Men Who Teach Young Children.* London: Institute of Education Press.

Coates, S. (2016), 'Leadsom: male carers might be paedophiles', *The Times*, 15th July. Accessed 4 January 2017 at https://www.thetimes.co.uk/article/leadsom-male-carers-might-be-paedophiles-btxfs8hx7

Department for Education (DFE) (2014) 'National Statistics, School Workforce in England: November'. Accessed 13 June 2016 at www.gov.uk/government/statistics/school-workforce-in-england-november-2014

Encyclopaedia Britannica (1998) 'Public opinion.' Accessed 13 April 2017 at www.britannica.com/topic/public-opinion

Equal Pay Act (1970) Accessed 13 April 2017 at www.legislation.gov.uk/ukpga/1970/41/pdfs/ukpga_19700041_en.pdf

Fawcett Society (2016) 'Gender Pay Gap and Causes Briefing Equal Pay Day – 10th November 2016.' Accessed 13 April 2017 at https://www.fawcettsociety.org.uk/Handlers/Download.ashx?IDMF=ae288cc4-81b0-4c11-a45b-a1bd4836c8e3

Gerhardt, S. (2014) *Why Love Matters: How Affection Shapes a Baby's Brain.* 2nd edn. London: Routledge.

Goudreau, J. (2012) 'A New Obstacle For Professional Women: The Glass Escalator.' Accessed 15 June 2016 at www.forbes.com/sites/jennagoudreau/2012/05/21/a-new-obstacle-for-professional-women-the-glass-escalator/#6d3a82b21135

Institute for Public Policy Research (2015) 'One third of mothers in working families are breadwinners in Britain.' Accessed 15 April 2017 at www.ippr.org/news-and-media/press-releases/one-third-of-mothers-in-working-families-are-breadwinners-in-britain

Jones, H. (2017) 'Maintained Nursery Schools Funding.' House of Commons Hansard. Accessed 3 January 2018 https://hansard.parliament.uk/Commons/2017-02-01/debates/60D822FE-9B15-4DE5-8649-A291034BF064/MaintainedNurserySchoolsFunding

Kandola, B. & Kandola, J. (2013) *The Invention of Difference: The Story of Gender Bias at Work.* Oxford: Pearn Kandola Publishing.

Kelly, B. (2016) 'Andrea Leadsom doesn't trust male nannies – and if you're honest, neither do you.' *The Telegraph,* 18 July. Accessed 19 November 2016 at www.telegraph.co.uk/news/2016/07/18/andrea-leadsom-doesnt-trust-male-nannies--and-if-youre-honest-ne

London Early Years Foundation (2012) 'Will Jimmy Savile case put men off working in childcare?' Accessed 13 April 2017 at www.telegraph.co.uk/women/mother-tongue/9684111/Will-Jimmy-Savile-case-put-men-off-working-in-childcare.html

Marshall, G. (2009) *Oxford Dictionary of Sociology.* Oxford University Press.

Maslow, A. H. (1954) *Motivation and Personality.* New York: Harper and Row.

McCombs, M. & Shaw, D. (1972) 'The agenda-setting function of mass media.' *Public Opinion Quarterly* 36(2), 176.

National College for Leadership (2013a) *Early Years Educator (Level 3): Qualifications Criteria.* Accessed 14 January 2017 at www.gov.uk/government/uploads/system/uploads/attachment_data/file/211644/Early_Years_Educator_Criteria.pdf

National College for Leadership (2013b) *Teachers' Standards (Early Years).* Accessed 14 January 2017 at www.gov.uk/government/uploads/system/uploads/attachment_data/file/211646/Early_Years_Teachers__Standards.pdf

Netmums (2012)'The changing face of modern UK families.' Accessed 1 October 2018 at https://www.netmums.com/coffeehouse/other-chat-514/news-12/766143-changing-face-modern-uk-families.html

Newsweek (2015) 'Extensive U.K. child abuse probe include high-profile figures.' Accessed 14 April 2017 at www.newsweek.com/extensive-uk-child-abuse-probe-includes-high-profile-figures-334222

Nickerson, M. & Femiano, S. (1989) 'How do Media Images of Men Affect Our Lives?' *Media & Values*, 48. Accessed 3 December 2016 at http://www.medialit.org/reading-room/how-do-media-images-men-affect-our-lives

Nutbrown, C. (2012) 'Foundations for quality: The independent review of early education and childcare qualifications – Nutbrown review' Ref: DFE-00068-2012. Accessed 14 April 2017 at www.gov.uk/government/uploads/system/uploads/attachment_data/file/175463/Nutbrown-Review.pdf

Professional Love in Early Childhood Education and Care (n.d.) Accessed 1 October 2018 at https://pleysproject.wordpress.com

Taylor, J. (2018) 'Just 8,700 new parents claimed shared parental leave in the last year.' Accessed 15 February 2018 at www.emwllp.com/latest/claimed-shared-parental

Terry, D.J. & Hogg, M. A. (2001) 'Attitudes, behaviour, and social context: The role of norms and group membership in social influence processes.' In J.P. Forgas and K.D. Williams (Eds) *Social influence: Direct And Indirect Processes*. New York: Psychology Press. (pp. 253–270)

The Telegraph (2009) 'Vetting and barring: This culture of suspicion needs to change.' Accessed 14 April 2017 at https://www.telegraph.co.uk/comment/telegraph-view/6807460/Vetting-and-barring-This-culture-of-suspicion-needs-to-change.html

Too Much Too Soon (2016) 'School Readiness.' Accessed 13 April 2017 www.toomuchtoosoon.org/school-readiness.html

Travis, A. (2010) 'Charities warn against scaling back vetting and barring scheme too far.' *The Guardian*. Accessed 15 April 2017 at www.theguardian.com/society/2010/jun/15/charities-warn-diltuing-vetting-scheme

Williams, C. L. (1992) 'The glass escalator: Hidden advantages for men in the "female" professions.' *Social Problems*, 39(3), 253–267.

World Health Organization (WHO) (1998) 'Gender and Health: Technical Paper 1998.' Accessed 13 June 2016 at www.who.int/reproductive-health/publications/WHO_98_16_gender_and_health_technical_paper/WHO_98_16.introduction.en.html

CHAPTER 3

What is it Like for Men Working in the Early Years?

SIMON BROWNHILL

Overview

Having investigated the low number of men working in the Early Years sector in Chapter 1 and the reasons for this in Chapter 2, we now explore what it is like for those men who do work with young children. Drawing on established thinking and new research that explores the 'lived experiences' of men in the field (Bryan and Browder 2013, p.142), we consider the reality for male practitioners who are employed in the Early Years sector in England. A balance of what we like to call 'positives and not-so-positives' are considered in an effort to facilitate critical discussion and reflection. We argue that men are likely to encounter a complex blend of opinions, responses and incidences which make working in the Early Years sector an enjoyable experience for most and a challenging one for some. The chapter initially explores some of the reasons why men choose to work with young children.

Why do men want to work with children in the Early Years?

It may be rather matter-of-fact but working with young children is, for most, a paid job. As such, men work in the Early Years sector for the simple reason of employment, 'being the breadwinner' (Focus Group Participant (FGP) 2) and earning a regular (if not small) wage. However, there is a widely held view that people who work in the Early Years do not do it 'just for the money'. So why do men choose to work in the Early Years sector? Established reasoning in the sector, as highlighted by Brownhill (2015), includes:

- actually liking children

- the satisfaction of the job

- being a role model for young children

- the constant variety that the Early Years provides for both children and adults ('No two days are the same!'), and

- 'wanting to make a difference' in children's lives. ('It's more than just playing!', FGP 4).

Additional reasoning by Romei (in Friedman 2010, p.42) advocates that early childhood '[t]eachers become teachers because of their love for children and their passion for the profession'. Our research suggests that men also choose to work in the sector because they:

- want to 'allow [children] to enjoy being a child' (Practitioners A and B), and

- have an 'interest in education [and] the challenge of teaching in another country and another culture' (Practitioners C and D).

All of the above show men choosing to work in the Early Years sector for what we consider to be the right reasons, with most of them focusing on the children, e.g. 'giving children opportunities that they might not have had before' and 'broadening the children's minds' (Practitioners A and B). For some men, however, choosing to work in the sector can simply be out of necessity due to issues of redundancy or unemployment; for others, it can be seen as a quick way for ambitious individuals to 'fast-track' up the professional ladder to a position of expertise and authority with financial benefits (Warin 2015). A rather disturbing reason, proffered by Andrea Leadsom, the former Secretary of State for Environment, Food and Rural Affairs, suggested that a man's desire to work with young children was 'for ulterior motives' (see Gaunt 2016). We strongly argue that this unfair association with wanting to harm children is one of the key reasons why men choose *not* to work or train in the Early Years sector for fear of being accused of 'sexual deviance and/or exploitation' (Petersen 2014, p.2).

An interesting reason offered by Participant E in our research suggested that he 'wanted to work in a natural relaxed environment without the pressures of grades or targets'. It is claimed that increased accountability measures are turning education settings in England into 'exam factories' (Hutchings 2015, p.67). This creates unnecessary stress on both learners and educators as they work tirelessly in a challenging, target-driven environment. We argue that the Early Years sector is becoming increasingly 'targeted' as a result of external top-down pressure to assess the value-add of teaching – this is clearly evident through the use of the Progress check at age two (see DfE 2017b, p.13–14) and the Early Years Foundation Stage Profile at the end of the EYFS (see DfE 2017b, p.14–15) which, whilst ostensibly implemented to ensure early identity of needs and the provision of appropriate support, have become in effect additional tests on children at an early age. Coupled with internal pressures to engage in ongoing baseline assessment and targeted observations of children, the demands and expectations on Early Years staff make it progressively difficult for them to practise in a 'stress-free' setting. With this in mind, whilst there are many positive reasons as to why men choose to work with young children, there are numerous reasons which can actually *deter* them from entering the profession or make it difficult or 'problematic' for them to effectively practise in the sector. But how do men who work in the Early Years actually 'get into it'?

How do men 'get into' the Early Years?

There are numerous routes or 'pathways' that men can take to work in the Early Years sector. This can be exemplified by examining the different routes that were taken by the two authors of this book.

CASE STUDIES

DAVID

David studied economics at a London university, followed by a 25–year career in computing. He joined his wife in their day nursery business in 2005, having retrained in child development via an NVQ Level 3 qualification followed by the achievement of Early Years Teacher Status. David has worked as a practitioner, nursery manager and as joint 'hands-on' owner of *Paint Pots*

Nurseries, Southampton, comprising (in 2017) of six day nurseries, three pre-schools and an after-school club.

SIMON

At the age of 18, Simon began a three-year BEd Primary teaching degree with a specialism in the 3–7 age range undertaken in the final year. He initially secured a Year One class teacher position which was then followed by a Reception (Foundation Two) post in a brand new primary school. After working in Higher Education as a Senior Lecturer for a number of years, Simon became an Assistant Head Teacher for the Early Years (3–6) in a large inner-city, culturally diverse primary school where he also served as a nursery teacher in a 120-place Foundation Unit.

Our research suggests that men follow one of two main routes to working in the Early Years sector – we refer to these as the *traditional* route and the *non-traditional* route. For those who followed the traditional route, a steady progression from school to further education to higher education (university) to full-time employment provided them with opportunities to practise with young children as part of their voluntary work or placements that were integral to their vocational courses. For others, the non-traditional route meant that some men *stumbled* into the Early Years as a result of dropping out of their AS levels (Practitioner F), doing supply work for a local agency (Practitioner E), or 'finding the passion through having a family' (Practitioners A and B). Practitioner G's journey into the Early Years supports the idea of a steady progression through his 'incremental gaining of Early Years experience', this being 'through voluntary play group roles, working as a parent of young children, into increasing responsibilities and professional training, e.g. EYPS and salaried pathway for School Direct'. For some men, working in the Early Years is simply a 'second chance career…following a period out of paid work and a review of options' (Rolfe 2005, p.8).

We acknowledge that there is seemingly no one way or 'best way' (Practitioners A and B) for men to get into the Early Years profession – the routes that people take are seemingly dependent on things such as circumstances, opportunities, awareness and motivation. In the case of Aaron Checkley at Westhill Corner Day Nursery & Pre-school (Wale 2017), we can clearly see the important role that exploration and guidance played in him becoming a nursery practitioner:

Why did you decide to choose a career in childcare?

I had always wanted to work with children since I was about 11. Originally, I had wanted to be a teacher but as I got older I explored different career options with children and decided on being a nursery practitioner.

Was childcare a career path that was ever suggested to you?

It was suggested to me by my teacher at school, Mrs Donohue. She thought I would work well with younger children.

(Interview extract)

What is considered important in all of the above is the support given to men by others as they follow their chosen pathway; male practitioners in our research, for example, recognised the influence of 'mentors and significant others (role models!) who made things happen [and] encouraged us' (Practitioner G). Clearly, the positive attitudes shown by these different individuals had some part to play in the successful recruitment and retention of these men in the sector. But are all attitudes towards men in the Early Years as positive?

What are people's attitudes towards male practitioners in the Early Years?

REFLECTION

In 1984, Robinson, Skeen and Coleman undertook a national study in the USA which assessed the attitudes of men and women 'toward the suitability, professional practice, and administrative capabilities of men in early childhood education' (p. 101). They found that men and women held similar views toward the capabilities and roles of male preschool teachers across all of these areas, thus challenging many of the popularly held beliefs and stereotyped attitudes about men in the early childhood field.

What do you think were some of these beliefs/attitudes and how do you think they compare to attitudes (perceived/actual) 30-plus years on? Compare your thoughts with the discussion below.

One of the most common and seemingly persistent opinions of 'other people...is that the Early Years is for women' (Practitioner H)

Unfortunately, this adds weight to the assertion that a job in the Early Years is 'women's work' (Peeters 2007, p.2) and is thus something that men should not or cannot do. We feel it necessary to critically unpick this widely-held view for it is one which we strongly oppose.

'Other people' – who might they be?

Bartlett (2015, p.4) suggests that these other people might include 'parents, colleagues and peers'. Indeed, international research efforts have been made to explore the attitudes of these different groups. A summary of interesting findings from three separate pieces of research are presented in the table below:

Table 3.1: Male practitioners in the Early Years and the perceptions of parent, colleagues and peers

Type of perception	Parental perceptions	[Female] colleagues' perceptions	Peer [friends'] perceptions
	Rentzou (2011)	Sak, Sahin and Sahin (2012)	Erden, Ozgun and Ciftci (2011)
Positive	'[M]ales can behave in the same ways as females and that they can be as nurturing as their female co-workers' (p.143)	Men are more 'professional' and 'objective' (p.588) in terms of their professionalism in the pre-school sector	No positive perceptions identified
Negative	'[P]arents in general are not supportive and accepting of males' (p.143)	'[S]ince preschool teachers should sometimes be a caregiver…males are not appropriate for this role' (p.589)	'My friends found [it] strange' (p.3202) 'They did not think that a male [caregiver could] do this job' (p.3203)

Some of the negative perceptions offered above mirror those drawn from our own research, with Practitioners A and B openly offering verbal comments that were made in response to them telling others of their employment in the Early Years sector:

We recognise that the attitudes of others towards men in the Early Years are not just limited to parents, colleagues and peers; the views of carers, head teachers/senior management teams, governors/committees and the local community should also be taken into consideration as well. But what are their attitudes and how do they compare to the perceptions of others?

ACTIVITY

Select one of the groups of people from the list below:

- Carers

- Head teachers/senior management teams

- Governors/committees

- The local community.

Using appropriately designed questionnaires, interviews or informal discussions, seek to find out their attitudes towards men in the Early Years sector either in your placement or your work setting. How do their views compare to your own personal/professional perceptions?

Is the Early Years really *'women's work'*?

In our view, the answer is quite simply *'no'*. Traditionally, caring for and working with children was seen as a predominantly female occupation (Owen 2003). However, radical changes in the family model and work patterns over the past few decades have resulted in more men actively caring for their children. As such, from our recent experiences of working with and supporting male professionals in the field, we firmly believe that men are just as capable as women in supporting the learning, development and care of young children;

they can 'read books, change nappies, fold laundry, prepare snacks, settle disputes, and so on' (Andrew 2010, p.12). This is evident in the case study below.

CASE STUDY

When Jamie, 23, joined an independent setting as an out-of-school play worker, his female colleagues were sceptical that he could actually do the job. Admittedly, his application was not the best, and his organisational skills were in need of development, but his ability to support children to follow their own play ideas and interests was instantly impressive. His careful questioning skills and enthusiastic manner meant that he could empower even the most reluctant of children to be creative, take risks and collaborate with others. He quickly became a competent team player, working hard to complete necessary paperwork on time and set up play areas, materials and equipment in safe and attractive ways. Liked by the children and the parents, Jamie 'won over' his female colleagues who relished his good sense of humour and commitment to promoting healthy food choices for children.

There are many positive attitudes towards men in the Early Years, examples of which include:

- they can help to make Early Years settings 'father-friendly' (Kahn 2006)

- they can establish a more balanced and diverse workforce (Envy 2013), and

- they have a 'positive influence' (Harty 2012) on children, particularly boys who are from single parent households, dysfunctional families or disadvantaged areas.

We argue that this positive influence can actually support *all* children – boys *and* girls – including those who come from stable, functional or affluent families (Canetto 1996). But how might this positive male influence benefit children? Suggestions from a learning perspective include:

- motivating reluctant learners (boys and girls)

- positively addressing behavioural difficulties (boys and girls), and

- helping to close the gender attainment gap between boys and girls, particularly in literacy and language development (see Read 2016).

Unfortunately, many settings are unable to reap these perceived benefits due to the absence of men who are actually employed in their workplace. One reason for this absence is down to negative stereotyping. With societal attitudes perceiving male practitioners as 'either homosexuals, p[a]edophiles or principals [head teachers/managers] in training' (King 1998, p.3), adverse attitudes of this nature can impact on men's wellbeing, causing them to develop a negative attitude towards themselves, their work and their employment in the Early Years sector. For some male practitioners this can be a contributing factor to them leaving the profession (see Manlove and Guzzel 1997). Clearly the way that people feel and are made to feel affects their perceptions of themselves and their work. So how does working in the Early Years as a man make them feel?

What does it feel like being a man in the Early Years?

As has been previously discussed, there are numerous reasons why men choose to work in the Early Years sector, with one of these reasons relating to how the job makes them feel – *satisfied*. We believe that men are likely to feel pride, joy, valued, worthwhile and energised when working in the sector; indeed, as Practitioner F puts it, 'I'm really proud of what I do as it's such a privelige [sic] to work with young children.' However, excessive workloads, stress, a lack of quality support (Crown 2015), and cultural, religious or social concerns about their employment in the sector inevitably results in many male practitioners feeling isolated, under suspicion or discriminated against.

REFLECTION

Consider the following comments made by different people to men who work in the Early Years, reflecting on how hearing these is likely to make male practitioners feel:

- 'None of the female colleagues in the setting are interested in football or cars I'm afraid.' (Room leader, Private Day Nursery)

- 'But why does *he* have to work in the Baby Unit? *Ugh!* It's just not right!' (Step-parent)

- 'We all hate the cold here so because you're the only bloke we'll timetable you for outdoor play duty till the spring, okay?' (Teaching Assistant, Reception class)

Consider how you might be able to effectively support men who hear/ are faced with these comments.

One of the most troublesome issues that men in the Early Years are likely to face is the suspicion that surrounds their presence in an Early Years setting. The 'more sinister undertones of people questioning their trust in men in an environment of children' (JJ 2016) are likely to fuel paedophilic assertions or accusations of abuse that unfortunately target men as the perpetrators. This is clearly felt by a male participant, as reported by Page (2015, p.11):

> What really bothers me is that those parents who argue that there are not sufficient men in Early Years settings, primary school settings, and child care, are also the first to accuse men of inappropriate behaviour towards (their) children. And only then these parents wonder why so many men shy away from working with children. Only then society comes to the conclusion that men are insensitive towards children and ignoring/neglecting/avoiding their duty of care towards children. As a male [practitioner] working with children I simply cannot win, and regardless of what I do I know it is only a matter of time before I get accused.

Coupled with 'sensational' national media coverage of child abuse cases involving male educators, e.g. Nigel Leat (BBC 2012) and Mark Maclennan (BBC 2015), men understandably have to be 'extra careful' (Clay in Cohen 1992, p.12) in their interactions with young children.

TAKE NOTE!

The Vanessa George abuse case (Plymouth Safeguarding Children Board 2010) not only highlighted the risk of abuse that could occur in a nursery setting, but also highlighted the fact that offenders could be female. However, statistics suggest that

'[t]he majority of reported abuse is carried out by male abusers'
(National Society for the Prevention of Cruelty to Children 2013,
p.3)

The effects of any allegations or accusations of child abuse, even when
unproven, can be extremely damaging for both the male practitioner
and the setting:

> The [setting] may suffer from adverse publicity with a resultant loss of
> reputation and business. For an employee accused of physical and/
> or sexual abuse…[d]etails of the police investigation can be recorded
> on the employee's [DBS] record which may have a profound effect on
> their future employment prospects (Clay 2012, p.1).

So, in what ways do settings help men to take 'extra care' in their work
with young children? Good practice suggests that settings develop
and use the following to not only protect young children but also
professionals, be they male or female:

- a range of policies, e.g. safeguarding, whistleblowing, intimate
  care, and positive handling and touch

- specific roles, e.g. safeguarding co-ordinators, and

- explicit practices, e.g. no mobile phones in the working
  environment, the use of security checks at the recruitment
  stage, and installing webcams/CCTV in the setting.

We feel that the effective implementation and review of the above,
along with regular training, can help to support men in feeling safe
and dispel some of the fear that surrounds their presence in the Early
Years, thus allowing them to effectively 'get on with the day job'.

In recognition of the measures highlighted in this chapter to date,
we strongly believe that there is a need for action from *all* Early Years
settings to positively address the issues of isolation, suspicion and
discrimination that many male practitioners may face when working
in the Early Years sector (Farquhar *et al.* 2006), particularly as there is a
sense in which men are constantly being watched, more so than their
female counterparts because of the underlying suspicion of the motives
of any man who willingly elects to work with young children. We
offer a suite of strategies in the Strategy Box below for professionals
and settings to select from, adapt and embrace as part of their own
positive practice we are calling for:

STRATEGY BOX

POSITIVELY ADDRESSING THE ISSUE OF MALE ISOLATION

- Pair male practitioners together in the work setting.

- Encourage male practitioners to join local/regional men support groups, e.g. the London Network of Men in Childcare or the Bristol Men in Early Years Network.

- Actively promote 'Dads and Lads' or DUGS (Dads, Uncles, and Granddads) sessions in the setting so that male practitioners can make professional connections with people of the same gender.

- Offer male mentoring of men students or newly appointed male members of staff.

- Facilitate 'practitioner swaps' between settings to give men the opportunity to work together in the same workspace.

POSITIVELY ADDRESSING THE ISSUE OF MALE SUSPICION (ADDITIONAL IDEAS)

- Ensure that all practitioners are made aware of and regularly review the policies and practices that are put in place to protect them and the children they work with.

- Actively raise awareness of the achievements of male practitioners through newsletters, photographs on displays, social media tweets, publicity and marketing materials.

- Use Open Days as a way of visually promoting the presence and work of male practitioners in the setting.

- Promptly address staff/parent/carer comments and concerns to show male practitioners that you are 'on their side' and that you are in total support of them.

- Encourage male practitioners to 'meet and greet' parents/carers at the start of the day/session in an effort to build positive relationships.

POSITIVELY ADDRESSING THE ISSUE
OF MALE DISCRIMINATION

- Ensure that male practitioners have equitable access to practise with children of all ages in the setting.

- Provide discrimination training for all staff members to highlight implicit and explicit discriminatory behaviours, attitudes and practices in the setting towards both men and women.

- Positively address intentional and unintentional discrimination towards male practitioners through private discussions, written communication and appropriate disciplinary action.

- Review and revise policies and practices in the setting that inadvertently promote discriminatory practices.

- Assure a balance of positive discrimination in relation to professional training, promotion and other opportunities for both men and women in the setting.

It is worth reminding ourselves that the overarching question driving the content of this chapter is 'What is it like for men working in the Early Years?' An intriguing aspect for consideration relates to what it is like to be a man (male) in the Early Years sector. It is to this topic of discussion that we now turn.

What is it like being a man (male) in the Early Years sector?

Many studies of male practitioners in the Early Years consider the issue of masculinity (see Brody 2015; Moosa and Bhana 2017). When we talk about this, we favour Vann's (2016) definition which sees masculinity as 'a socially constructed concept that people selectively use to describe what a man *should* be and how he *should* act' [original emphasis]. But what should a man be like and how should he act? We recommend that you engage with the activity below before reading on.

ACTIVITY

Note: We suggest that you undertake this activity with a colleague or a peer where possible.

1. Working individually, make a list of the qualities/characteristics and behaviours that you consider a man (any man) should exhibit.

2. Compare your list with your colleague/peer – how similar or different are they?

3. Look again at the qualities/characteristics and behaviours that you have both identified. Group these into types of qualities/characteristics and behaviours, and then reflect on whether these types are more masculine or feminine in nature. Use the examples below to help you make a judgement of the qualities/characteristics and behaviours that you have both identified:

   - **Masculine** Strong, aggressive, dominant, macho, drinks beer, brave, rational, likes football, independent, competitive, leader.

   - **Feminine** Soft, kind, emotional, reflective, thoughtful, sensitive, caring, patient, tolerant, flexible, empathetic, a good listener, cooperative.

The qualities/characteristics and behaviours you have generated are likely to present a rich cocktail of similarities and differences between people's thinking. This is inevitable because of the way that different 'contexts, situations and expectations' shape our thoughts and opinions (Brownhill 2014, p.256). The purpose of the Activity above was to highlight the fact that there is no one construct of a man (or a woman). We argue that this applies to men who work in the Early Years and the forms of masculinity that they individually exhibit (see Brownhill, Warin and Wernersson 2016).

Examination of the masculine qualities/characteristics and behaviours presented in the Activity show a strong subscription to *conventional masculinity* (Connell 2002) or what stereotypically embodies 'a typical bloke'. The unprofessional nature of some of these characteristics means that they are inappropriate for men to exhibit when working in the Early Years. However, in an effort to promote *bravery, independence* and *rational thought* in young children, we believe these to be suitable traits/behaviours for male practitioners to exhibit. Previous research has found that some men in the Early Years sector are keen to demonstrate their 'blokeyness' or 'maleness' (Cameron 2006) by engaging in rough-and-tumble play, construction activities, outdoor provision and physical tasks to combat the commonly held assumption that men who work with young children are gay, or at least effeminate due to their 'sensitive/caring nature' (FGP 5). This undertaking of masculine activities resonates with the research of Brownhill (2015) who found that men in the Early Years were *expected* to practise in masculine ways; this was in relation to the following aspects:

- *Play:* male practitioners were expected to engage in more physical activity with children, e.g. 'rough and tumble, chasing/running, throwing, football' (p.173); male practitioners were also expected to engage in more boys' play, e.g. 'army, soldiers, guns, tools, fixing things, bikes…nature garden, hunting' (p.173).

- *Behaviour management:* male practitioners were expected to serve as 'a disciplinarian' (Brownhill 2013), embracing a strict style of management to effectively deal with the behaviour of children, especially boys.

- *Risk:* male practitioners were expected to encourage children to take more risks in their play, e.g. using real tools and 'resources that give the sensation of instability' (Tovey 2014, p.23).

- *'Dad' figures:* male practitioners were expected to serve as 'surrogate fathers' (Mills, Martino and Lingard 2004, p.363) or the 'father model' (Tsigra 2010, p.6) for children who came from single-parent, dysfunctional or social disadvantaged families.

- *Manual labour:* male practitioners were expected to collect and carry heavy things, e.g. boxes and equipment, due to their physical strength.

We are concerned about the existence of expectations like these as they place unnecessary restrictions on the practices of men with a rather one-dimensional view of masculinity. Given that quality Early Years practice is underpinned by values that are synonymous with feminine traits – 'patience, empathy, flexibility, tolerance, kindness, compassion…and affection' (Balchin 2002, p.31) – our research suggests that there are men who show strength in character and conviction through their alternative presentations of what they believe a man to be:

> I tell the children my favourite colour is pink, that it's okay to cry, everything in my power to combat what a man should be. (Practitioner F)

By engaging in activities such as cooking, talking on the telephone, arts and crafts and 'home corner' role play, it is clear that some active male practitioners are keen to show the children they work with what we like to call 'varied versions' of masculinity:

> I am particularly conscious that I am a male [practitioner] and I recognise that I need to display multiple masculinities, e.g. caring, sensitive, strong, calm, dominant, more subordinate, perhaps to show that there is more than one kind of man-identity dissonance. (Practitioner F)

The idea of multiple masculinities (Connell and Messerschmidt 2005) recognises the fact that there is no one way of being masculine; as such, we believe that a suite of masculinities is favourable for the offering in the Early Years in an effort to show young children diversity and recognition that there are different ways of being a man. However, we believe that the masculinities exhibited by men should be part of who they really are; as such, men should demonstrate *natural* dispositions, traits and behaviours so that they 'feel like themselves' as opposed to trying to be someone that they are not, largely because this is likely to be an impossible task to sustain. With this in mind, we acknowledge that being a man in the Early Years sector brings with it added pressure, as highlighted by the expected masculine practices detailed earlier. Brownhill's (2015, p.179–180) research offers further support for this assertion, recognising additional pressures that some men feel when working in the Early Years sector (0–8 years); these relate to:

- having to be a role model

- the demands of being professional at all times

- parental pressures, and

- the issues surrounding physical contact with children.

CASE STUDY

Max, 25, began working as a teaching assistant in a nursery class that was part of a primary school in a deprived area of the North East of England. Initially excited about his new role, Max was informed on his first day that he would be expected to deal with the many behavioural difficulties exhibited by the boys with SEND so that the class teacher could focus on the 'real job of teaching the others'. By the end of the first week Max had been called into the head teacher's office where he was told that the governors were expecting him to lead two or three after-school sports clubs for the children in Key Stage Two 'as everyone else in the school is too busy to run them'. With no financial incentive offered, Max reluctantly used his lunch times to plan activities for the newly formed football, hockey and basketball clubs. Parents who came to watch their children in the different clubs became increasingly demanding as they wanted their child to play in the most important positions when preparing for the inter-school competitions that were to take place later on in the school year. One single parent (female) also saw Max as a potential partner, expecting him to not only be her boyfriend but also 'take on' her two boys who were both at the school and who 'needed a father figure' so that they would 'toe the line' at home.

Sadly, Max handed in his resignation near the end of his second term at the school. His decision came as rather a shock to the head teacher, governors, nursery class teacher, parents and children.

The case study above highlights the importance of professional roles, responsibilities and expectations being discussed, negotiated and agreed/shared out as opposed to them being *forced* on individuals who may not be able, capable or willing to carry them out. We stress this point as we remain mindful of the concerning turnover of staff in the Early Years sector (National Day Nurseries Association 2016) which is likely to be prompted by the unnecessary pressures felt by practitioners, be they male or female. The process of discussion and negotiation can be facilitated through having open and honest lines of communication between staff members. These lines of communication are also important if professional and productive relationships are going to be established and sustained between colleagues. But what kind of relationships do men have with different people in the Early Years sector?

What kind of relationships do men have with different people in the Early Years sector?

One of the overarching principles that shapes quality practice in the Early Years is 'children learn to be strong and independent through positive relationships' (DfE 2017b, p.5). The importance of positive relationships for children *and adults* cannot be underestimated – our interest in this focus stems from our experiences of working in the Early Years sector where our professional relationships with parents/ carers and colleagues can be described as being warm, supportive and constructive, or reserved, tense and rather challenging!

Initially, when male practitioners enter an Early Years setting they may 'upset the apple cart' in the sense that they do not fit the norm, i.e. they are not female. As a result, men are likely to find some parents/ carers and colleagues a little distant, quiet or wary of them – *what is a man doing here? Is he any good? Will he directly be working/caring for my child? Has he had a DBS check?* In the case of 'Mark' (Robert-Holmes and Brownhill 2011) and *Childcare worker, nursery, 28* (Cooke and Lawton 2008), these negative reactions can make for an uncomfortable experience:

> There's one dad in particular – I can feel him staring at me as he leaves his daughter in my class. Sometimes he looks me up and down as if to say 'I'm watching you' – it makes me a bit paranoid to tell the truth. (Robert-Holmes and Brownhill 2011, p.123)

> I've had ones before…you can tell, they don't trust me. And it's fine, you give it a month down the line and they're fine… For men… they maybe feel a bit weird and think that people aren't going to trust me, they're going to question my motives. (Cooke and Lawton 2008, p.21)

Much 'concern…caution or even worry' (King 2015) from parents/ carers and male practitioners themselves relates to them touching children (Jones 2007) and offering children intimate care. Whilst this is understandable, particularly in light of recent high profile child abuse cases, we feel that it is important that men should be seen as 'one of the team'; as such, parents/carers need to know right from the start that their child's nappy will be changed by a practitioner irrespective of their gender. By doing this, settings are presenting a very clear message about their policies, their trust in the male practitioners who work there, and their commitment to equality in the workplace. For one male practitioner in our research, addressing parental concerns about intimate care 'head on' actually prompted a very positive outcome:

> A parent wasn't happy for me to change her daughter's nappy. I did it anyway and actually became close to the child and family'. (Practitioner D)

Our research suggests that the relationships male practitioners have with parents/carers and colleagues in the Early Years are 'really influenced by how long we have worked somewhere' (Practitioner G). By 'demonstrating professionalism' and 'an interest' (Practitioners C and D) in their work and the children, our findings suggest that 'views tend to change once people get to know you and realise your passion for children gaining a decent upbringing' (Practitioners A and B). There are simple ways that male practitioners can use to break down any negative view or perceptions that parents/carers may particularly have of them which we advocate as good practice:

GOOD PRACTICE

- Acknowledging parents/carers as they bring their child to the setting/collect them, e.g. by their surname ('Mrs X' or 'Mr Y').

- Showing a genuine interest in both the parent/carer and their child, e.g. 'Did you both enjoy seeing Peppa Pig on stage at the weekend?'

- Making time at the start and the end of the session/day to talk with parents/carers about everyday matters, addressing any issues or concerns that they may have.

- Seeing parents as partners (https://www3.havering.gov.uk/Documents/Education/PIPS/pips-good-practice-guide.pdf), seeking their knowledge and advice when addressing any difficulties involving their child in the setting.

- Inviting parents/carers as volunteers into the setting (this gives them first-hand experience of seeing men working in the Early Years sector, thus quickly dispelling their concerns).

- Sharing observations with parents/carers, e.g. photos/videos of their children interacting with male practitioners.

The DfE (2017a, p.24) highlights how a 'survey conducted in 2012 by Pre-school Learning Alliance and other major providers showed that 98 per cent of parents wanted men to be involved in childcare', a figure that matches the percentage of female nursery workers who said they wanted to work with male colleagues (Bartlett 2015). As such, there are likely to be parents/carers and colleagues who are pleased at the prospect of a man working with their young children/them, with men being welcomed with smiles, warm 'hellos' and even handshakes/hugs! This positive attitude towards men was clearly felt by a good number of the men involved in our research; for example, feedback from parents at events like Parents Evenings ('they talk about you and mention your name') made male practitioners feel they were 'getting better' in their practice which spurred them on to 'do more' (Practitioners C and D). However, it is important to recognise that these positive relationships with parents/carers and colleagues are not an automatic given; clearly it is a 'two-way street' with male practitioners having to earn the trust of parents/carers by exhibiting the kinds of characteristics that Colker (2008) considers to be reflective of effective Early Years educators; these include being patient, respectful, authentic (self-aware) and having a sense of humour.

Whilst the importance of positive relationships with parents/carers and colleagues cannot be underestimated, it is the relationships with the children that are clearly of the utmost significance. Indeed, Joseph and Strain (2004) assert that '[b]uilding positive relationships with young children is an essential task and a foundational component of good teaching'/practice. Our research suggests that men have 'good feelings with lots of positive attitudes' when working with young children on a daily basis; this is seemingly achieved by 'working with the children on their interests, being very patient, and being a good listener' (Practitioners C and D). Numerous other strategies can be embraced by practitioners, irrespective of their gender, to help build positive relationships with young children (see Durden 2011). As word limitations prevent us from exploring this further, we recommend that you engage in the following Activity to find out about the kinds of relationships that children have with male practitioners in your work setting/placement.

ACTIVITY

Seek opportunities to talk with young children about their relationships with male practitioners in your setting when on placement or in the workplace. Questions you might choose to adapt and ask to include:

- Do you like 'Matt'? Why/not?

- What do you like doing with 'Mr Trimbee'?

- Which practitioners do you like playing with? Why?

- How does 'Malcolm' make you feel when you work with him?

- In what ways does 'Mr Hallsworth' help you with your work?

- Is there anything you would change about 'Alan'? What would it be and why?

These questions could be asked during child-initiated play activities or during focused adult-led tasks. Carpet time and circle time opportunities may provide a useful time for children to contribute to a whole group discussion.

We bring this chapter to a close by considering some of the main ideas which have been discussed in it. There are many positive reasons why men choose to work in the Early Years sector. Attitudes from a range of people highlight a mixture of both encouraging and critical opinions in relation to the presence of men in the sector. The very nature of these views is likely to affect the ways in which men perceive themselves and their role in the Early Years sector; feelings of isolation, suspicion or discrimination are likely to result in a good number of men leaving the profession. However, the building of positive relationships with parents/carers, colleagues and children is seen as an important way of addressing any issues associated with their motives to work with those aged 0–5. The extent to which they are permitted, validated and supported in their ability to exhibit natural and varied forms of masculinity is likely to help male practitioners feel safe and respected in a collaborative working environment where differences are celebrated and different perspectives enrich both provision and practice.

References

Andrew, Y. (2010) 'I'm not a man, I'm a teacher'. *Every Child*, 16(1), 12–13.

Balchin, T. (2002) 'Male teachers in primary education.' *Forum*, 44(1), 28–33.

Bartlett, D. (2015) 'Men in childcare: How can we achieve a more gender-balanced Early Years and childcare workforce?' Marlborough: Fatherhood Institute. Accessed 23 June 2017 at www.fatherhoodinstitute.org/wp-content/uploads/2015/04/Men-into-Childcare-PDF.pdf

BBC (British Broadcasting Corporation) (2012) 'Nigel Leat sex abuse: "Lamentable failure" of school management.' *BBC News*, 26 January. Accessed 25 June 2017 at www.bbc.co.uk/news/uk-england-somerset-16725849

BBC (2015) 'Nursery abuse trial hears interview with three-year-old boy.' *BBC News*, 27 January. Accessed 25 June 2017 at www.bbc.co.uk/news/uk-scotland-highlands-islands-31007404

Brody, D. (2015) 'The construction of masculine identity among men who work with young children: An international perspective.' *European Early Childhood Education Research Journal*, 25(3), 351–361.

Brownhill, S. (2013) '"Build me a role model!" A critical exploration of the perceived qualities/characteristics of men in the Early Years (0–8)'. Seminar presentation given at Lancaster University as part of the Department of Educational Research Seminar Series 20 March. Accessed 13 August 2017 at www.lancaster.ac.uk/fass/doc_library/edres/13seminars/brownhills_20.03.13.pdf

Brownhill, S. (2014) 'Build me a male role model!' A critical exploration of the perceived qualities/characteristics of men in the Early Years (0–8) in England.' *Gender and Education*, 26(3), 246–261.

Brownhill, S. (2015) *The 'brave' man in the Early Years: The ambiguities of being a role model.* Saarbrücken, Germany: LAMBERT Academic Publishing.

Brownhill, S., Warin, J. and Wernersson, I. (Eds) (2016) *Men, Masculinities and Teaching in Early Childhood Education: International Perspectives on Gender and Care.* London: Routledge.

Bryan, N. and Browder, J. K. (2013) '"Are you sure you know what you are doing?"– The lived experiences of an African American Male kindergarten teacher.' *Interdisciplinary Journal of Teaching and Learning*, 3(3), 142–158. Accessed 26 June 2017 at files.eric.ed.gov/fulltext/EJ1063219.pdf

Cameron, C. (2006) 'Men in the nursery revisited: Issues of male workers and professionalism.' *Contemporary Issues in Early Childhood*, 7(1), 68–79. Accessed 27 June 2017 at journals.sagepub.com/doi/pdf/10.2304/ciec.2006.7.1.68

Canetto, S. S. (1996) 'What is a normal family? Common assumptions and current evidence.' *The Journal of Primary Prevention*, 17(1), 31–46.

Clay, J. (2012) *Child Safeguarding*. BLM (Berrymans Lace Mawer) Manchester. Accessed at 2 October 2018 at https://doctiktak.com/child-safeguarding.html

Cohen, D. (1992) 'Why there are so few male teachers in early grades.' *Education Digest*, 57(6), 11–14.

Colker, L. J. (2008) 'Twelve characteristics of effective early childhood teachers.' *Young Children*, March, 1–6. Accessed at 2 October 2018 at http://www.fbcherndon.org/weekday/docs/article_BTJ_Colker.pdf

Connell, R. W. (2002) *Gender*. Cambridge: Polity Press.

Connell, R. W. and Messerschmidt, J. W. (2005) 'Hegemonic masculinity: Rethinking the concept.' *Gender & Society*, 19(6), 829–859. Accessed 2 October 2018 at https://student.cc.uoc.gr/uploadFiles/181-%CE%9A%CE%9C%CE%9C%CE%9A397/Connell%20and%20Messerschmidt-Hegemonic%20masculinity.pdf

Cooke, G. and Lawton, K. (2008) *For Love or Money: Pay, Progression and Professionalization in the 'Early Years' Workforce*. London: ippr. Accessed 13 August 2017 at www.ippr.org/files/images/media/files/publication/2011/05/for_love_or_money_1633.pdf

Crown, H. (2015) 'Nursery workers consider leaving profession due to workload.' *Nursery World*, 23 October. Accessed 27 June 2017 at www.nurseryworld.co.uk/nursery-world/news/1154397/nursery-workers-consider-leaving-profession-due-to-workload

DfE (2017a) *Early Years Workforce Strategy*. March. Accessed 28 June 2017 at www.gov.uk/government/uploads/system/uploads/attachment_data/file/596884/Workforce_strategy_02-03-2017.pdf

DfE (2017b) *Statutory Framework for the Early Years Foundation Stage: Setting the Standards for Learning, Development and Care for Children from Birth to Five*. Accessed 25 June 2017 at www.foundationyears.org.uk/files/2017/03/EYFS_STATUTORY_FRAMEWORK_2017.pdf

Durden, T. (2011) *Making it Happen: Building Positive Relationships with Children. HEF601 Participant Guide*. University of Nebraska–Lincoln Extension. Accessed 13 August 2017 at http://digitalcommons.unl.edu/cgi/viewcontent.cgi?article=1042&context=cyfsfacpub

Envy, R. (2013) 'Developing the Children's Workforce.' In Envy, R. and Walters, R. *Becoming a Practitioner in the Early Years* London: Learning Matters, pp. 1–15.

Erden, S., Ozgun, O. and Ciftci, M. A. (2011) '"I am a man, but I am a pre-school education teacher": Self- and social-perception of male pre-school teachers.' *Procedia – Social and Behavioral Sciences*, 15, 3199–3204.

Farquhar, S. *et al.* (2006) *Men at Work: Sexism in Early Childhood Education*. New Zealand: Childforum Research Network. Accessed 28 June 2017 at www.childforum.com/images/stories/men.at.work.book.pdf

Friedman, S. (2010) 'Male voices in early childhood education.' *Young Children*, May, 41–45.

Gaunt, C. (2016) 'Outrage over Leadsom's comments that male childcarers might be paedophiles.' *Nursery World*, 15 July. Accessed 14 June 2017 at www.nurseryworld.co.uk/nursery-world/news/1158237/outrage-over-leadsoms-comments-that-male-childcarers-might-be-paedophiles

Harty, A. (2012) 'An exploration of the influence male childcare workers have when working with children.' In *Childlinks: Men in Early Years Care and Education.* Issue 1 (pp.22–26) Barnardos. Accessed 14 June 2017 at www.barnardos.ie/assets/files/publications/free/childlinks_body28.pdf

Hutchings, M. (2015) 'Exam factories? The impact of accountability measures on children and young people.' National Union of Teachers. Accessed 14 June 2017 at www.teachers.org.uk/files/exam-factories.pdf

JJ. (2016) 'Men battling gender imbalance in Early Years education.' *1 Big Database*, 24 February. Accessed 25 June 2017 at www.1bigdatabase.org.uk/blog_articles/433-men-battling-gender-imbalance-in-early-years-education

Jones, D. (2007) 'High risk men: Male teachers and sexuality in Early Years contexts.' *International Journal of Adolescence and Youth*, 13(4), 239–255. Accessed 13 August 2017 at www.tandfonline.com/doi/pdf/10.1080/02673843.2007.9747979

Joseph, G. E. and Strain, P. S. (2004) 'Building Positive Relationships with Young Children. Module 1 Handout 1.5: Building Relationships and Creating Supportive Environments.' The Center on the Social and Emotional Foundations for Early Learning, Vanderbilt University. Accessed 13 August 2017 at http://csefel.vanderbilt.edu/modules/module1/handout5.pdf

Kahn, T. (2006) *Involving Fathers in Early Years Settings: Evaluating Four Models for Effective Practice Development.* Report prepared for the Department for Education and Skills. Accessed 26 June 2017 at https://shop.pre-school.org.uk/document/751

King, D. (2015) 'Exploring parental attitudes towards male early childhood educators in the Republic of Ireland today.' *Researching Early Childhood: Children's Research Digest*, 2(2). Accessed 25 June 2017 at www.childrensresearchnetwork.org/knowledge/resources/exploring-parental-attitudes-towards-male-early-childhood-educators-in-the-republic-of-ireland-today

King, J. R. (1998) *Uncommon Caring: Learning from Men Who Teach Young Children.* New York: Teachers College Press.

Manlove, E. and Guzzel, J. (1997) 'Intention to leave, anticipated reasons for leaving and 12 month turnover of child care center staff.' *Early Childhood Research Quarterly*, 12(2), 145–167.

Mills, M., Martino, W. and Lingard, B. (2004) Attracting, recruiting and retaining male teachers: Policy issues in the male teacher debate. *British Journal of Sociology of Education*, 25(3), 355–369.

Moosa, S. and Bhana, D. (2017) 'Men managing, not teaching Foundation Phase: Teachers, masculinity and the Early Years of primary schooling.' *Educational Review*, 69(3), 366–387.

National Day Nurseries Association (NDNA) (2016) *Early Years Workforce Survey: England 2016.* Huddersfield: NDNA. Accessed 28 June 2017 at www.ndna.org.uk/NDNA/News/Reports_and_surveys/Workforce_survey_2016.aspx

National Society for the Prevention of Cruelty to Children (NSPCC) (2013) 'Child sexual abuse: An NSPCC research briefing.' July. Accessed 25 June 2017 at www.nspcc.org.uk/globalassets/documents/information-service/research-briefing-child-sexual-abuse.pdf

Owen, C. (2003) *Men's work? Changing the Gender Mix of the Childcare and Early Years Workforce.* London: Daycare Trust. Accessed 26 June 2017 at www.meninchildcare.co.uk/Mens%20Work.pdf

Page, J. (2015) *Professional Love in Early Years Settings: A Report of the Summary of Findings.* University of Sheffield Innovation, Impact and Knowledge Exchange (IIKE) in collaboration with Fennies Nurseries.

Peeters, J. (2007) 'Including men in early childhood education: Insights from the European experience.' *NZ Research in Early Childhood Education*, 10, 1–13. Accessed 23 June 2017 at http://stop4-7.be/files/janpeeters10.pdf

Petersen, N. (2014) 'The "good", the "bad" and the "ugly"? Views on male teachers in foundation phase education.' *South African Journal of Education*, 34(1), 1–13. Accessed 13 August 2017 at www.sajournalofeducation.co.za/index.php/saje/article/viewFile/772/394

Plymouth Safeguard Children Board (2010) *Serious Case Review. Overview Report. Executive Summary in respect of Nursery Z.* Accessed 27 June 2017 at www.cscb-new.co.uk/downloads/Serious%20Case%20Reviews%20-%20exec.%20summaries/SCR_Archive/Plymouth%20SCR%20-%20Nursery%20Z%20(2010)pdf

Read, C. (2016) *The Lost Boys: How Boys are Falling Behind in their Early Years.* London: Save the Children. Accessed 28 June 2017 at www.savethechildren.org.uk/sites/default/files/images/The_Lost_Boys_Report.pdf

Rentzou, K. (2011) 'Greek parents' perceptions of male early childhood educators.' *Early Years: An International Research Journal*, 31(2), 135–147.

Robert-Holmes, G. and Brownhill, S. (2011) 'Where are the men? A critical discussion of male absence in the Early Years.' In Miller, L. and Cable, C. (Eds.) *Professionalization, Leadership and Management in the Early Years.* London: Sage Publications, pp.119–132

Robinson, B. E., Skeen, P. and Coleman, T. M. (1984). 'Professionals' attitudes towards men in early childhood education: A national study.' *Children and Youth Services Review*, 6(2), 101–113.

Rolfe, H. (2005) *Men in Childcare.* EOC Working Paper Series, No. 35. Manchester: Equal Opportunities Commission. Accessed 27 June 2017 at www.koordination-maennerinkitas.de/uploads/media/Rolfe-Heather.pdf

Sak, R., Sahin, I. T. and Sahin, B. K. (2012) 'Views of female preschool pre-service teachers about male teaching colleagues.' *Procedia – Social and Behavioral Sciences*, 47, 586–593.

Tovey, H. (2014) 'All about…risk.' *Nursery World*, 13–26 January, pp.21–24. Accessed 25 June 2017 www.nurseryworld.co.uk/digital_assets/291/LDAllaboutRisk.pdf

Tsigra, M. (2010) 'Male teachers and children's gender construction in Preschool Education.' Paper given at the 26th World Congress, August 11–13, Göteborg, Sweden. Accessed 13 August 2017 at www.koordination-maennerinkitas.de/uploads/media/OMEP_2010_Tsigra_01.pdf

Vann, J. (2016) 'What is masculinity, exactly?' *HuffPost*, 23 November. Accessed 24 June 2017 at www.huffingtonpost.com/entry/what-is-masculinity-exactly_us_581e290be4b044f827a78dd1

Wale, L. (2017) 'Why aren't more men in childcare?' *Tommies Childcare*, 12 January. Accessed 13 August 2017 at www.tommieschildcare.co.uk/reading-corner/why-arent-more-men-in-childcare

Warin, J. (2015) 'Pioneers, Professionals, Playmates, Protectors, "Poofs" and "Paedos": Swedish Male Pre-school Teachers' Construction of their Identities.' In Brownhill, S., Warin, J. and Wernersson, I. (Eds) *Men, Masculinities and Teaching in Early Childhood Education: International Perspectives On Gender And Care.* London: Routledge, pp.95–106.

CHAPTER 4

Do We Need Men? Do They Make a Difference?

DAVID WRIGHT

Overview

We believe that having more men as part of the Early Years workforce is a good thing. However, does our opinion reflect the view of others, be they parents/carers, practitioners and children? In this chapter we consider the case for a more gender-balanced Early Years workforce in general and whether there is evidence that it makes a difference in the Early Years profession. We also look at the implications of the 2010 Equal Opportunities legislation in the English context with respect to positive action to redress the gender imbalance.

In Chapter 1 we noted the very low numbers of men working in the Early Years sector and examined some of the many reasons as to why this is the case in Chapter 2. We have also considered what motivates and fulfils those men who do make a successful career working with young children, recognising some of the challenges that they face in their continued practice. We believe it is also valid and necessary to ask the following questions: *So what? Does it actually matter that so few men currently work in the Early Years sector? What support is 'out there' for more men to work in the sector?* We aim to answer these questions in this chapter, initially by examining the views of society.

What does society want?

In Chapter 2, we considered the culture of groups, the concept of public opinion, the role of the media, and how data from surveys has been used to provide a representative voice for the 'man (and woman) on the street'. In Chapter 3 we explored the perceptions of 'other people' about men in the Early Years and the notion that they are engaged in 'Women's Work' (Nutbrown 2012, p.40). Rhetoric, survey results, policy and tabloid headlines do not necessarily accord with one another. For example, publicised concerns (Kelly 2016) expressed through the media about the potentially higher risk of child abuse through employing men suggests that society is fearful and averse to the idea, and yet as we have seen, survey results by the likes of Owen (2003) and MORI (2002) indicate that there is a strong desire from parents for their children to be cared for by both men and women. The Major Providers' Group Survey (cited in Pre-school Learning Alliance 2011) showed that 97.8 per cent of female Early Years practitioners in day nurseries support the notion of mixed gender teams. The key suggestion from the Early Years Workforce Strategy (DfE 2017, pp.25–26) that 'quality contact time with men' is seen as 'vital' underpins the DfE's belief in and commitment to a mixed gender Early Years workforce. At one level then, society, as represented by our government's published policy, acknowledges there is an issue here. It expresses a desire for children to interact with both men and women.

In an official capacity, as expressed in its government's policy document, society in England believes that children are missing out by not engaging with men and women in the Early Years; this implies that men can make a difference. Considering the available evidence from existing parent surveys, current policy statements and sensational media stories, perhaps the conclusion to be drawn is that, as a society, many of us are conflicted in our thinking about the efficacy of children experiencing Early Years care and education from both men and women. There appears to be support for the general principle but also continued unease about men's motives for entering what has been long thought of as a traditionally female role (Nutbrown 2012). It is our contention that initiatives and policy to effect change (be it at a local, national or international level) must address these areas explicitly in public relations campaigns in an effort to provide reassurance and demonstrate the benefits of having men working in the sector alongside their female colleagues. The promotion of positive images and testimonials of men working in the Early Years is a powerful tool for mitigating the fear and uncertainty that is generated from oppositional press stories. There are examples of organisations in England such as the London Early Years Foundation (www.leyf.org.uk), Kids Allowed (www.kidsallowed.com), Chapel House Day Nursery (http://chapelhousedaynursery.co.uk), Bright Horizons (www.brighthorizons.co.uk) and Tops Day Nurseries (www. topsdaynurseries.co.uk) successfully employing men and women together to provide childcare. We feel that these need to be publicised to raise awareness and promote diversity in the workplace.

ACTIVITY

Select images and profiles of male Early Years practitioners from any of the following suggested sources:

- Profiles of male practitioners (visit www.menteach.org/mens_stories)

- Podcasts recorded at the 2016 UK national Men in Early Years conference (visit www.samey.uk/conference and scroll to the bottom of the page)

- London Men in Childcare video (visit www.youtube.com/watch?v=u1owCB53zgo)

- Podcasts recorded by individual practitioners (visit www.kathybrodie.com/men-in-childcare-podcast)

- Toad Hall nursery group male practitioner profile (visit https://tinyurl.com/ycqmswgv)

Reflect on the messages conveyed. How might these be useful and applicable to your context/situation? How could you use these to support and encourage men and women in your professional team? How might these be used as recruitment resources? How could you use these to promote the benefits of a mixed gender team to:

- Parents/carers of the children you care for/teach?

- The local community/media/social media?

- Local primary and secondary schools?

- Careers advisors?

Society comprises all of us. We use this collective noun in representing our opinions and attitudes towards men working in Early Years but we also understand that there are various constituencies within society who may have different needs and wants. We examine some of these, starting with the children who are the recipients of Early Years care and education.

What do children want?

What children want and what they need is not necessarily the same thing! Returning to Maslow's Hierarchy of Needs (Maslow 1954), in the basic model, human necessities are stratified according to classification as *physiological, safety, care, esteem* and *self-actualisation*. Most adults, regardless of their gender, are capable of providing these for young children. Considering the typical Early Years practitioner's job description, the duties of the role are not differentiated for a man or a woman. Both are equally expected to care for and educate the children that they are responsible for. In our experience, young children do not express a preference for relationships or time spent with particular adults based solely on their gender. Boys and girls relate to men and women dependent on the 'fit' of their character, and crucially whether he or she pays attention to the child as an individual in a respectful, sensitive and supportive relationship that acknowledges his or her interests and needs. This accords with the guidance laid out in the Children Act (2004) requiring all adults working with children to promote their needs and wellbeing above everything else, and for Early Years settings to promote anti-discriminatory practice within their work.

In 2012, the London Early Years Foundation (LEYF) conducted research, albeit on a very small population – 56 staff and 23 children aged 3 and 4 years – to test the notion that children express a preference undertaking perceived gender-specific activities with different practitioners based on their gender, e.g. boys wanting to play football with men rather than with women. Conclusions in the resulting report ('Men working in childcare: Does it matter to children? What do they say?') did not support the hypothesis:

> The level of importance placed on a variety of activities by staff and whether or not they felt men could offer different and enhanced experiences to the children did not usually match the evidence provided by the children's choices. Some of the results show examples

of social stereotyping yet others are the opposite of what one might have anticipated. One cannot, of course, rule out that children's choices were made because of their personal preferences for certain staff members. (Chambers and O'Sullivan 2012)

FURTHER READING

Read this newspaper article on research into preference expressed by children aged seven to eight years on the gender of their teachers: www.theguardian.com/education/2006/jun/22/schools.uk3

Do you consider the findings of this research are applicable to children aged five years and under?

How do you feel these findings affect the case for recruiting men into the Early Years workforce?

We endorse the finding that children express 'personal preferences for certain staff members'. In our professional experience, some children relate better to certain individuals than to others – this is human nature. But do children want or need these individuals to be male or female? In the absence of male carers, we believe that we are not actually giving them the option. We have effectively restricted the available spectrum of Early Years practitioners, thus reducing the chance of meeting these children's needs. Diversity is not solely a gender issue. We believe that the Early Years workforce should reflect the true diversity of the community in terms of gender, race, sexual orientation, age, culture and character type.

Children may or may not express a desire to interact with both male and female carers but we believe it is necessary that they do so, particularly in their formative years. According to the Center on the Developing Child at Harvard University (2009), 'The Early Years matter because, in the first few years of life, more than 1 million new neural connections are formed every second. Neural connections are formed through the interaction of genes and a baby's environment and experiences, especially interaction with adults.' The first five years of a child's life are foundational in terms of physical brain development. At this stage the brain is 'plastic' – highly responsive and adaptive to successive stimuli:

> Almost everything in the brain is shaped by experience. It's true that every time we learn something, that learning physically changes our brains. (Gopnik 2016)

During this crucial phase of brain development, it can be argued that boys and girls need to build relationships with both men and women if they are to create a balanced inner model of the world. Where there are diminishing opportunities for children to interact with men, particularly where there is no father present in the home, boys and girls can potentially reach well beyond the first five years of life being cared for exclusively by women at home and in their Early Years settings. During this period, when the brain is most in need of repeated positive interactions with adults to determine how to respond to them (Mastergeorge 2014), the chance is gone for developing foundational neural pathways that guide children in how to interact with and respond to men. In this sense then, we would argue that whilst children may or may not express a desire or preference for interaction and relationship building with men as well as women, it is important to their development that they are given the opportunity to do so.

As the primary users of Early Years services, children's voices must be pre-eminent in shaping them. From the limited research that does exist, we conclude that children are less interested in the gender of their carers more than personal preference for individual characters, but how does this compare to what their parents think?

What do parents/carers want?

Available data concerning parents' views on men working in Early Years is becoming rather dated. The Major Providers' Group survey (cited in Pre-school Learning Alliance 2011) is, at the time of writing, six years old and the Men in Childcare survey (MORI 2002) is from 15 years ago. To ascertain what parents' attitudes are now, we conducted our own research for this book during November and December 2017 using a short online survey. We received 440 responses from parents of children attending a range of Early Years providers across England. Details about the survey can be found in the Introduction to this book.

We present select findings from our research in an effort to draw critical comparison between the findings of earlier surveys held in

2002 and 2011. In the discussion below, references to individual survey responses are identified as (nxxx) where xxx refers to the observation number, or (Parent, Observation number, Sex (M or F)).

Select findings from the survey

When asked, 92 per cent (n405) of respondents believed it is beneficial for children to be cared for by men as well as women in Early Years settings. This result is consistent across male and female respondents. Comments noting the benefits of a mixed gender Early Years workforce included:

> Having a mixed gender workforce would provide children with a more accurate reflection of the gender mix of their community and the world around them. It would provide my son with another male role model to look up to. (Parent 291, F)

> Less stereotyping, varied role models. (Parent 429, M)

> Children see a balanced approach, rather than thinking that childcare is something that just a female [practitioner] does. (Parent 414, M)

> I feel this is important to show our children that men and women can be caring. It also changes the dynamic of the Early Years workforce as males can bring a different perspective and way of thinking. It confirms equality which is what we are trying to teach children. (Parent 315, F)

Ninety-five per cent (n413) of respondents are happy for their child to be cared for by a male Early Years worker. This result is consistent across both genders of respondents. However, 14 per cent (n59) of respondents have concerns about men working in Early Years. Twelve per cent (n48) of female respondents indicate that they have concerns whilst 21 per cent (n11) of male respondents have concerns, a significantly greater percentage than the female respondents. Various reasons were identified in relation to the concerns parents had about men working in the Early Years. Of significance are the perceptions linked to fears about potential abuse, professional capabilities, media portrayal of men and what several individuals referred to as instinctive uncomfortable feelings:

> I am probably old fashioned but, according to the National Crime Agency, 1 in 35 men have sexual urges relating to children. This is

a terrifying prospect. I appreciate women are also capable of this however, I feel that some men can present a greater risk. (Parent 3, F)

Having worked for 10 years in child protection I am aware of the much higher ratio of male to female child abusers. (Parent 48, F)

My concern is it is unusual to see men in Early Years childcare. Media and society portrays men as being predatory where as women will inevitably come across as motherly. (Parent 392, M)

Children tend to be more scared of men. Men don't tend to want to work in this role and so I am suspicious of men that do. (Parent 50, F)

Due to lack of experience surrounding men in childcare, I am wary of the unknown also media portrayal of men and selfishly lack of trust although I know this is wrong. (Parent 434, F)

I do not believe that men instinctively have the same level of empathy as women to deal well with young children. (Parent 33, M)

Media cases have led to my nervousness around men working in Early Years. (Parent 401, M)

Select findings from the data are in line with previous surveys of parent/carer opinions such as the Major Providers' Group survey (cited in Pre-school Learning Alliance 2011) and the Men in Childcare survey (MORI 2002). The data shows overwhelming support from parents for a mixed gender Early Years workforce, however individual comments provide interesting insight into the reasons that reflect the sense of fear felt by some. There is a strong emotive element to these collective responses, as evidenced by the words used – 'terrifying', 'wary', 'predatory', 'child abusers', 'sexual urges', 'nervousness'. These findings confirm our assertion that some parents continue to subscribe to the prevailing culture of suspicion that surrounds men who work in the Early Years. Despite this, the overall support by respondents for more men to work in the Early Years is very encouraging.

CASE STUDY

We asked Nick Corlett, a male nursery manager at Chapel House Day Nursery in Norwood, to share with us the views of parents and prospective parents of children about the setting's mixed gender workforce. Nick says:

Just being a male manager is very bizarre because a lot of parents will come in and say, 'Oh, it's amazing isn't it? We've been to 20 nurseries this week and you're the first male manager.' We have quite a few parents on show-round saying that they like how many men are around. It's more of a gender-neutral environment. There's a different type of atmosphere with men in the room. They still have the nurturing side but it's a different type of nurturing side. Parents enjoy the fact that there's men around and females around. It's a more homely environment. Quite a few parents will come through and say, 'There's so many men here, it's great, isn't it?'

Nick says that the issue of parents not wanting male practitioners to change their child's nappies does come up and that they initially choose to respect parents' wishes and not to make it a point of principle. Their team is large enough to enable children to have nappies changed by willing female colleagues. He reports that once the parents have got to know the nursery and have built a relationship with the individuals in the team, they are then happy for the men to carry out intimate care routines for their child. Nick says it is a question of building trust and demonstrating that the men are safe and capable of doing this as part of an integrated team.

Nick's repeated description of his nursery is that it is a 'gender-neutral' environment. He refers to their homelike and extended family ethos which encompasses staff diversity in terms of age, race and sex. Their current oldest worker is 76! There is a demonstrable established culture where it is normal for men and women to work together as professional Early Years practitioners. Parents are aware of this and indeed express a choice for it by placing their children at the nursery.

REFLECTION

- How far do the views expressed by Nick reflect your own experience as a professional or parent/carer and the views of those you work with?

- Are there any ways in which your practice or opinions differ from those of Nick and his team? If so, what are the reasons for this?

We have examined the views of service users – children and their parents. We now turn our attention to those who deliver these services, the practitioners.

What do (male and female) practitioners want?

This is not a straightforward question to answer. In Chapter 2 we discussed the idea of women serving as potential gatekeepers. The fact that 98 per cent of the English Early Years workforce continues to be female suggests that there is little in the way of positive action to encourage more men to apply for jobs. This raises an important question: *In all-female teams, could this be the result of unconscious bias?* For clarification purposes, we turn to Notebaert (2017) who defines unconscious biases as 'assumptions, preferences or habitual thinking patterns that often surface as stereotypes and unconsciously can lead to incorrect decisions... People who we perceive as similar to us ... are quickly and unconsciously connected with positive emotions.' Given established conventions in the Early Years, it can be seen how unconscious bias could shape recruitment practice to perpetuate a female-only workforce by implicitly discounting men as potential candidates.

REFLECTION

- What assumptions, preferences or habitual thinking patterns might you or your team have about potential applicants for a vacant role in your Early Years organisation/setting?

- How might this affect your expectations of those who apply and your approach to the recruitment process?

What steps could be taken to mitigate the influence of any unconscious bias in your team?

Settings with male practitioners that we have spoken to have noted the benefits of having other men working as part of a mixed gender team. For example, Practitioner H said, 'I don't think a male [practitioner] brings anything specifically different than a female [practitioner] brings except for their presence'. Practitioner I suggested that 'Men have nurturing instincts. We have protective instincts. Why shouldn't we work with children? Why shouldn't we want our children to have the very best?' This is also reflected in the following case study.

CASE STUDY

The Sky High Achievers group of day nurseries has at one time managed to achieve 10 per cent of its workforce being male. Owner Fiona Atkinson refers to the complementary characteristics men and women bring to her Early Years staff team, in terms of enhanced experiences for children, improved team dynamics and cross-fertilisation of skills and confidence across different areas.

Fiona says:

Having men in my team is hugely important because there are a number of my families who don't have any male role models in the home or the ones that are in their children's lives, in some cases, are not necessarily positive. The dynamic that men bring to the team and to the nursery setting is so different and so beneficial to the children. Where you have a group of women, you do tend to get competitive gossiping and tittle-tattle. It is amazing how much this reduces with a male presence. Men are less tolerant to it, so it doesn't happen as much. They tend to be the problem solvers and those who calm situations down. They have a different outlook on certain situations in my experience.

We have seen a lot more physical play from our men, a lot more outdoor play and a lot more construction. Different language is used. They are setting themselves up as really good role models to the children who may not experience these types of interactions with men in the same way outside the caring and nurturing setting of the nursery environment.

We find that having that male member of staff in the setting can enhance what we offer children in various areas of development particularly, in our experience, in ICT, mathematics, the more practical areas and physical play. Men use a lot more construction specific language around building, making and lifting. They encourage the children to take more risk than maybe a woman would do. They tend to manage risky situations really well whereas the women would be worried that someone would get hurt. It's good that men model this because it gives female staff the confidence to take more risk themselves which results in far better types of play and far more 'in the moment' opportunities for learning.

I think there is definitely cross-over both ways between male and female characteristics with the example above of more risk taking by the women and also in terms of the nurturing approach role-modelled for the men by the women.

With regard to the recruitment and retention of men in the workforce, the notion of 'critical mass' (Kramer *et al.* 2006) is cited as a determining factor in an individual's decision to join, stay with and to influence an organisation. However, we question what percentage of the workforce needs to be male in order for men to feel comfortable and to establish a normal culture where they are not regarded as 'outsiders' and which will, in turn, encourage and support other men to apply and remain. Implicit in the question 'What do male practitioners want?' is the concomitant issue of the critical mass needed to achieve a self-sustaining balance in the Early Years workforce gender mix. This cannot be an absolute number. Clearly it must be somewhere between 0–50 per cent of the organisation workforce, but we would suggest that the critical mass is different for an organisation that has only a few employees to that which employs tens or hundreds. Some men that we interviewed are content to be the only male in their team, but Kramer *et al.*'s (2006) research suggests that a figure of three or more individuals of the same gender represents a critical mass. A chief executive officer (CEO) of one major Childcare Group agrees, saying that 'once there are a few men, it makes it easier for the others'.

We move on from considering the opinions and experience of the men and women who work in the Early Years workforce, to turn our attention to those who recruit, manage and support them, their managers.

What do managers want?

In Chapter 2 we discussed the notion of culture at different levels and the factors that influence it. We firmly believe that leaders create the organisational culture. They do so through:

a) What they pay attention to

b) Their actions and behaviours

c) Their allocation of attention and resources, and

d) What they reward and punish

(Schein 2010)

In Early Years settings, organisation leaders are typically the manager or the head teacher. As individuals responsible for the management of day-to-day operations, it can be seen that their actions, behaviours and priorities directly affect the culture by delivering strong messages about the relative importance of procedural elements. These are the people who are, under the direction of setting owners and governing bodies, responsible for staff recruitment and development. How these leaders direct recruitment initiatives, and where and who they target job adverts at, provides evidence of the culture they wish to develop or maintain in terms of the diversity of the workforce. As a male manager at Chapel House Day Nursery, Nick Corlett says that he does not have an explicit strategy or target for balancing gender within his team, and yet it is evident from talking to him that he not only welcomes applications from men as well as women but that he cultivates an environment where it is normal for men and women to work together and where appropriately skilled men are wanted, welcomed and supported. Out of the applications he receives from recruitment agencies, one in five is from a man. Chapel House Day Nursery also uses its own network of contacts to recruit from and this provides another source of male applicants. There is a public awareness of the culture in Chapel House Day Nursery, at least at a local level. Agencies and contacts respond accordingly. There is a ready supply of job applications from men as well as women in response to a perceived demand for them. So how is it that Chapel House Day Nursery has a choice of male and female candidates to select the best person for the job from where others are not receiving any applications from men? The nursery seemingly fosters a culture which clearly signals that what this manager wants is men and women working together and to receive applications from both genders.

REFLECTION

- What do I as a manager or what does my organisation manager want in terms of a gender-mix in our Early Years team?

- How explicit is this?

- What are the implications of this?

- Do we publicise/signal this externally? Why/why not?

- How could this be achieved more effectively?

- If we do not currently have any men working in our team, what leadership actions might be taken to positively address this?

Having examined the wants and needs of various Early Years stakeholders, we now consider the effects of a gender-mix within staff teams in relation to group dynamics.

Group dynamics

One of the questions we posed to organisations in our research was whether they had noticed any difference in team behaviours attributable to the gender make-up of the group. Despite the relatively small sample of responses that we analysed (n12), several characteristics and behaviours were repeatedly mentioned:

- a reduction in 'bitchiness/gossip'

- a more relaxed attitude to children's risk-taking and building independence skills

- a gender-neutral environment

- mutual professional respect.

The operation of group dynamics (Lewin 1948) is of interest from a sociological perspective within the Early Years workforce. In any group, there can be a tension between the need to fit in and maintaining one's individuality and distinctiveness. A male Early Years practitioner joining an existing all-female team encounters a system of established behaviours and psychological processes. 'In-group' members (Tajfel and Turner 1986) show a tendency to identify and comply with the informal rules used to regulate group behaviours and practices. Where the Early Years team is all female, a man must decide how to relate to the in-group. As Warin (2016, p.96) points out, 'gender is a key element of the construction of personal identity and related social awareness of others around us' and 'awareness of one's gender group membership is thrown into relief when our immediate social reference group is mainly, or entirely, made up by members of the opposite sex'.

Some of the male Early Years practitioners we interviewed attested to feelings of isolation as the only male in an otherwise all-female team. As men, they found it challenging to be expected to join in with and conform to the implicit cultural habits of an all-female group. Practitioner H described his first work placement experience in a day nursery as, 'feeling like I was stuck in an alien world'. This is supported by Acker (1992, pp.252–253) who refers to 'the interactions among individuals and the symbols, images, and forms of consciousness' that create and justify gender divisions within gendered organisations. This could be, for example, what topics of conversation are held in the staffroom.

Much has been written about stereotyping, expected gender roles and hegemonic masculinity, defined as practices that serve to normalise men's dominance and women's subordination (Demetriou 2001; Donaldson 1993). Where a man is the only representative of his gender in a team, it is easy to see how preconceptions about his nature could be projected onto him – it is assumed he will act according to assumptions about his gender. On the other hand, Sargent (2005, p.252) classes men who care for young children in the category of subordinate masculinity, characterised by behaviours and presentations of self that could threaten the legitimacy of hegemonic masculinity. The single, isolated man in the Early Years team has only his own instincts from which to draw on in determining how to act in relation to his female colleagues.

Where there is more than one man in an Early Years team, both men and women typically describe their common purpose and group identity in professional terms as working together for the benefit of the children. Jennie Johnson, CEO of Kids Allowed nursery group, expresses the benefits of a mixed gender team by saying, 'Just like a mixed board, different perspectives are always good. A blended workforce gives richer experiences to other colleagues.' Balanced gender teams seemingly provide 'richer experiences' for both children and colleagues. The greater the balance, the more gender preconceptions and stereotypes are broken down and mutual respect is established. The 'in-group' has thus expanded its definition to encompass diversity and an appreciation of men and women bringing their unique character to the collective role of Early Years educator.

Managers of mixed gender teams attest to the benefits of men and women working together in terms of them

- tempering perceived extremes of behaviour

- fostering a culture of mutual respect and fairness, and

- improving morale.

Provider A in our research describes the benefits they have experienced from their perspective from having mixed gender teams [presented in the form of a list]:

- 'Role models for the children.

- A male influence where there may not be one in a child's life.

- Different ideas and influences on the team.

- Celebrating differences between everyone in the human race whether short, tall, African American, male, female or whoever you may be.'

We now focus our discussion to consider the importance of equal opportunities to both policy and actions aimed at addressing diversity issues in the Early Years workforce. We begin with a formal exploration of current UK legislation.

Equal opportunities

The Equality Act (2010a) (Chapter 1, Section 4) defines protected characteristics as:

- age

- disability

- gender reassignment[1]

- marriage and civil partnership

- pregnancy and maternity

- race

- religion or belief

- sex, and

- sexual orientation.

The Equality Act Explanatory Notes (2010c) expand on the definition of sex as a protected characteristic to mean 'being a man or a woman,

---

1   While gender reassignment is the term used in the legislation, the preferred term is now 'gender transition' which we have used in this book.

and that men share this characteristic with other men, and women with other women'. Section 13 of the Equality Act (2010b) states that: 'A person (A) discriminates against another (B) if, because of a protected characteristic, A treats B less favourably than A treats or would treat others.' The Act provides a legal definition for discrimination against an individual. For example, where a person can prove that he has been treated less favourably than others by another person because, for example, he is a man, it can be claimed that he has been discriminated against.

REFLECTION

–   Which of the protected characteristics above do you think are relevant to men in the Early Years workforce?

–   In what ways could a man entering or working in the Early Years workforce be treated less favourably than others because of any relevant characteristics he possesses?

Returning to our discussion of mutual professional respect, it can be seen that where this arises as a benefit of professional relationships developing in mixed gender teams, there is less chance of discrimination, e.g. person A treats person B less favourably than person A treats or would treat others because of a protected characteristic. Tolerance, respect for and acceptance of all protected characteristics are more likely to develop in a diverse workforce that represents and reflects the community it serves. This is exemplified in the non-education-based case study below.

CASE STUDY

Croda is a producer of highly specialised chemicals for a wide range of sectors including health, beauty and engineering. Its diversity and inclusion programme is explicitly focused on increasing the number of those with under-represented characteristics within its workforce including women who have previously been a small minority in what has been seen traditionally as a male-dominated industry requiring STEM (Science, Technology, Engineering and Mathematics) expertise. Positive action by Croda has resulted in 'an increase in the percentage of women across the business to 33 per cent and a 50/50 gender balance in their North America graduate scheme in 2015'.

Croda's focus on diversity and inclusion is targeted at 'supporting, valuing and respecting difference in their workforce, and ensuring that all employees feel empowered and included'.

Croda attests to the result of this focus in terms of benefits for their team who report that they feel 'respected and that their opinion counts'. As a consequence, they enjoy 'greater career satisfaction, feel invested in and have more opportunity to fulfil their potential'. Greater diversity has allowed Croda to 'better represent the diversity of the communities in which they operate'. It has 'driven innovation through widening the scope of ideas from men and women, producing better outcomes. This has generated mutual respect within the company's teams'. (Croda 2015)

Treating people equally acknowledges their intrinsic value as individuals regardless of their characteristics. This is a fundamental human right which we believe is vital to foster and to model in Early Years settings if we are to see children develop into tolerant, humane and open-minded adults. Those working with these young children need to experience this for themselves and to demonstrate equal opportunities impartiality. Not only is this enshrined in statute but there is a moral imperative to do so. Men working in Early Years settings should have the opportunity and the privilege of bringing their unique talents, character and skills to their professional job role. It is the responsibility of the Early Years sector to ensure they are allowed to do this and are respected for being themselves. In such an environment, diversity is valued, difference is respected and stereotypes are rejected. In the case of gender impartiality, men and women regard one another as professional colleagues with complementary skills, experience and mutual trust. Recruitment and promotion are conducted based solely on merit. The best person for the job is appointed. Whilst equal opportunity law provides challenge to and ultimate protection against discrimination, the successful development of tolerance and respect in diverse teams means that it is not necessary to use it. In other words, equal opportunities make a strong case for a mixed gender Early Years workforce. When asked about their approach to equality, Provider A responded, 'Our culture is that everyone is respected for their own talents and personality whether female, male, transgender or anything else. One of our male team members said, we are treated fairly and no differently to any other team member – it's the same for everyone, I like it that way'.

There is explicit provision within Section 158 of the Equalities Act (2010b) for 'Positive Action' to achieve greater participation in an activity for those with a protected characteristic whose representation is disproportionately low. When applying the Act to the Early Years workforce and the specific protected characteristic of sex, it is the case that men are under-represented (disproportionately low) working in Early Years (participation in an activity). Paraphrasing slightly, the Act does not prohibit (and therefore allows) any (proportionate) action to enable or encourage such persons to participate in the activity (working in the Early Years). Our interpretation of this clause is that it supports positive action to address imbalances in the diversity of the Early Years workforce. Perhaps the contentious or equivocal terms are 'proportionate' and 'enabling or encouraging'. Stipulating that applications from men only will be considered for a job vacancy, whilst undoubtedly enabling and encouraging men to apply, would not be considered a proportionate means of achieving this. It would be classed as discrimination since equal opportunity is not being afforded to women to apply. It would be appropriate and acceptable, therefore, to promote a vacancy by stating that applications are welcome from men as well as women or to use pictures and case studies of both men and women as examples to promote career opportunities in Early Years. This is exemplified in the case study offered below.

CASE STUDY

On its company website, Toad Hall nursery group has a separate 'men in childcare' information link from its main careers page – see www. toadhall-nursery.co.uk/nursery-jobs/men-in-early-years/. Whilst the process for submitting a job application is the same, regardless of gender, the explicit reference to men is appropriate positive action to encourage more applications from them. The introductory text reads:

> We believe children need both male and female role models in life. Thus, at Toad Hall we do our utmost to recruit more men in childcare, to help guide children through their Early Years and beyond. If you're a male childcare professional, or you're interested in childcare as a career,

read on to find out more about the benefits and perks of this unique and exciting profession.

REFLECTION

- Do you believe it is necessary or helpful to provide specific career information on company websites for men seeking jobs in the Early Years?

- What actions could your organisation consider to encourage job applications from men as well as women?

We believe that it is valid and appropriate to raise the issue of the need for more men in the Early Years. This serves as the primary focus of this book! By definition, the aim to achieve a more gender-balanced workforce is in line with the principle of equal opportunity. As we have argued, positive action is most definitely needed to address the current gender imbalance in the Early Years workforce. We must be careful, however, as to how we go about achieving this, ensuring that every job is open to the best candidate, regardless of gender. We explore multiple ways that this could be achieved in Chapter 7.

In Chapter 2 we noted that gender as a characteristic is sometimes problematic in the public perception of the appropriateness of an individual to work with young children. Homosexuality and gender transition are also often confused/associated in the media with potential child abuse. We now examine some of the attitudes and issues relating to these characteristics.

Sexual orientation and gender transition

Whilst sexual orientation and gender transition are not a topic of extensive discussion in this book, we note that they are explicitly included as separate protected characteristics within the Equal Opportunities Act list. UK law affords protection to its citizens with respect to employment and participation in activities, irrespective of not only sex but also sexual orientation and gender transition.

SCENARIO

As a manager of a day nursery, one of your team confides in you that he/she is proposing to embark on the process of confirming their gender.

- How would you consider listening to and supporting the team member through their transition?

- What would you need to consider with respect to informing colleagues, parents/carers and children connected with your nursery?

In considering workforce diversity and the need for children to experience interactions with adults who have a wide range of characteristics, we argue that it is beneficial for them to be cared for and educated by individuals who represent the character mix of the community; this will allow children to learn how to relate to different types of people, to tolerate, value and to respect difference and to normalise responses to them. This is acknowledged in the theme of 'Positive Relationships' laid out in the English Early Years Foundation Stage (EYFS) curriculum.

Development Matters (Early Education 2012) provides non-statutory guidance to support the implementation of the EYFS. For the theme of 'Positive Relationships' under the specific area of learning 'Understanding the World', the guidance prompts practitioners to 'Be positive about differences between people and support children's acceptance of difference. Be aware that negative attitudes towards difference are learned from examples the children witness' (Early Education 2012, p.37). The Development Matters guidance thus encourages Early Years organisations in their efforts to provide children with examples of diversity. Whilst activities, resources and experiences can all provide examples, unless the workforce is diverse, it is difficult for teams to model positive attitudes towards difference themselves on a day-to-day basis. We need to mitigate the stereotypical attitudes held regarding male and female gender characteristics, as highlighted by Colangelo (2017):

Sex and gender are much more complex and nuanced than people have long believed. Defining sex as a binary treats it like a light switch: on or off. But it's actually more similar to a dimmer switch, with many people sitting somewhere in between male and female genetically, physiologically, and/or mentally. To reflect this, scientists now describe sex as a spectrum.

We believe that adults in Early Years settings should be free to be themselves with the confidence to recognise their own self-worth and the intrinsic value they have to offer as carers and educators without being constrained in their behaviours by the pressure to conform to the set heterosexual norm or the male/female sex binary. The National Scientific Council on the Developing Child (2009) reminds us that 'Healthy development depends on the quality and reliability of a young child's relationships with the important people in his or her life, both within and outside the family.' It is the quality of consistent relationships with individual carers that actually matters. Indeed, Cushman (2008, p.125) is explicit in attesting that 'studies have found the qualities learners value in teachers are non-gender specific'.

Transgender and gay male Early Years practitioners in particular can come under suspicion from some parents/carers and possibly from colleagues as to their motives for working in the sector. For example, Stephanie Nordt is a spokeswoman for Queerformat, a German organisation which provides classes on gender and sexuality in education. Stephanie is quoted as saying, 'The general suspicion against males becomes even more potent against gay educators.' (The Local 2017). The same article in the German edition of an English-language news publication leads with the headline, 'Muslim parents take kids out of Berlin nursery after discovering teacher is gay'. The article goes on to report, 'The parents of preschool children in the northern district of Reinickendorf threatened to gather names for a petition against the kindergarten when they found out that one of the (male) nursery teachers was gay.' Here we have the tricky balance between religious and cultural beliefs versus the right of the individual to protection under the law upheld by the centre in recognition of the human rights of the staff member and the benefits he bestows by virtue of performing his professional role as carer and educator. Depending on the circumstances, perhaps there are limits to how far it is possible to confront discrimination and effect immediate change but we believe the principles of equality, and protecting diverse characteristics within the workforce must take precedence. Thankfully in this example, 'the management of the preschool put their foot down and gave the parents the choice: either accept that a gay man would look after their children, or put their kids into a different preschool'.

Early Years settings that foster and support an inclusive culture provide the conditions for diversity to be accepted and celebrated within the workforce, providing children, their parents and team members with the opportunity to form relationships with and to become tolerant of non-binary individuals. They are well-placed to challenge any negative thinking and to positively contribute to a more inclusive and diverse society. However, this will take time and it must acknowledge the cultural context of each locale.

ACTIVITY

Conduct an inclusion, diversity and equality audit across all stakeholders in your organisation (see http://www.acas.org.uk/media/pdf/2/q/Prevent_discrimination_June_2018.pdf or http://www.naceweb.org/uploadedfiles/files/2017/resources/nace-diversity-inclusion-self-assessment.pdf).

Possible questions to reflect on include:

- To what extent does your team reflect the community it serves in terms of the protected characteristics listed in the Equal Opportunities Act?

- What opportunities do you provide for your children to interact with individuals of differing characteristics?

- How far do you reflect, celebrate and value diversity

  - in your practice, activities and routines?

  - in your resources?

- What rules or expectations do you have that might limit any individual's freedom of expression?

- What is the reason for these rules or expectations? Could/should you consider reviewing them?

We recommend that the audit should consider the views of all team members, parents/carers and children. On completion, it is good practice to analyse practice and to discuss the results as a team, developing a plan for the implementation of any actions identified.

We bring this chapter to a close by briefly considering some of the main ideas which have been discussed in it and addressing the questions that we opened the chapter with having examined the available evidence – do we need men in Early Years and do they make a difference? We have considered the expressed wants and needs of various groups involved and who hold an interest in the Early Years sector with respect to having more men in the workforce. Provided that it is always the best person for the job who is appointed, we conclude that there are benefits to be gained through a more gender-balanced workforce in terms of the richness of experience and opportunity available to children as they develop through interactions with individuals who have the widest spectrum of characteristics.

The parents we surveyed overwhelmingly support the need for more men in the Early Years workforce and recount the benefits they bring. Leaders and teams within more gender-balanced Early Years settings attest to improvements in group dynamics, behaviours and morale. We have also noted the capacity that Early Years settings have to reflect the diversity of the communities they inhabit through those who interact with children as carers, educators and visitors. The exercise of inclusive practice which supports equality and diversity in action, not just as protected characteristics in law, has the potential to increase tolerance, fairness and acceptance, within the settings themselves and also out into society through changing people's attitudes, beliefs and thinking.

Our evidence indicates that we do indeed need more men in the Early Years workforce and there are benefits to be gained from their inclusion.

References

Acker, J. (1992) 'Gendering Organizational Theory.' In Mills, A. J. & Tancred, P. (Eds.), *Gendering Organizational Analysis.* Newbury Park, CA: Sage.

Center on the Developing Child (2009) 'Five Numbers to Remember About Early Childhood Development.' Accessed 16 October 2017 at https://developingchild. harvard.edu/resources/five-numbers-to-remember-about-early-childhood-development/#cps

Chambers, S. and O'Sullivan, J. (2012) 'Men working in childcare: Does it matter to children? What do they say?' London Early Years Foundation. Accessed 12 July 2017 at https://issuu.com/leyf/docs/leyf-research-report-men-working-in-childcare-2012

Children Act 2004. Accessed 16 October 2017 at www.legislation.gov.uk/ukpga/2004/31/pdfs/ukpga_20040031_en.pdf

Colangelo, J. (2017) 'The myth that gender is binary is perpetuated by a flawed education system.' Accessed 1 October 2017 at https://qz.com/1007198/the-myth-that-gender-is-binary-is-perpetuated-by-a-flawed-education-system

Croda (2015) 'Diversity & Inclusion. Embrace and empower all individuals.' Accessed 23 October 2017 at www.croda.com/en-gb/sustainability/material-areas/diversity-and-inclusion

Cushman, P. (2008) 'So what exactly do they want? What principals mean when they say "male role model".' *Gender and Education*, 20(2), 123–136.

Demetriou, D. Z. (2001) 'Connell's concept of hegemonic masculinity: A critique.' *Theory and Society*, 30(3), 1–25.

DfE (2017) *Early Years Workforce Strategy*. Accessed 12 July 2017 www.gov.uk/government/uploads/system/uploads/attachment_data/file/596884/Workforce_strategy_02-03-2017.pdf

Donaldson, M. (1993) 'What is hegemonic masculinity?' *Theory and Society*, 22(5), 643–657.

Early Education (2012) 'Development Matters in the Early Years Foundation Stage.' Accessed 19 October 2017 at https://foundationyears.org.uk/files/2012/03/Development-Matters-FINAL-PRINT-AMENDED.pdf

Equality Act (2010a) Part 2 Chapter 1. Accessed 31 August 2017 at www.legislation.gov.uk/ukpga/2010/15/section/4

Equality Act (2010b) Part 2 Chapter 2. Accessed 31 August 2017 at www.legislation.gov.uk/ukpga/2010/15/part/2/chapter/2

Equality Act (2010c) Explanatory Notes. Accessed 19 October 2017 at www.legislation.gov.uk/ukpga/2010/15/notes/division/3/2/1/8

Gopnik, A. (2016) *The Gardener and the Carpenter: What the New Science of Child Development Tells Us about the Relationship Between Parents and Children*. London: The Bodley Head.

Kelly, B. (2016) 'Andrea Leadsom doesn't trust male nannies – and if you're honest, neither do you.' *The Telegraph*, 18 July. Accessed 19 October 2017 at www.telegraph.co.uk/news/2016/07/18/andrea-leadsom-doesnt-trust-male-nannies--and-if-youre-honest-ne

Kramer, V. W., Konrad, A. M. and Erkut, S. (2006) 'Critical Mass on Corporate Boards: Why Three or More Women Enhance Governance.' The Wellesley Centers for Women's Publications Office. Accessed 2 October 2018 at http://www.wcwonline.org/pdf/CriticalMassExecSummary.pdf

Lewin, K. (1948) *Resolving Social Conflicts; Selected Papers On Group Dynamics*. New York: Harper & Row.

Maslow, A. H. (1954) *Motivation and Personality*. New York: Harper & Row.

Mastergeorge, A. (2014) 'The Importance of Everyday Interactions for Early Brain Development.' *Huffington Post*, 14 April. Accessed 17 October 2017 at www.huffingtonpost.com/dr-ann-mastergeorge/the-importance-early-brain-development_b_4696877.html

MORI (2002) 'Men and Childcare'. Accessed 17 October 2017 at www.ipsos.com/ipsos-mori/en-uk/men-and-childcare

National Scientific Council on the Developing Child. (2009) 'Young children develop in an environment of relationships. Working Paper No. 1.' Center on the Developing Child at Harvard University. Accessed 17 October 2017 at http://developingchild.harvard.edu/wp-content/uploads/2004/04/Young-Children-Develop-in-an-Environment-of-Relationships.pdf

Notebaert, K. (2017) 'CFA Institute Talk: What is unconscious bias and how can it sabotage diversity?' Accessed 2 October 2018 at Notebaert, K. (2017) 'How Unconscious Bias in Our Brain Counteracts Diversity' Accessed 16 October 2017 at https://eic.cfainstitute.org/2017/09/05/how-unconscious-bias-in-our-brain-counteracts-diversity

Nutbrown, C. (2012) 'Foundations for quality: The independent review of early education and childcare qualifications – Nutbrown review.' London: DfE.

Owen, C. (2003) *Men's Work? Changing The Gender Mix Of The Childcare And Early Years Workforce.* London: Daycare Trust. Accessed 12 July 2017 at www.meninchildcare.co.uk/Mens%20Work.pdf

Pre-school Learning Alliance (2011) 'Parents "want men to work as childcarers in day nurseries"' 21 July. Accessed 12 July 2017 at https://shop.pre-school.org.uk/media/press-releases/255/parents-want-men-to-work-as-childcarers-in-day-nurseries

Sargent, P. (2005) 'The gendering of men in early childhood education.' *Sex Roles,* 52(3–4), 251–259.

Schein, E. H. (2010) *Organizational Culture And Leadership* (4th ed.). San Francisco: Jossey-Bass.

Tajfel, H. and Turner, J. C. (1986) 'The Social Identity Theory of Intergroup Behaviour.' In Austin, W G. and Worchel, S. (Eds) *Psychology of Intergroup Relations* (2nd ed.). (pp.7–24). Chicago: Nelson-Hall.

The Local (2017) 'Muslim parents take kids out of Berlin nursery after discovering teacher is gay'. Accessed 19 October 2017 at https://www.thelocal.de/20170329/muslim-parents-protest-after-gay-berlin-man-hired-to-raise-their-kids

Warin, J. (2015) 'Pioneers, professionals, playmates, protectors, "poofs" and "paedos": Swedish male pre-school teachers' construction of their identities.' In Brownhill, S., Warin, J. and Wernersson, I. (Eds.) Men*, Masculinities and Teaching in Early Childhood Education: International Perspectives on Gender And Care.* London: Routledge, pp.95–106.

CHAPTER 5

Exploring the Perceived Benefits of a Mixed Gender Early Years Workforce

SIMON BROWNHILL

Overview

In Chapter 4 we considered the expressed wants of various stakeholders in the Early Years sector with respect to men working in it. In this chapter we now focus our attention on the perceived benefits of a mixed gender Early Years workforce by exploring the views of various groups of people with reference to relevant literature and recent/new research findings. For the purpose of clarification, an emphasis will be placed on discussing the benefits of more men participating in the Early Years sector. Whilst Rolfe (2005: vi) asserts that these perceived benefits are 'widely recognised and include demonstrating gender equality to children, and enriching children's experiences of care', we aim to raise awareness to a suite of tensions and dilemmas that are associated with these benefits. The chapter initially highlights some of the broad arguments for a mixed gender Early Years workforce at a macro, mesa and micro level.

In March 2017, the Department for Education (DfE) published its Early Years Workforce Strategy. As a consequence of lobbying and representation from men in Early Years groups, *Diversity of the workforce* was identified as one of the five focus areas of the Strategy, with the DfE (2017, p.24) stating that '[w]e want children in Early Years provision to have both male and female role models to guide them in their Early Years, and we want more men to choose to work in the Early Years sector'. In support of this, several assertions were made:

> A diverse Early Years workforce, which better reflects wider society, helps to enhance children's experiences. Encouraging increased gender diversity amongst those joining the Early Years sector would have two main benefits; an increased pool of applicants for the sector to recruit from and male role models for young children. (p.24)

It would appear that the more-men-in-Early-Years agenda is being promoted at a macro level in light of perceived benefits for both employers and, more importantly, young children. We remain mindful, however, of the fact that this agenda is not solely targeted at a national level as recent/current policy making in numerous European countries and beyond demonstrates an international calling, largely in the western world, to increase the number of men who work in the Early Years sector (see Oberhueme 2011; McCormack and Brownhill 2014; Moreau and Brownhill 2017).

In support of the government's Strategy, local authorities such as Bristol City Council and the City of York Council advocate the perceived benefits of men in the Early Years workforce in relation to both provision and practice, e.g.:

> Children can benefit from the different experiences and styles of caring men bring, which can result in more positive behaviour. Having a diverse workforce also enhances children's experiences and better reflects the real gender mix of the world. (Surrey County Council (2017)

These views are supported at a mesa level by regional support groups, district branches of professional bodies, and projects led by education and care societies that collectively work to 'promote the positives' and get men involved in the Early Years, be it as a volunteer, a trainee or an employee/employer. The case study below aims to exemplify some of the many activities undertaken by an active network group.

CASE STUDY

The Southampton Area Men in Early Years (SAMEY) network has developed relationships with key contacts in individual schools and colleges in the local area. Through this network they regularly provide personnel to man stalls at careers events, engaging with children/students from primary level through to Further Education colleges with display boards, banners, photographs of men interacting with children, a large stuffed giraffe and a quiz on baby brains! The intention is to raise awareness of Early Years career opportunities for both genders.

In an effort to consider the perceived benefits of a mixed gender Early Years workforce at a micro level (this includes individual settings, clusters of settings, neighbourhood special interest groups and community organisations), we encourage readers to engage with the Reflection task below which considers the perceptions of 'shop-floor' service providers in the form of Early Years practitioners (male and female) and service users in the form of parents/carers.

REFLECTION

'The Pre-school Learning Alliance MPG [Major Provider Group] survey asked parents and men and women working in childcare what benefits more men working in childcare and early education could bring' (Baker 2012a). Read the responses reported below, indicating your own/your colleagues' level of agreement using the suggested Key:

SA = Strongly Agree

A = Agree

N = Neither Agree or Disagree

D = Disagree

SD = Strongly Disagree

Response (as reported in Baker 2012a)	Level of agreement
More men would end the stereotype of childcare being seen as 'women's work'.	
Having more men involved in Early Years childcare would increase the status of the work (and possibly salaries as well), as childcare is traditionally seen as a low-pay, low-status sector.	

Response (as reported in Baker 2012a)	Level of agreement
The presence of more men in Early Years settings would make it easier for fathers and other men to feel more at home there and be more involved with their children's childcare.	
Men would bring 'added value' to pre-schools and day nurseries, including a different perspective, different ways of working and being with children, such as 'rough and tumble' play with boys.	
The importance of male role models to young children, both boys and girls, particularly for those children growing up in families with little or no contact with men.	
A number of co-parenting parents and single parents spoke of the value their children (often sons) had from them having a male Early Years or primary school teacher.	

Critically reflect on your responses by taking them to a team meeting for discussion. Alternatively, think about canvassing parents'/ carers' opinions to draw critical comparisons of your thinking. Might these findings help you/your setting to review its values, ethos and practice?

As opposed to subscribing to a multitude of individual benefits (as highlighted above), The Fatherhood Institute (2017) offers four main advantage (benefit) areas for a mixed gender Early Years workforce which we particularly favour:

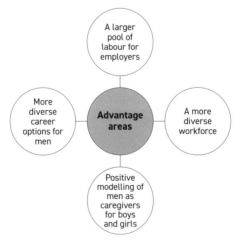

Figure 5.1: Advantage (benefit) areas for a mixed gender Early Years workforce

Given the strong support at a local, regional, national and international level, there would appear to be little argument to oppose the active recruitment of men in the Early Years sector. With education charities such as Men in Childcare and London Early Years Foundation, coupled with international organisations such as the Organisation for Economic Co-operation and Development advocating a 'mixed gender, diverse workforce' (OECD 2006, p.15), we acknowledge the widely-held view that more men in the Early Years sector is 'a good thing' [our words].

But is there another side to this discussion? What disadvantages are there to having a mixed gender Early Years workforce, and how do they challenge the 'beneficial bounty' that policy makers, associations and professionals in the sector claim 'more men' to be? We aim to answer these questions by drawing the reader's attention to an array of tensions and dilemmas that are associated with many of the perceived benefits, as identified by different groups of people. These include:

- male practitioners

- female practitioners

- managers, head teachers, senior management members, and governors and committees, and

- parents and carers.

NOTE!

We fully recognise that there are many advantages (benefits) and disadvantages (tensions and dilemmas) which overlap between the groups of people identified above. We have made the conscious decision to avoid repetition in this chapter by presenting selected benefits in relation to the most prominent group based on our research, academic reading and professional judgement.

We initially explore the views of men who are either rooted in active Early Years practice or who are associated with the sector in an effort to give their perceptions a much needed 'voice' in the discourse that surrounds the perceived benefits of a mixed gender Early Years workforce.

The benefits of having a mixed gender Early Years workforce: the male practitioner perspective

A commonly held view by male Early Years practitioners relates to the notion of *variety* and the advantageous nature of this for both Early Years practice and the work setting. Brandes *et al.* (2015, p.326) suggest that this refers to the ways in which 'male ECE workers can positively affect the diversity of learning activities' for young children. This is recognised by David Stevens (2011, p.47), a manager at a nursery setting in London:

> Within my setting we have four male staff, as well as three female LSAs, a nursery officer and an apprentice. We come from a wide mix of backgrounds, experiences and ages, which I feel leads to a diverse melting pot of ideas and activities, not to mention a great atmosphere within the nursery.

It is of interest that Stevens' thinking resonates with findings from our own research where male practitioners argued that one of the benefits of having a mixed gender Early Years workforce was that it was 'good for the staff dynamic – there are differences between the genders and diversity brings a range of perspectives' (Practitioner H). Whilst this was seen as a way of helping to contribute to a positive working environment, Practitioner F saw this 'diversity' as being of particular benefit for young children as this would allow them to 'understand new experiences and not conform to the binaries of stereotyped roles currently seen in society'.

ACTIVITY

Download a copy of Aina and Cameron's (2011) interesting article 'Why does gender matter? Counteracting stereotypes with young children' (available at tinyurl.com/prbqv89).

Reflect on the discussion and ideas offered, considering how you/your colleagues could address gender biases in your setting to positively influence young children's development and the opportunities that will help them to lead successful lives.

We believe that having more than one male employee in an Early Years setting (as per Stevens' nursery) is noteworthy seeing as male practitioners typically find themselves to be *one-of-a-kind* in the workplace. Warin (2015, p.99) argues that these men are seen as representing 'something different' (or at least some*one*) given their 'rarity value'. The perceived benefits of this are illustrated by another nursery manager, Andrew Baker (see Lyndon 2016), in relation to children's reactions to these 'novelty figures' [our words]:

> The children's response to seeing a male [practitioner] within nursery was unbelievable – they loved to see a father like figure. You had preschool [children] wanting to play football only with me, 'Daddy's girls' settling with myself and nobody else…

For some male practitioners this positive response is of personal benefit as it helps them to feel 'of value' and offers what some might call 'an ego boost'. Indeed, findings from our research suggest that some men are 'elevated to "superhero status"' (FGP 1) as a result of working in an Early Years setting. Professional egos are likely to be stroked further by 'employers and colleagues [who] tend to regard [male practitioners] as something to brag about and show off as if they are a trophy or prized asset' (Alexander 2012). We believe that men who feel they are an important part of the Early Years workforce are likely to be motivated and remain in the profession, which is clearly of benefit for this can help to lower the turnover of staff in the sector (Walker 2016).

The reaction of children towards men in the Early Years is of particular interest, especially when considering the perceived benefits of male practitioners for young boys and their levels of attainment. The issue of boys' underachievement in the Early Years remains a prevalent one in both professional and public discourse (see Richardson 2016), and we acknowledge that we would need a separate book to do critical justice to this 'hot topic'! In an effort to focus our discussion, we highlight the concern that surrounds standards of young boys' language development in comparison to that of young girls (see Moss and Washbrook 2016). Engaging boys in communication and language activity is deemed problematic by some professionals in the sector, but when interviewed, David Francis (a Pre-school Learning Alliance Early Years team leader) said that when he worked in a nursery in Peckham 'young boys would excitedly chat to him about the latest pop stars and their favourite football team in a way they wouldn't chat to the female nursery staff' (cited in Baker 2012b). Being able to positively respond to this desire to talk, and engage boys further in this kind of activity, is clearly of benefit as male practitioners are in a positive position to support boys' learning and development by capitalising on and promoting the principles and repertoires associated with dialogic teaching (see Alexander, n.d.). However, we believe that the discussion above raises an important question: Do all young boys only want to talk to male practitioners? From our observations of practice in the Early Years, we certainly do not think that this is the case given that in some settings there may be:

- a personality clash between the child and the practitioner,

- more of a desire on the part of the child to 'play rather than say',

- difficulties in communication as a result of the child speaking English as a second language, or

- no male practitioners present in the setting.

This suggests that the participation of men as part of a mixed gender Early Years workforce is not necessarily of benefit to every young boy as some may feel more comfortable talking to and being around female practitioners. With this in mind, we present a select number of tensions and dilemmas that are associated with some of the perceived benefits raised in this chapter to date for readers to critically reflect on and discuss with their colleagues/peers:

TENSIONS AND DILEMMAS 1

Just for the boys?: If gender does make a difference to boys' learning, we question what the perceived benefits are for having more men in the Early Years workforce for young girls, a topic which is rarely discussed in public/professional discourse or research (Brownhill 2015b).

The pressure of attention: For some men in our research, the attention they received from the children, the parents/carers and the staff 'install[ed] a level of fear in me' (FGP 2), not just because they found working in the Early Years to be 'quite isolating' to begin with (FGP 3), but because of the constant anxiety of feeling that they 'had to be liked' (FGP 2) by different groups of people in the setting.

'*Same old practice*': Brownhill and Oates (2017) found that the contributions of male practitioners in Early Years settings were typically 'confined' to stereotypical male activities, e.g. outdoor play, 'rough and tumble', and sports. This research challenges assertions of 'diversity' in relation to practice that many people argue men are able to bring to the Early Years setting.

Gender matching madness: The idea of matching educators and learners by gender – male Early Years practitioners and young boys – to benefit learning and attainment is a practice that is strongly contested by Francis *et al.* (2006) and validated by Smyth (as reported in Lang 2015): 'no [research] studies have indicated improved achievement of pupils (regardless of stage, age, ethnicity or social class) where their gender was matched with that of their teachers'.

ACTIVITY

Visit tinyurl.com/yb9nb7t5 for an interesting research report by the Gants Hill Partnership Teaching Alliance (n.d.) entitled 'Would a "Gender Balanced" workforce within an Early Years setting increase the attainment of boys, closing the gender gap in attainment?' Reflect on the findings presented in the report, considering how the discussion and conclusions challenge the claim made by Smyth (see 'Tensions and Dilemmas 1' above).

As our discussion has considered some of the perceptions of male practitioners in the Early Years sector, it is important that we offer readers what we like to call a gender-balance of viewpoints by considering the perceived benefits of having a mixed gender workforce as proposed by female practitioners.

The benefits of having a mixed gender Early Years workforce: the female practitioner perspective

Bartlett (2015, p.4) reports that '98 per cent of female nursery workers say they want [to work with] male colleagues'. With such strong support, there would appear to be numerous benefits that help to substantiate this claim. Drawing initially on our informal discussions with former female colleagues in the Early Years sector, we recall some women seeing men as being able to communicate more effectively with fathers/male carers as they [male practitioners] were regarded as being able to relate better to them (Neugebaurer 1999). This is of benefit for it helps men and their young sons/boys to 'feel more comfortable' [our words] when entering the Early Years environment, both at induction and on a daily basis. In contrast, Wardle (2004: page unknown) asserts that women in the Early Years 'are more comfortable working with women'. With this in mind, a male presence in the sector has the potential to not only engage fathers/male carers with the services offered by the setting, but also to encourage more men to volunteer/ work in the sector as they have someone to look up to and learn from. Indeed, research by Potter and Carpenter (2008, p.761) found that the 'high level of skill and persistence demonstrated by a dedicated [male practitioner]' can increase male involvement in the Early Years significantly. We believe that this is a key point for recruitment and retention. In our view, the 'successful' male practitioner represents an example to aspire to for other men, particularly in modelling a professional role as an educator who is making a difference. We argue that these are the kinds of case studies that need to be actively publicised (see Chapter 7).

RECOMMENDED READING

The National Literacy Trust (2007) published a valuable magazine entitled *Getting the Blokes on Board: Involving fathers and male carers in reading with their children*. We strongly recommend that you download a copy (available at https://tinyurl.com/ycmf56kr, identifying and reflecting on the practical literacy strategies suggested that could be embraced as part of your practice/the practice of the setting you work/volunteer in to improve adult male engagement levels, both at home and in the Early Years setting.

A curious benefit is drawn anecdotally from a memorable conversation that was overheard on a bus journey between a group of female early childhood student practitioners. It was claimed that Early Years settings benefitted from having men because 'they are so good for advertising, like', men thus being seen as a model to help visually promote not only the setting but also the profession. We believe that many male practitioners are likely to be subjected to this marketing role, as highlighted by the Scenario below.

SCENARIO

Jackson, 42, is a 'second-career' newly qualified Reception teacher in a small village infant school. During the 'Meet the new teacher day' at the school, Jackson is introduced to various colleagues he will be working with. The EYFS Lead makes the passing comment that Jackson is going to be 'useful PR for the school', claiming that he will 'look good on the website banner'. Jackson's TA also suggests that he is likely to find his face 'splashed all over the front of the new school prospectus'.

Take a moment to reflect on your thoughts about these comments made.

- Do you think that male practitioners should be used as a 'publicity aid' to promote education and care settings? What equity issues are highlighted by this practice?

- Do you think that there could be any negative aspects to using male practitioners for publicity, e.g. a deterrent to prospective parents/carers who are suspicious of male practitioners?

- Do you think it should be assumed that all male practitioners are happy to be used as a 'publicity aid' based on their gender?

For our next small collection of perceived benefits, we turn to the research of Jones (2006, pp.68–70) who identified five 'factors' (which we interpret as benefits) from discussions held with 13 female teachers. Two of these are of particular interest to our discussion:

- *Family:* There is a 'need for children to experience a positive male influence. This, it was argued, was not present in many families due either to absent fathers or to those who were, in themselves, poor role models' (p.69), male professionals thus serving as father figures or positive male role models for children.

- *The notion that men are 'better for boys'*: 'Another common response was that male teachers have more authority over boys than females do' (p.69), male professionals thus being seen as a disciplinarian figure.

Support for Jones' findings can be found in the responses offered by female practitioners who were asked what they thought the benefits of a mixed gender Early Years workforce were as part of a recent online special interest group post in 2017. Of particular interest were the perceived benefits 'that children are looked after by a team that reflects society as a whole, that they don't end up thinking caring is a purely female attribute or role, that they get to see men and women working together, bringing different energies and approaches to learning and playing' ('Margo').

Whilst these perceived benefits are clearly positive in nature, we feel it is important to draw the reader's attention to a number of additional tensions and dilemmas which threaten the apparent advantageous nature of having a mixed gender Early Years workforce. Again, we offer these below for readers to critically reflect on and discuss with their colleagues/peers:

TENSIONS AND DILEMMAS 2

A capabilities issue: Despite 'the gradual professionalisation of the Early Years workforce' over the last 20 years (Faulkner and Coates 2013, p.250), there are still female practitioners who work in the Early Years sector who believe that women are better at taking care of children than men, as recognised by Craig (2006).

Uneven distribution of attention: Given the investment of time and energy in recruiting and retaining men, some female practitioners question why little is being done by policy makers and senior management members to address the low pay and low status which affects morale and retention of women in the Early Years workforce (Brownhill and Oates 2017).

Men as role models: Much has been written to challenge the idea of male practitioners serving as role models for children (see Wood and Brownhill 2018). Walker (2007, pp.515–16), for example, argues that for role models to be of value to children 'these need to be geographically, generationally and experientially close to their own lives', aspects which male practitioners in the Early Years do not match. The ambiguity which surrounds the term 'role model' exacerbates criticism of this as a concept, as verbally discussed by Brownhill (2017).

Underestimating women: Assertions of men being able to offer something that women cannot do undermine the wealth of competences and capabilities that we believe female practitioners undoubtedly bring to the Early Years sector, perpetuating the bifurcation of stereotypical gender characteristics.

Men as father figures: Researchers such as Brownhill (2015b, p.32) challenge the 'imposition' of male practitioners having to act as father figures for young children on the grounds of personal experience: 'As a practitioner in the infancy of my teaching career I did not feel ready, able, nor was I particularly willing to assume this father figure role, largely due to my age [early 20s] and my lack of experience of working in the education sector'.

Another important voice we feel needs airing in the exploration of perceived benefits of a mixed gender Early Years workforce is that of professionals who are in positions of authority, e.g. centre managers, head teachers, senior management team (SMT) members, and governors and committees. For ease of reference, we use the term 'management team' to encompass all of these different roles.

The benefits of having a mixed gender Early Years workforce: the management team perspective

At a very basic level, having a mixed gender Early Years workforce is seen as helping to contribute to a more gender-balanced sector which Envy (2013, p.11) strongly calls for 'to ensure that the needs of all children are met'. A common view is that this is of benefit at an institutional and strategic level in achieving male recruitment targets (Jones 2009). This is recognised by Cushman (2008, p.124) from whose research we draw several interesting benefits. Her exploration of the perceptions of principals [head teachers/managers] in New Zealand in relation to the term 'male role model' yielded numerous findings which are of adapted relevance to our discussion:

- Increasing the number of male practitioners would help to 'lessen the visibility, and therein vulnerability, of each man' in the Early Years sector (p.129).

- 'A more equitable staff gender balance would also help to challenge the widely held belief that schools [and settings] are feminised institutions' (p.130).

- More men in the Early Years workforce would help to 'deconstruct stereotypes and demonstrate that men can be gentle, caring, compassionate, talk about feelings and show emotions' (p.132).

As the joint owner of a family-owned group of nursery settings in England's south coast, David [lead author of this book] firmly believes that a mixed gender Early Years workforce can have a positive impact on the ethos of a setting. David argues that this is based on feedback and observations over many years of the effects of a mixed gender team:

> Parents and carers have been universally supportive of and grateful for a combination of men and women working together to care for their children. Parents often comment how their children speak enthusiastically about their male carers. Whilst the recruitment and retention of men into the company remains a challenge, my wife and I attest to a positive change in team dynamics where men and women do work together, and in the case where there is a more equal balance of genders within the team, a normalisation of culture with more equal representation of mentors, professional teachers/carers and 'role models' across both genders. In this context, new male team members are not isolated and have support and validation from the other men and women around them.

Carrington and Skelton (2003, p.264) support David's views, arguing that there is little doubt that men (from a primary school perspective) contribute to the ethos of the learning space through their roles as mentors, advocates for the teaching profession and 'inspirational figure roles'. But does this thinking resonate in the Early Years sector? The case study below would seem to suggest so!

CASE STUDY

Nick Corlett works as a manager at a nursery setting in London where seven of the 22 members of staff are men (see Jones Russell 2017). He sees numerous benefits in having a gender-balance, many of which have already been considered in this chapter. Of particular interest are his thoughts relating to differences and the benefits of these:

> [E]veryone has a different approach, a different energy, and all bring different influences. It is most important to have as many different personalities as possible (p.24–25)…[as] [d]ifferences in opinion and ideas give children a broad range of activities and learning experiences. I think as the number of men…has grown, it has had a really positive impact on the setting. (p.25)

Critically reflect on whether you think increasing the number of men in your setting would have a 'really positive impact' or not. Why do you think this? How might you measure this impact? Share your thoughts with colleagues/peers.

Mistry and Sood (2013) suggest that male teachers progress more quickly to leadership positions when they enter the Early Years context. One of the perceived benefits of a mixed gender Early Years workforce is that men are more likely to want to 'take on a leadership role in [the Early Years] in the first few years of their…career' (p.67) due to their heightened levels of ambition, as highlighted in our research focus group. This helps to address the issue that management teams face in the recruitment of female practitioners to positions of authority – their reticence to take on these roles is likely to be due to family commitments, low pay, and the fear of the job 'tak[ing] them away from their preferred status as educators and child developers' (Mistry and Sood 2012, p.28).

For some male members of the management team, a poignant benefit of having a mixed gender Early Years workforce is that this helps to ease the loneliness of 'being the only man about the place' [our words]. The adage of it being 'lonely at the top' is seemingly valid when one reflects on the perceptions of male school principals in Turkish elementary schools and the social isolation that they experience (Korumaz 2016). As such, the presence of more men in the Early Years can be seen as a positive way of addressing this unfortunate phenomenon.

However, it is important that we consider 'the other side of the coin' by raising awareness to further tensions and dilemmas that exist in relation to some of the perceived benefits suggested by management team members. These are presented below for readers to critically reflect on and discuss with their colleagues/peers:

TENSIONS AND DILEMMAS 3

Quantity over quality. Cushman (2008, pp.132–3) suggests that less than a third of the principals involved in her research 'added the proviso that a male role model needed also to be a good teacher [which] might indicate that some principals were prepared to compromise good quality teaching in order to increase the number of man teachers'. We firmly believe that men should be employed in the Early Years sector based on their pedagogical merit and not their gender.

'Not a job for the boys': Worryingly, some settings are unwilling to employ men. David King, a male pre-school teacher in Ireland, reflects on the difficulties of getting his first job in the Early Years (as reported by Wayman 2016): 'Having completed a postgraduate diploma in Montessori, he reckons he applied for about 50 jobs and some openly told him that they would not hire a man to work with young kids.'

It's how you look at things: We believe that tensions are likely to exist between staff members as a result of the different ways that women and men think and operate in the setting, and how they discuss and implement policies and practice. Management teams may have to 'step in' to deal with 'cross words' and uncomfortable situations (Kimberley 2015).

*A rise in complaint*s: With Early Years settings facing an ever increasing number of 'pushy, aggressive parents' (Learner 2014), management teams may have to handle an increase in verbalised/written concerns and accusations in relation to the toileting of young children and the changing of babies' nappies by male practitioners.

The final tension offered above relates to the 'very real' concerns that are raised by parents/carers (Millam 2011). But do parents/carers not see men who work in the Early Years as being 'of benefit'? Our discussion, which serves as the final section of this chapter, strives to answer this important question.

The benefits of having a mixed gender Early Years workforce: the parent/carer perspective

In 2009, Gaunt reported that '[f]ifty-five per cent of parents questioned by the Children's Workforce Development Council (CWDC) said they would like their child to have a male childcare worker in their Early Years setting'. Two years later and research conducted by the Major Providers' Group (cited in Pre-school Learning Alliance 2011) found that 98 per cent of parents who used day nurseries were in favour of men caring for their children as trained childcare professionals. We consider this dramatic increase, in part, to be in recognition of the perceived benefits of having men in the Early Years workforce. Comments made by parents reported in the research by the Major Providers' Group suggest specific advantages:

Comment (cited in Pre-school Learning Alliance 2011)	Benefit
'I have been pleased when there have been male staff at my children's nursery as I believe they often offer a more active style of care, which my son in particular liked.'	Men provide different styles of care for children
'The right man in the right setting could be a positive role model to both female co-workers and children.'	Men provide a positive role model for colleagues, not just for children
'I think (having men in childcare) can have a huge positive impact.'	Men are of benefit, full stop!

The final comment above is gratifying but does not offer any clarity as to what constitutes this 'huge positive impact'. Our research suggests that one of the benefits of having a mixed gender Early Years workforce is that it helps to address what Practitioner H refers to as the 'unhealthy environment' that is as a result of there only being one professional gender in the workplace. By having a mix of men and women in the sector, Practitioner H (himself a parent) asserts that we are likely to promote 'a more positive culture of listening/collaborating', a culture which is strongly advocated by Ofsted (2015).

ACTIVITY

Download a copy of 'Collaborating to support Early Years teaching and learning: Broomhall Nursery School and Children's Centre' from http://dera.ioe.ac.uk/23469/1/Broomhall_Nursery_School_ and_Children_s_Centre_-_good_practice_example.pdf. This is a good practice case study which shows how 'learning from others can successfully enhance the quality of Early Years provision [and] how highly effective teamwork and strong collaboration with a range of Early Years professionals results in high quality teaching and learning'. (Ofsted 2015, p.1)

Consider how this practice mirrors your own professional practice/ the practice modelled by colleagues in your setting, irrespective of gender. Are there any collaborative lessons that can be learned from this case study to enhance your/your setting's provision and practice?

An interesting benefit of having a mixed gender Early Years workforce is derived from the views of a male parent, as reported in the research of King (2015):

> As a busy man who owns a business, I'm afraid that I do not get much contact time with my kids during the week. I was delighted when I found out that there were male teachers at the school that would be able to set a good male example for my kids.

The assertion is made that having more men in the sector will increase the 'exposure' to a positive male figure that some young children might not have close contact with during the working week. With '66 per cent [of lone mothers] saying they would like a man to be involved in their child's development' (CDWC in BBC 2009), another perceived benefit of a mixed gender Early Years workforce is that the participation of men helps to meet the needs of single-parent families. Research by Brownhill (2015b, p.155) builds on this idea of family types, suggesting that a mixed gender Early Years workforce is seemingly of benefit for different groups of parents:

You have an impact on parents…particularly young parents and… you know, parents who might have unstable relationships. My children [at the school where I am the head teacher] come from very socially disadvantaged backgrounds…they come from dysfunctional families…parents will come to me and say 'Mister Hughes,[1] can you talk to them because you're a man; they'll listen to you?' ('Will', head teacher and parent)

By serving as a 'stable male' (Jones 2007, p.184), it is thus argued that male practitioners can be a source of support for parents/carers, especially those who may struggle in the effective management of their children.

In light of these numerous benefits, we consider a final selection of tensions and dilemmas which relate to the perceived benefits put forward by parents/carers. These are presented below for readers to critically reflect on and discuss with their colleagues/peers:

TENSIONS AND DILEMMAS 4

You can't always get what you want!: Despite the majority of parents/carers being in favour of men working in nurseries, 'most male students would not consider childcare as a career' (Morton 2011). This challenges the idea of parents/carers actually *seeing* many men in the Early Years workforce, particularly those who are young and new to the profession.

Take another look at the stats!: The research by the Major Providers' Group (cited in Pre-school Learning Alliance 2011) found that the percentage of parents in favour of men working in day nurseries with two-year-olds actually *fell* to 95.7 per cent; with babies and toddlers under the age of two the percentage stood *at just* 93.5 per cent. It would appear that the younger the child the less likely parents are to want male practitioners to care for their children (see Walshe and Healy-Magwa 2012, pp.4–6).

Cultural challenges: Parents and carers from certain cultures have difficulty accepting some men (and women) as carers for their children based on their (the practitioners') sexual orientation. Whilst this should have absolutely no bearing on their ability to

---

1   Pseudonym used

practise effectively, publicised cases in Birmingham (Osbourne 2014) and Berlin (The Local 2017) highlight the unpleasantness that this creates for male (and female) professionals.

It's too much of a risk: Sandseter (2013, p.437) argues that 'because male ECEC practitioners are themselves greater risk-takers they may handle children's risk-taking behaviours in a different manner than do female ECEC practitioners'. This can be troublesome for some parents/carers as they worry about the safety of their children when engaged in risky play activity led by male practitioners.

We bring this chapter to a close by considering some of the main ideas which have been discussed in it. We have highlighted the fact that the perceived benefits of a mixed gender Early Years workforce are advocated on different platforms, be they at a setting, local community, district or national level. The perceived benefits are wide-ranging and are not solely focused on young children; benefits also relate to the workforce and parents/carers. However, we have acknowledged an assortment of tensions and dilemmas which raise critical questions about the validity of some of the positive assertions made by policy makers, education charities and professionals in the Early Years sector.

We are keen to make our position on this topic clear: we firmly believe that the employment of more men in the Early Years sector is of benefit. In support of this, we subscribe to the thinking of Tayler and Price (2016: ch.6) whose professional views mirror our own:

> Our position is that we fully support the inclusion of men into the Early Years workforce. We feel that children need to have people caring for them who *represent the society* that is around them and that includes men. Having men in the workforce also means that the work of the caring for children is seen by society as a *higher status job* that can be carried out by men and women and is not just an extension of the childcare role that can be seen as 'natural' to women and therefore not a skill. [our emphasis]

However, we argue that more quality empirical research needs to be undertaken at both a policy and practice level to validate or disprove the 'gain claims' proposed. We make this request in light of Rolfe's (2005: vi) assertion that the 'evidence is limited [or] simply absent' when considering the benefits of a mixed gender Early Years workforce.

We feel that greater effort is needed in the research community to undertake empirical research studies which are:

- less speculative, anecdotal and attitudinal, and more objective, measurable and definitive

- substantial in terms of numbers of men involved rather than being based on 'the few'

- long term rather than short term

- large scale so that it is representative of the whole sector, and

- critically analytical of any effects on the outcomes for children and settings.

In doing so, we are of the opinion that this will help to confirm and strengthen arguments for a mixed gender Early Years workforce so that we are in no doubt that employing more men in the sector is of benefit.

Our final comment openly recognises the absence of a valuable voice in this discussion – that of young children. Efforts to capture their thinking about complex topics such as the one that this chapter focuses on are notoriously problematic due to issues of age, maturity levels, comprehension and understanding, and language limitations. However, impressive efforts have been made to counter these difficulties, and so we recommend that readers download a copy of Chambers and O'Sullivan's (2012) 'Men working in childcare: Does it matter to children? What do they say?'.[2] reflecting critically on the interesting discussion and research findings presented. We would be intrigued to know what the young children in your setting think are the benefits of having a mixed gender Early Years workforce if you take up the challenge of asking them!

References

Aina, O. E. and Cameron, P. A. (2011) 'Why Does Gender Matter? Counteracting Stereotypes With Young Children.' *Dimensions of Early Childhood*, 39(3), 11–19.

Akerman, R. (Ed.) (2007). *Getting the Blokes on Board*. London: National Literacy Trust.

Alexander, R. (n.d.) 'Dialogic teaching essentials.' Accessed 15 July 2017 at www.serwis. wsjo.pl/lektor/1316/FINAL%20Dialogic%20Teaching%20Essentials.pdf

---

2   Available at http://tinyurl.com/ydc2n8kh

Alexander, S. (2012) 'Recruitment and employment of men in early childhood teaching, childcare, kindergarten and home-based early childhood education.' *ChildForum*, January. Accessed 10 July 2017 at www.childforum.com/management/staffing-and-employment-relations/232-spotlight-on-the-recruitment-of-men.html

Baker, R. (2012a) '"Childcare is not just a woman's job" – why only two per cent of the day nurseries and childcare workforce is male.' *Daynurseries.co.uk,* 10 September. Accessed 5 July 2017 at www.daynurseries.co.uk/news/article.cfm/id/1557858/childcare-is-not-just-a-womans-job-why-only-two-per-cent-of-the-day-nurseries-and-childcare-workforce-is-male

Baker, R. (2012b) 'Men reveal the highs and lows of working in childcare.' *Daynurseries.co.uk*, 10 September. Accessed 5 July 2017 at www.daynurseries.co.uk/news/article.cfm/id/1557857/men-reveal-the-highs-and-lows-of-working-in-childcare-and-day-nurseries

Bartlett, D. (2015) 'Men in childcare: How can we achieve a more gender-balanced Early Years and childcare workforce?' Marlborough: Fatherhood Institute. Accessed 15 July 2017 at www.fatherhoodinstitute.org/wp-content/uploads/2015/04/Men-into-Childcare-PDF.pdf

BBC (2009) 'Call for more male nursery staff.' *BBC News* 20 January. Accessed 15 July 2017 at http://news.bbc.co.uk/1/hi/education/7838273.stm

Brandes, H. *et al.* (2015) 'Does gender make a difference? Results from the German "tandem study" on the pedagogical activity of female and male ECE workers.' *European Early Childhood Education Research Journal*, 23(3), 315–327.

Brownhill, S. (2015) 'The "brave" man in the Early Years (0–8): The ambiguities of being a role model.' Saarbrücken, Germany: LAMBERT Academic Publishing.

Brownhill, S. (2017) 'Podcast: Bristol Men in Early Years – Simon Brownhill.' SoundCloud. Accessed 15 July 2017 at https://soundcloud.com/bristolmeninearlyyears/simon-brownhill

Brownhill, S. and Oates, R. (2017) 'Who do you want me to be? An exploration of female and male perceptions of "imposed" gender roles in the Early Years.' *Education 3–13*, 45(5), 658–670.

Carrington, B. and Skelton, C. (2003) 'Re-thinking "role models": Equal opportunities in teacher recruitment in England and Wales.' *Journal of Education Policy*, 18(3), 253–265.

Chambers, S. and O'Sullivan, J. (2012) 'Men working in childcare: Does it matter to children? What do they say?' *London Early Years Foundation*. Accessed 12 July 2017 at ttps://issuu.com/leyf/docs/leyf-research-report-men-working-inchildcare-2012

Craig, L. (2006) 'Does father care mean fathers share? A comparison of how mothers and fathers in intact families spend time with children.' *Gender & Society*, 20(2), 259–281. Accessed 12 July 2017 at www.policy.hu/takacs/courses/matters/Childcare06.pdf

Cushman, P. (2008) 'So what exactly do you want? What principals mean when they say "male role model".' *Gender and Education*, 20(2), 123–136.

DfE (2017) *Early Year Workforce Strategy*. Accessed 3 July 2017 at www.gov.uk/government/uploads/system/uploads/attachment_data/file/596884/Workforce_strategy_02-03-2017.pdf

Envy, R. (2013) 'Developing the Children's Workforce.' In Envy, R. and Walters, R. *Becoming a Practitioner in the Early Years*. London: Learning Matters, pp.1–15.

Fatherhood Institute (2017) 'Men In The Early Years (#MITEY)' 12 May. Accessed 3 July 2017 at www.fatherhoodinstitute.org/2017/men-in-the-early-years-mitey

Faulkner, D. and Coates, E. A. (2013) 'Early childhood policy and practice in England: Twenty years of change.' *International Journal of Early Years Education*, 21(2/3), 244–263.

Francis, B. *et al.* (2006) 'A Perfect Match? Pupils' and teachers' views of the impact of matching educators and learners by gender.' Paper presented at the British Educational Research Association Annual Conference, University of Warwick, 6–9 September. Accessed 7 July 2017 at www.leeds.ac.uk/educol/documents/160644.doc

Gants Hill Partnership Teaching Alliance (n.d.) 'Would a "Gender Balanced" workforce within an Early Years setting increase the attainment of boys, closing the gender gap in attainment?' Accessed 5 July 2017 at www.ghpta.co.uk/research/excellence-in-the-early-years/would-increasing-the-number-of-men-working-within-an-early-years-setting-increase-the-attainment-of-boys-closing-the-gender-gap-in-attainment

Gaunt, C. (2009) 'Parents want to see men in the nursery, says CWDC.' *Nursery World* 20 January. Accessed 15 July 2017 at www.nurseryworld.co.uk/nursery-world/news/1104922/parents-nursery-cwdc

Jones Russell, M. (2017) 'In proportion.' *Nursery World*, 29 May-11 June, pp.24–25. Accessed 12 July 2017 at www.nurseryworld.co.uk/digital_assets/1487/024_NW_PR_men-in-childcare.pdf

Jones. D. (2006) The 'right kind of man': the ambiguities of regendering the key stage one environment. *Sex Education*, 6(1), 61–76.

Jones, D. (2007) 'Millennium man: Constructing identities of male teachers in Early Years contexts.' *Educational Review*, 59(2), 179–194.

Jones, J. (2009) 'Briefing paper: Men in early childhood education.' *New Zealand Journal of Teachers' Work*, 6(1), 28–34.

Kimberley (2015) 'Dealing with conflicting practitioners in the Early Years.' *Early Years Careers*, 14 November. Accessed 13 August 2017 at www.earlyyearscareers.com/eyc/latest-news/dealing-with-conflicting-practitioners-in-the-early-years

King, D. (2015) 'Exploring parental attitudes towards male early childhood educators in the Republic of Ireland today.' *Researching Early Childhood: Children's Research Digest*, 2(2). Accessed 8 July 2017 at www.childrensresearchnetwork.org/knowledge/resources/exploring-parental-attitudes-towards-male-early-childhood-educators-in-the-republic-of-ireland-today

Korumaz, M. (2016) 'Invisible barriers: The loneliness of school principals at Turkish elementary schools.' *South African Journal of Education*, 36(4), 1–12. Accessed 7 July 2017 at www.scielo.org.za/pdf/saje/v36n4/15.pdf

Lang, K. (2015) 'When men are given a hard time for being teachers it's no wonder there are so few of them in the profession.' *MenTeach*, 19 October. Accessed 5 July 2017 at www.menteach.org/news/when_men_are_given_a_hard_time_for_being_teachers_it_s_no_wonder_there_are_so_few_of_them_in_the_profession

Learner, S. (2014) 'Nurseries forced to deal with rising number of pushy, aggressive parents.' *Daynurseries.co.uk*, 3 April. Accessed 8 July 2017 at www.daynurseries.co.uk/news/article.cfm/id/1563140/nurseries-deal-with-rising-number-pushy-aggressive-parents

Lyndon, D. (2016) 'The influence of male practitioners in childcare settings'. *Early Years Careers*, 10 March. Accessed 5 July 2017 at www.earlyyearscareers.com/eyc/latest-news/the-influence-of-male-practitioners-in-childcare-settings

McCormack, O. and Brownhill, S. (2014) '"Moving away from the caring": exploring the views of in-service and pre-service male teachers about the concept of the male teacher as a role model at an early childhood and post-primary level.' *International Journal of Academic Research in Education and Review*, 2(4), 82–96. Accessed 16 July 2017 at www.academicresearchjournals.org/IJARER/PDF%202014/May/McCormack%20and%20Brownhill.pdf

Millam, R. (2011) *Anti-Discriminatory Practice:* A *Guide For Those Working With Children And Young People.* 3rd edn. London: Continuum.

Mistry, M. and Sood, K. (2012) 'Challenges of Early Years leadership preparation: A comparison between early and experienced Early Years practitioners in England.' *Management in Education*, 26(1), 28–37. Accessed 12 July 2017 at http://irep.ntu.ac.uk/id/eprint/24241/1/217998_PubSub1185_Sood.pdf

Mistry, M. and Sood, K. (2013) 'Under-representation of males in the Early Years: The challenges leaders face.' *Management in Education*, 27(2), 63–69. Accessed 7 July 2017 at http://irep.ntu.ac.uk/id/eprint/20789/1/212794_1177.pdf

Moreau, M-P. and Brownhill, S. (2017) 'Teachers and educational policies: Negotiating discourses of male role modelling.' *Teaching and Teacher Education*, 67, 370–377.

Morton, K. (2011) 'Parents want men in nurseries but male school leavers "not interested" in childcare.' Nursery World, 26 July. Accessed 14 July 2017 at www.nurseryworld.co.uk/nursery-world/news/1105507/parents-nurseries-male-school-leavers-childcare

Moss, G. and Washbrook, L. (2016) 'Understanding the Gender Gap in Literacy and Language Development.' Bristol Working Papers in Education #01/2016. Bristol: Graduate School of Education, University of Bristol. Accessed 5 July 2017 at www.bristol.ac.uk/media-library/sites/education/documents/bristol-working-papers-in-education/Understanding%20the%20Gender%20Gap%20working%20paper.pdf

Neugebaurer, R. (1999) 'Recruiting and retaining men in your center.' In *Inside Child Care.* Trend Report. Redmond, WA, pp. 151–154.

Oberhueme, P. (2011) 'The Early Childhood Education Workforce in Europe Between Divergencies and Emergencies.' *International Journal of Child Care and Education Policy*, 5(1), 55–63. Accessed 15 July 2017 at https://link.springer.com/article/10.1007/2288-6729-5-1-55

OECD (Organisation for Economic Co-operation and Development) (2006) 'Starting Strong II: Early Childhood Education and Care: Executive summary.' Paris: OECD. Accessed 9 July 2017 at www.oecd.org/edu/school/37417240.pdf

Ofsted (Office for Standards in Education, Children's Services and Skills) (2015) 'Collaborating to support Early Years teaching and learning: Broomhall Nursery School and Children's Centre.' Accessed 8 July 2017 at http://dera.ioe.ac.uk/23469/1/Broomhall_Nursery_School_and_Children_s_Centre_-_good_practice_example.pdf

Osbourne, L. (2014) 'Gay teacher who writes books challenging homophobia has resigned after parents complained they did not want him to teach their children.' *Daily Mail,* 6 April. Accessed 8 July 2017 at www.dailymail.co.uk/news/article-2598231/Gay-teacher-writes-books-challenging-homophobia-resigned-parents-complained-did-not-want-teach-children.html#ixzz4mFV1n2Od

Potter, C. and Carpenter, J. (2008) 'Something in it for dads': Getting fathers involved with Sure Start. *Early Child Development and Care,* 178(7–8), 761–772.

Pre-school Learning Alliance (2011) 'Parents "want men to work as childcarers in day nurseries", 21 July.' Accessed 8 July 2017 at https://shop.pre-school.org.uk/media/press-releases/255/parents-want-men-to-work-as-childcarers-in-day-nurseries

Richardson, H. (2016) 'Boys "twice as likely to fall behind girls" in early years.' *BBC*, 18 July. Accessed 20 September 2018 at https://www.bbc.co.uk/news/education-36803400

Rolfe, H. (2005) *Men in Childcare*. EOC Working Paper Series, No. 35. Manchester: Equal Opportunities Commission. Accessed 9 July 2017 at www.koordination-maennerinkitas.de/uploads/media/Rolfe-Heather.pdf

Sandseter, E. B. H. (2013) 'Early childhood education and care practitioners' perceptions of children's risky play: Examining the influence of personality and gender.' *Early Child Development and Care*, 184(3), 434–449.

Stevens, D. (2011) 'A job for the boys.' *Teach Nursery*, 46–48. Accessed 5 July 2017 at www.teachearlyyears.com/images/uploads/article/what-male-practitioners-have-to-offer-children.pdf

Surrey County Council (2017) 'How men in Early Years can benefit you and your child. Family Information Service.' Accessed 3 July 2017 at www.surreycc.gov.uk/people-and-community/family-information-service/choosing-childcare-for-children-and-young-people/choosing-and-arranging-childcare/help-and-advice-on-choosing-childcare/how-men-in-early-years-can-benefit-you-and-your-child

Tayler, K. and Price, D. (2016) *Gender Diversity and Inclusion in Early Years Education*. London: David Fulton.

The Local (2017) 'Muslim parents take kids out of Berlin nursery after discovering teacher is gay.' 29 March. Accessed 8 July 2017 at www.thelocal.de/20170329/muslim-parents-protest-after-gay-berlin-man-hired-to-raise-their-kids

Walker, B. M. (2007) 'No more heroes any more: the "older brother" as role model.' *Cambridge Journal of Education*, 37(4), 503–518.

Walshe, D. and Healy-Magwa, N. (2012) 'Men in childcare in Ireland.' In *Childlinks: Men in Early Years Care and Education*, 1, 2–6. Accessed 14 July 2017 at www.barnardos.ie/assets/files/publications/free/childlinks_body28.pdf

Wardle, F. (2004) 'Men in early childhood: Fathers & teachers.' *Early Childhood News*, 16(4), 34–42. Accessed 15 July 2017 at www.earlychildhoodnews.com/earlychildhood/article_view.aspx?ArticleID=400

Warin, J. (2015) 'Pioneers, professionals, playmates, protectors, "poofs" and "paedos": Swedish male pre-school teachers' construction of their identities.' In Brownhill, S., Warin, J. and Wernersson, I. (Eds) *Men, Masculinities And Teaching In Early Childhood Education: International Perspectives On Gender And Care*. London: Routledge, pp. 95–106.

Wayman, S. (2016) 'Why we need more men working in our crèches.' *The Irish Times*, 9 August. Accessed 7 July 2017 at www.irishtimes.com/life-and-style/health-family/parenting/why-we-need-more-men-working-in-our-creches-1.2737234

Wood, P. and Brownhill, S. (2018) '"Absent fathers" and children's social and emotional learning: an exploration of the perceptions of "positive male role models" in the primary school sector.' *Gender and Education*, 30(2), 172–186.

CHAPTER 6

Building and Normalising a Mixed Gender Culture

DAVID WRIGHT

Overview

In previous chapters we have examined the experience of male Early Years practitioners and some of the reasons for their continued minority status within the workforce. We have also presented reasons why we believe it would be beneficial to have more men in the Early Years workforce. We now turn our attention to possible ways to build a mixed gender Early Years workforce. By examining select case studies of existing mixed gender teams, we look to identify principles and strategies that might be applicable to other settings and contexts. We consider what, if anything, distinguishes these settings from those employing all-female staff and what actions have been taken by them in terms of attracting, retaining and developing male practitioners.

Note: in contrast to previous chapters, the main body of evidence presented in this chapter comprises the profiles of three Early Years providers in their own words. We recognise that this represents a change in writing style but we felt it was helpful within our book to give a voice to these representatives of settings with mixed gender teams in order to demonstrate their approach to building and normalising a culture which supports men and women working together to provide Early Years care and education. In our analysis we will consider 'how culture constrains, stabilizes, and provides structure and meaning to the group members' (Schein 2004, p.1). We invite the reader to reflect on the characterisation of each of these settings and we summarise our own findings in the conclusion to the chapter.

A fundamental point that we reiterate throughout this book is the need for the best people to be employed in the Early Years sector regardless of their gender. We are definitely not advocating any actions to increase the number of men in an Early Years team based purely on their biological sex. Every employee must be appointed on merit as the best person for the job. This is germane to the notion of a mixed gender Early Years workforce. A team where 50 per cent of the positions are populated by unsuitable male Early Years practitioners is clearly not desirable. Highly passionate, skilled and motivated individuals, irrespective of whether they are male or female, are required to 'build warm relationships with young children' which are 'at the heart of the quality of learning that is subsequently co-constructed between the practitioner and the child' (Fisher 2016, p.12).

The phrase 'mixed gender Early Years workforce' does not quantify ratios. For example, a team could comprise 1 man and 29 women. It is mixed gender but we would argue that it is also unbalanced. A numerically balanced team would comprise 50 per cent men and 50 per cent women. But we need to ask ourselves an important couple of questions: *Is this achievable and is it desirable?* Many consider a gender-balanced Early Years team to be the goal but there may not be enough suitable men available or having the desire to fill the vacancies. These are just some of the issues to be considered as part of any plan to improve gender-balance in a team.

So what does a mixed gender workforce look like?

As we discussed in Chapter 4, group dynamics is just that – *dynamic!* Generally, teams change over time. The way in which a team operates is dependent, at any given time, on a number of factors including, significantly, the individuals who make up that team. Changing a member can alter the way in which a team acts since a new individual team member may exhibit very different characteristics and behaviours. The extent to which teams are affected by a change in one of its members depends on its size. In a team of two, such as a childminder with an assistant, his or her resignation represents a 50 per cent change in the team which could represent a 50 per cent change in gender-balance in this Early Years workforce. A strong culture of equal opportunities mitigates the effects of such changes. Schein (2004, p.17) defines organisational culture formation as 'a striving toward patterning and integration'. Once this culture is established, subsequent changes in personnel have less impact. An Early Years practitioner joining an established team is entering into a paradigm of values, expectations, social behaviours and operational methods based on experience and shared history. This is an area of interest in considering how culture develops within an Early Years organisation that manages to build and sustain mixed gender in its workforce.

REFLECTION

In contemplating a goal of recruiting male practitioners to your team, consider the following points:

- Where are you starting from and what do you intend to achieve?

- What size is your team?

- What would the notion of a mixed gender team look like in your setting?

- Is this different from your concept of a gender-balanced team?

- How will you know that you have achieved the desired level of gender balance?

Would you consider success to be measured by the relative number of men and women in your workforce or the enabling of all suitable male and female candidates to have the opportunity to apply for positions in it? Why/not?

The very obvious impediment faced in attempting to describe the mixed gender Early Years workforce is the relatively small number of examples from which to draw characterisation. Nevertheless, it has been possible to identify some that do exist. As such, this has allowed us to interview stakeholders and to identify the nature and some of the benefits and challenges of creating and sustaining such a team.

For the purposes of our examination of the nature of mixed gender Early Years teams, we have included organisations where the number of male Early Years practitioners is significant, depending on the size of the team. This is not a specific number or percentage but it is somewhere between 40 and 55 per cent of the workforce.

The following table summarises some of the characteristics of the three organisations we intend to focus on:

Interview	Location	Number of Settings	Number of children	Number of staff	% male staff
1 Leanna Barrett, Owner, Little Forest Folk Nurseries	South London, England	5	120	53	(51%, n27)
2 Anders Farstad, Director, Hval Gård and Vepsebolet Kindergartens	Asker, Norway	4	160	36	(40%, n14)
3 Practitioner K, Childminder	Hampshire, England	1	6	2	(50%, n1)

Our first two interviewees gave permission for their details to be included along with the transcript of their interview. The third interviewee preferred to remain anonymous. In the interviews that follow, we have included the full transcript to provide context to the evidence of culture and practices in each setting. We encourage you to refer to the research section of the Introduction to this book for information about the interview process and details of each setting. Whilst we planned a standard set of questions with which to conduct the interviews, these were subsequently adapted in response to the direction that the interviewee's responses led the interview.

Interview 1

The first interview examines practices within the Little Forest Folk group of outdoor Forest Nurseries located in South London, founded and owned by Leanna Barrett. The interview begins by investigating the origins of the group.

Can you tell me about how you started as an organisation?
I have three children who are now six, four and two years old. We opened our first nursery in 2014 because we wanted our eldest two children to have a better childhood. We did not think the local nurseries offered what we wanted for them. We didn't want to move

to Scandinavia so we looked to recreate their outdoor lifestyle here in the UK. At that time, we had no experience of Early Years education and so it didn't take us by surprise that men were attracted to work with us. It is only now we have been going longer than we realise how unusual it is to have so many men working for us in Early Years and how lucky we are.

What strategies did you employ when you started to recruit men and how many men did you have when you opened?
I opened with three staff, two of them were men.

Where did you get them from?
They both came from the Forest School Association.

So you started with a mixed gender team?
Yes.

What are your current staffing numbers?
Across our company, we currently have 53 staff of which 27 are men. In our Barnes nursery, for example, we have a team of seven of which six are men whilst in our Chiswick nursery we only have one man in that team. It very much depends on what role we are recruiting for at the time.

What characterises the culture in your mixed gender teams? Does the gender make-up of the team make any difference to the culture?
It doesn't make any difference. We have a balance in each setting. We don't try to attract men. We try to attract good people. We employ the best person that comes to us to fit the vacancy that we have at the time. It has just happened that over the last couple of years, half of the best people who have applied for these positions have been men.

Are men attracted to you because you are a Forest School?
I think it's partly because we are a Forest School, but also that they are looking for a career rather than a job and they can see development opportunities with us. A lot of our men are actually primary school teachers who have had enough of 'education'. They see our organisation as somewhere they can teach and continue their career.

What makes it attractive to primary school teachers?

They tell me that in the primary sector, they started to feel like conduits. They are not allowed to teach children the way they want to. They are given a book and the list of instructions. They are expected to filter information through their heads and into the children's heads. We empower them as much as we can and give them as much freedom as we can. We say – here is our ethos, here is our pedagogy, take that and do with it what you think is best for each child. They really appreciate having the freedom to take charge of children's learning and to help them individually by personalising everything. The men really enjoy that, as do the women.

How did these men know that you had vacancies that they would be interested in applying for? How would they find out?

We place adverts in the usual places – trade publications such as *Nursery World*, on recruitment sites including Indeed and using our own social media channels.

How do you refer to the positions?

Forest nursery educator, curriculum leader, third-in-charge, deputy, manager. We have five managers across our five settings, of these two are men. Three of our deputies are men, two of our curriculum leads are men and three of our third-in-charge are men. Men are quite heavily represented in our management. We actually reject a lot of applications from men because we receive more than enough applications. I think we are attractive because we are out-of-doors with a different style of teaching that appeals more to men.

How would you say your role as leader influences your organisation's determination to achieve gender balance in your workforce?

I think enormously. My standpoint has a huge impact. In the early days when we first opened, we had those parents who would say, 'Oh, I'm not sure I feel quite comfortable with him changing my child's nappy.' As leader, how you respond to that comment very definitely demonstrates your position on everything. My response to those parents would be, 'In that case, we are probably not the setting for you. Would you object to a woman changing a boy's nappy?' We are very clear in every message we give that we will not accept any type of sexism at all. The fact that we do this and that this is the message I'm giving to all parents gives the staff confidence. They know that I've got their backs and that I want equal opportunities for all of them.

Interestingly, things have changed. When we first opened in Wimbledon, there weren't many men working in Early Years in the area. So there was a lot of, 'Oh, you've got men working in your nursery. What about changing nappies?' There was a lot of that. We would say, 'This is the way it is.' Now we just had one of our men resign. He left us at Christmas, and all the parents are saying, 'I hope you're going to replace him with another man. We don't want to have one less man in the setting.' They're coming from seeing men as an unknown quantity to now thinking they are an enormous asset to the nursery. That's an interesting shift in their mental attitude.

If a parent comes to me with any concerns, I speak to them and go through their issues and come out the other side. If they come to me with anything about men not being suitable, I don't even open the conversation. I immediately shut it down and say, 'I'm not going to discuss this with you because this is not a concern.' That makes them realise they are pulling this out of nowhere. There's nothing actually wrong. We are not going to talk about, 'Is it this particular person's first time to change a nappy, or could he be a paedophile?' I am not going to dignify that with a discussion because I refuse to allow any hint of anything like that against my educators. I will protect my guys with everything I've got; I will never let any accusation or anything like this come near them unless they are founded.

Have you ever had any false allegations made against any member of your team?
No.

What would you say about the sense of professional identity of your team members?
They are all absolutely amazing; they see themselves as part of an incredible team. They feel that they have a purpose. They are very tight knit. No one is working with us because they just want a job. This is their passion. They feel purposeful. They're not doing this just for money. No one would work in Early Years for money! They feel

like they've got a calling to a bigger thing, bigger than themselves. They feel like they're changing the world.

So they feel like they have a status?
Yes, absolutely. Partly because we are a bit different, our parents idolise them. They are like rock stars to the children. They know that they are changing a child's life. The amount of positive feedback they get makes them so proud of what they are achieving.

Are the experiences and outcomes for your children any different due to having a mixed gender team?
I wouldn't like to say that any particular sex affects anything but it is a different kind of play with men. There's no denying it. It's a completely different kind of play. Not that all our women are false nails and extensions types; they are out in the forest as well, but it's a different kind of play. In particular, for the children where we are, they don't get many male role models. Dads are working full-time. They go early in the morning and come back late at night. These children don't spend much time with men. To have male role models around is, I think, incredibly beneficial for them. What I love is that they don't notice the difference between men and women. We try to teach them to not see the difference between children and adults and men and women. Everyone in the setting is equal. It's amazing to see that they take that on board. I would hate for my own children to be in a setting with only women or only men. I want them to get models for how men and women should behave in society and I want them to learn that first-hand.

What would you say children gain from the experience of being with mixed genders?
They get an all-round balance of society, they learn how to talk to men, they learn how to talk to women, they learn how to interact and to be natural. We don't have children who are timid around men.

Overall, what would you say are the benefits of having a mixed gender team?
It just feels natural, it feels right. We've got 50-50 children; why shouldn't we have 50-50 staff? When you walk into our settings, it feels right.

Any top tips?

If you're an excellent setting and providing an excellent experience for the children, then you'll attract men and women. That's been our experience. I would like to set up an apprentice scheme that really targets young men. We just need to give these young men exposure to the world we've got, for them to come and work with four or five men in the forest for the day. I would love to start giving them the opportunity so that they can see it as a viable career, and how much fun it is.

I feel that people don't really understand that Early Years is about education, not babysitting. I think that exposing young people to the fact that this is a career, not a time-filler job, would really help. It would also be helpful to promote men in Early Years with profiles and images that show that they are just normal men.

ACTIVITY

Read through the interview above and summarise its key messages in five bullet points.

Jot down anything in this interview you find particularly inspiring or challenging.

Identify and record one quote that stands out for you.

We will return to these notes at the end of the chapter.

Interview 2

Our second interview explores the Norwegian experience to try and understand what has been achieved and how the context differs from England. Anders Farstad is the director of the Hval Gård and Vepsebolet kindergartens in Asker, Norway. Anders qualified as a kindergarten teacher in 1977 and has been the director of the kindergartens for the last 29 years. He has worked in kindergartens for 40 years and has led the Men in Childcare (MIC) organisation in the Asker Municipality since 1996. Forty per cent of Anders' team working with the children in his kindergartens are currently male. We asked Anders about the path taken to achieve the current gender balance in his team and to see if there are any lessons learned which might be transferable from the Norwegian experience into our English context.

Could you start by giving some of the history and background to your current situation?

There were already three male teachers working in our kindergarten when we started the MIC organisation 20 years ago. In 1996 there was a national government initiative to recruit more men into Early Years. This gave us the incentive to create a local organisation in Asker. We received very good support from the local council along with finance to enable us to carry out our own initiatives. The project resulted in the recruitment of an additional 14 men in the community's kindergartens in 1997 rising to over 100 men, four years later. This represents the most successful recruitment initiative in the history of our municipality. We continue to receive financial support and the project is continuing.

How do you maintain the level of male teachers in the workforce?

We have explicit political and financial backing to ensure male representation in Early Years settings in Asker. About 13 per cent of the total Early Years workforce in our community is male at the moment. We organise at least two gatherings each year for our male practitioners, one of which includes an overnight stay. These events include the sharing of good practice, practical lessons and child development theory teaching alongside social activities. We also have an ongoing work experience programme for male students from secondary schools to provide them with exposure to our kindergartens and to raise their awareness of the career opportunities available to them in Early Years.

What was it like for the first few men?

I would say it was difficult. The men experienced feelings of isolation, suspicion and challenge to their identity as men. We promoted our cause through the media by challenging gender stereotypes and, as a result, we started to see attitudes changing. It was a big step forward when we recruited more men to work together and to support one another. We started to see changes in the way they were accepted in the workplaces.

**What would you say is the critical mass that normalises
the culture, in other words when men are no
longer considered a novelty, minority group?**

We believe that the ultimate target should be 50 per cent but acceptance of men as a 'normal' element of the workforce increases significantly where they are at least 10 per cent of the team. We have succeeded in establishing a target of 30 per cent men in the Early Years workforce in the kindergartens in Asker. The national goal in Norway is 20 per cent.

What strategies have worked in recruiting and retaining men?

You have to work on short-term and long-term recruitment goals and strategies. Retention is also a key focus. We don't want to lose the men who have already joined us.

**Do you work with local schools, colleges/
training organisations to recruit men?**

Yes, we are working in partnership with local secondary schools and training providers to arrange placements for male students in our kindergartens.

**How much does your role as leader influence
the organisation's determination to achieve
gender-balance in the workforce?**

It means everything. If you don't have a leader who sees the importance, you will never succeed. Remember that it is all about children's rights to have relationships with both men and women in their daily life.

**What would you say characterises the culture
of a mixed gender team such as yours?**

It gives a mixed female and male culture, with the best of both sides, providing you are open to it. I would say it produces more open discussions and direct communication, increased physical activities and better understanding of boys' behaviour when you can recognise what is happening from your own experience as a man.

**Has it impacted on the sense of professional
identity of those who work there?**

It has given the profession a 'new face' and an acceptance of male Early Years workers at the same level as their female colleagues.

How are the men viewed by parents and their acceptance of them as teachers/carers? Has it reduced levels of suspicion?
Parents accept male staff in exactly the same way as they see the female staff. They know that in our kindergartens we aim for balance in the gender make-up of our teams and that if they want their children to attend they must accept this as normal. This is natural in Norwegian culture. There are low levels of suspicion. In our experience it is parents of foreign origin who are most likely to express any concern.

What actions, if any, have you taken to protect men against false allegations? Do you offer any specific guidance on keeping themselves safe from potential allegations?
We have worked together with our local authority on rigorous safeguarding protocols which set out the process to follow in situations where someone is accused of any kind of abuse, regardless of gender. We also advise the men on how to conduct themselves and to protect them from situations that could provoke or lead to suspicions.

Are the experiences and outcomes for children any different in a centre with a mixed gender team?
It is difficult for me to comment on this as we are a mixed gender team and I can only speak about our experience. From what I have observed, we have a lot of activities that lie outside the 'normal' kindergarten box, at least in our kindergartens. We also believe that there is a deeper understanding of boys' behaviour and that what is important for them is recognised and valued. The girls benefit from interacting with different male role models, to experience that not all men are like daddy.

Overall what would you say are the benefits?
We are enabling the children to be taught, cared for and build relationships in an environment that reflects society in a truer way. We are meeting children's rights to meet both men and women in their daily lives. I am certain that a mixed gender staff gives a much better working environment if it is open to mixing the best from male and female cultures.

Do you have any top tips?

When working on recruitment, you have to consider at least three areas: short-term recruitment, long-term recruitment, and how to keep those you have already recruited.

REFLECTION

In the interview above, highlight three ideas from Ander's fascinating responses, using a highlighter, pen or pencil. Consider how these relate to your setting and their applicability to the English Early Years context and culture. Compare the ideas you have highlighted in this interview with your bullet points from interview 1 and look for any common themes.

Interview 3

As a contrast to the group setting context, as noted in the first two interviews, for our third interview we were interested in the experiences relating to the practice of a male Early Years practitioner in a small setting. Practitioner K works as a registered childminder in his own home, alongside his wife who is also a registered childminder. We again asked about the route taken to the current situation, the characterisation of practice, and attitudes and any specific attributes of a mixed gender Early Years team.

Could you tell us about your current role and your journey to it?

I previously worked in the leisure industry. Following my marriage and the arrival of our first baby, I was finding my shifts were conflicting with our family commitments. My wife left her job, retrained and qualified as a childminder. She registered with Ofsted and started caring for children in the September. By the following February, demand was such that she required an assistant. At that time, we saw the opportunity for me to leave my job, which I was not enjoying, to join my wife as an assistant. I worked as an assistant childminder over the next two years whilst I also trained and qualified as a childminder, enabling me to register as a childminder in my own right. This removed the restriction on how long I was able to supervise children on my own, for example on outings. Our business has flourished since.

We have gone from strength to strength. We care for children up to age five during the day, as well as dropping-off and collecting children from school. I also teach paediatric first aid courses as an additional income stream.

What has been the reaction of parents and others to you as a male Early Years practitioner?

Our parents are all totally behind us. Most parents express surprise – a pleasant surprise – on their initial visit to learn that I am here as a childminder in my own right. We have three (female single-parent) families who chose us specifically because they were looking for a male child carer. We currently have one boy who relates to and wants to spend time with me in preference to my wife.

I have encountered some negative attitudes from other female Early Years staff. For example, when collecting children from local pre-schools, there have been incidents when discussion has arisen over areas of the EYFS curriculum and care framework relating to the children we care for. Staff at the pre-school have expressed surprise that I, as a childminder, have knowledge of this. I have seen that my wife experiences a different, more positive response when collecting children.

There was one incident when a child we were caring for hurt herself by falling on a balance beam and had to be taken to hospital to be checked. Subsequently, a doctor phoned us to clarify the circumstances surrounding the accident. I answered the phone but it was evident that the doctor only wanted to speak to my wife even though we share joint responsibility working together.

As part of our duties, we attend various toddler groups in local churches with the children in our care. Apart from the occasional grandfather, I am the only male in attendance. It has taken time for me to become accepted into the group. This improved after we took over the running of one of the groups when the leader announced that she was stepping back from doing so. Subsequently, the other attendees now relate to me as one of the group leaders. This has helped build relationships and acceptance across all the groups as most of those in the group we lead also attend the others. We have been leading the group for coming up to four years now and relationships have built up over this time.

How do you work as a husband and wife childminding team?
We have complementary skills. I can be quite direct in handling conversations with parents about their children's development. My wife is more sensitive in these situations. I can be more 'level-headed', providing an alternative view of things. In working with the children, my strengths and preferences lie in being outdoors, such as garden duty. I am less comfortable with craft or messy activities. I would say I am more confident in engaging in physical or rough and tumble play with the children. Because of my relative physical strength, I am able to push boundaries more. Whilst our approach to risk is the same, I am able to provide more support and challenge, for example catching children jumping from climbing bars.

Have you experienced any suspicion or negative reactions to your job role due to your gender?
There was one occasion when I was minding a one-year-old and a nine-month-old on my own in a soft-play centre. As the children were of different races, it was evident that I was not their father. Both children repeatedly got up to play and then returned to sit on my lap. The other person present in the area was a [woman] who viewed me very suspiciously. I talked to her and explained that I was childminding the children. Having broken the ice, her attitude changed and we had a friendly conversation.

What do you get out of doing this role?
I enjoy watching the children flourish. I love it when I hear them using my own phrases in the right context, for example, 'No way, Jose!' We are still in contact with a child who came to us aged 18 months and stayed with us until he started school. He is now in Year 2 at school, aged seven, and he is a lovely boy. It gives me a lot of satisfaction knowing the input we have had into his Early Years development.

Childcare has become a way of life for us, more than just a job. Comparing it to my previous employment, this is a much better job. It is a lot less stressful. Every day is different and there is more practical involvement doing active things every day rather than just admin on a computer. As our own bosses, we get to choose how we organise our time.

What can be done to increase the number of men working in Early Years?

I do not think it is an issue just for men. There is a stigma associated with the role and alternative jobs are better paid. Childcare needs wider promotion as a career opportunity. We need to offer work experience opportunities and promote Early Years to children in schools. There needs to be more funding for training. We need to create opportunities for people to understand the skills needed in working in child development and the fulfilment of doing so.

Any final comments/advice?

Unless I had experienced this job role, I wouldn't have believed how rewarding it is and how hectic at times! I am very happy telling people what I do for a living. A lot of my oldest friends find it hard to believe I work in childcare for a living. I try to explain that we are not just 'babysitting' children and the breadth of knowledge and skills needed to do our job.

I would recommend it to anyone with an aptitude for childcare.

ACTIVITY

Read through this interview again noting any points or quotes that particularly stand out for you. Compare this summary with the points you have identified in the previous two interviews, noting similarities and differences between the three interviews. Ask a colleague to do the same and discuss your findings between you. Compare your thoughts with our short analysis which follows.

- What can you learn from reflecting on this analysis in relation to your own situation?

- What actions might you consider planning as a consequence, in developing a mixed gender team?

Analysis

The settings of the leaders we selected for interview represent different contexts – geographically, culturally and in terms of their age and size. We chose two settings based in England whilst Anders' Norwegian forest-based kindergartens provide a model of established practice in a society which has traditionally demonstrated support for male involvement in the Early Years sector. As a childminder, Practitioner K's home-based setting is a contrast to the group settings in terms of team size and numbers of children. Nevertheless, the responses regarding his experiences as a male practitioner in terms of interactions with children, professional colleagues and parents highlight similar challenges and rewards to those men working in larger teams.

A comparison of these three interviews identifies common themes. In the table below we have listed identified various attributes of a mixed gender Early Years team, some of the supporting evidence from the interviews, and our summary finding based on it.

Main theme	Interview	Quotes (examples)
Leadership	1	'[male practitioners] know that I've got their backs.' 'I will protect my guys with everything I've got.'
	2	'We received very good support from the local council, along with finance.' 'We have explicit political and financial backing.' 'If you don't have a leader who sees the importance, you will never succeed.'
	3	'It has taken time for me to become accepted into the group. This improved after we took over the running of one of the groups.'
Main finding	Both internal and extrinsic leadership are significant elements in building trust, commitment and sustainability.	
Professional Identity	1	'[male practitioners] feel like they've got a calling to a bigger thing. They feel like they're changing the world.' 'Our parents idolise [the male practitioners].' 'This is [the male practitioners'] passion.'
	2	'More open discussions and direct communications.' 'Parents accept male staff in exactly the same way as they see the female staff.' 'It has given the profession a "new face" and an acceptance of male Early Years workers at the same level as their female colleagues.' 'There are low levels of suspicion.'
	3	'It gives me a lot of satisfaction knowing the input we have had into [the child's] Early Years development.'
Main finding	These settings have established a common professional identity for their Early Years team members across genders. This has resulted in a decrease of suspicion, a sense of professional pride, status, shared ownership and fulfilment.	

Equal Opportunities /Diversity	1	'We don't try to attract men. We try to attract good people.' 'Everyone in the setting is equal.' '[The children] don't notice the difference between men and women.' '[The children] get an all-round balance of society.' 'When you walk into our settings, it feels right.'
	2	'We are enabling the children to be taught, cared for and build relationships in an environment that reflects society in a truer way.' 'I am certain that a mixed gender staff gives a much better working-environment if it is open to mixing the best from male and female cultures.'
	3	'Most parents express surprise – a pleasant surprise – on their initial visit to learn that I am here as a childminder in my own right.' 'We currently have one boy who relates to and wants to spend time with me in preference to my wife.'
Main finding	Greater gender-balance in the Early Years workforce provides a wide spectrum of character types for children to experience and within which their needs are met. The character mix and shared professional responsibilities are a reflection of adult relationships in society and models from which children can learn.	
Pedagogy/ Agency	1	'We empower [the male practitioners].' '[The male practitioners] really appreciate having the freedom to take charge of children's learning.' 'I think we are attractive because we are out-of-doors with a different style of teaching that appeals more to men.'
	2	'We have a lot of activities that lie outside the "normal" kindergarten box.'
	3	'In working with the children, my strengths and preferences lie in being outdoors, such as garden duty.' 'Unless I had experienced this job role, I wouldn't have believed how rewarding it is.'
Main finding	The freedom, empowerment and agency of practitioners and their ability to express their character through an unrestricted curriculum are incentives for men and women to join these organisations. In particular, outdoor or forest-based activities are repeatedly identified as a common attraction.	

Gender Attributes	1	'A different kind of play with men.'
	2	'Increased physical activities.'
	3	'I am more confident in engaging in physical or rough and tumble play with the children. Because of my relative physical strength, I am able to push boundaries more. Whilst our approach to risk is the same, I am able to provide more support and challenge.'
Main finding		Acknowledgement is given to a wider scope of activities on offer to children in these settings, attributable to the added dimension (different kind of play) that men bring. This is typically described as physical play.

Interviewing each of the three professionals featured in this chapter was a positive and enriching experience. Their sense of pride, passion and achievement in what they have accomplished as an organisation is evident in all three transcripts. Their stories are affirming and inspiring. Comparing the narratives and their contexts reveals commonality in the culture of each setting from which we can draw conclusions about the nature of mixed gender Early Years settings. We will now consider each of the common themes identified in our analysis, in turn.

Leadership

Schien (2004, p.223) asserts that 'leaders begin the culture creation process'. In the examples presented in this chapter, leadership is characterised by passion, confidence and a commitment bordering on zeal to the development and maintenance of a mixed gender Early Years workforce. Anders, for example, refers to 'meeting children's rights to meet both men and women in their daily lives'. For these leaders, it is a question of rights and therefore a moral imperative for them. All three interviewees recognise and attest to the primacy of their own leadership in enabling and sustaining the mixed gender Early Years team through their support. Leanna asserts that 'I will protect my guys with everything I've got; I will never let any accusation or anything like this come near them unless they are founded.'

Professional identity

Professional identity in the Early Years is determined by 'how pedagogues see themselves as individuals and as a group' (Ringsmose and Kragh-Muller 2017, p.238). Brock (2006, p.4) proposes that it is based in 'knowledge, education and training, skills, values, ethics, autonomy and reward – influence, status, power and vocation'. All three interviews refer to the establishment of a common professional identity for the role of Early Years teacher within their settings, which transcends gender differences. They reference, either directly or indirectly, elements of Brock's seven dimensions, particularly with regard to autonomy and reward. Leanna is clear that her staff see their role as a vocation; that they are empowered by being given the 'freedom to take charge of children's learning'. She says, 'This is their passion.' 'They feel purposeful.' 'They feel like they're changing the world.' Leanna's teams have the autonomy 'to take charge of children's learning by personalising everything'.

Anders comments that the mixed gender team represents a 'new face' for the profession. Leanna says her male and female educators 'see themselves as part of an incredible team', whilst Practitioner K talks about the satisfaction he shares with his wife, 'knowing the input we have had into [a child's] Early Years development'. In these settings, where mixed gender teams have been established, men and women see themselves as professional educators, both as individuals and as a group. This identity is based on shared values, respect and influence that recognises complementary skills and knowledge.

Equal opportunities

The strong sense of professional identity within the team appears to be key to the development of equal opportunities. Our interviewees highlight the licence men and women are given as educators within their organisations to express their individual character and to pursue their interests within each setting. Leanna refers to, 'primary school teachers who have had enough of "education"' and the opportunity they have been given to be themselves in adapting the Early Years Foundation Stage curriculum to meet the needs of the children they teach in the Forest Nursery. Practitioner K notes the complementary roles he and his wife play deploying their individual characteristics to meet the needs of children: 'Whilst our approach to risk is the same, I am able to provide more support and challenge.' The sum of the parts thus provides a richer experience than the separate individual components. The men and women working together to perform these roles recognise one another and are acknowledged by parents as equals.

Agency

The evidence from our interviews identifies strong leadership in all three organisations providing support for teams and the establishment of a common professional identity across Early Years teachers of both sexes. This combination of support and professional identity has eliminated suspicion and false allegations from parents. The corollary of this is a sense of personal confidence and freedom of expression within the team members and mutual professional trust between stakeholders. Given the traditional suspicion towards men working with young children that we have described in earlier chapters, and which is still evident in responses to our parent questionnaire detailed in Chapter 4, the fact that this issue has effectively been addressed within these three settings removes a significant barrier to entry. This makes these job opportunities particularly attractive to men, many of whom are fearful of the consequences of potential false allegations against them due to unfounded suspicion. The ability to be themselves provides them with the opportunity to fully express their character, talents and interests when teaching children. The resulting pedagogy is fulfilling for the practitioner and enriching for the children.

Our interviews do not provide any information on the impact that a mixed gender team has on children's attainment. There is very limited data available on this. What has been published does not provide unequivocal correlation between the presence of male Early Years educators and improvement in outcomes for children. As noted in Chapter 1, a recent study from Norway suggests that male staff may be important for the development of both boys and girls (Drange and Rønning 2017) whilst research from Austria concludes that '[b]oys have a fundamental need for same-gender exchange and identification' [with their teachers] (Huber and Traxl 2017 p.15). On the other hand, focusing specifically on influences on academic achievement in the primary and preschool sectors, Carrington and Skelton (2003) say that 'research has shown that matching young people and their teachers by gender and ethnicity makes little impact on pupil's attainment', whilst Cushman (2008) cites several studies that have found that the qualities learners value in their teachers are non-gender specific (Lahelma 2000; Skelton 2001 and Sumsion 2000).

Clearly further research is needed in this area to substantiate any claims. We would recommend that any initiatives targeted at recruiting more men into Early Years should include a longitudinal study of the effects of a mixed gender teaching team on children's attainment.

Gender attributes

A study by Lindsey, Mize and Pettit, (1997), found that depending on their gender, 'there is some evidence to indicate that parents may engage in different types of play with their children'. In our interviews, all three of the organisation leaders and the practitioners themselves referred to the 'different kind of play' that men bring. These examples suggest that this mostly takes place outside and is both practical and physical in nature. As we have previously stated, this characteristic and mode of engagement with children is not unique to men. Women are equally capable of engaging in physical activities outdoors. Leanna acknowledges this, stating that '[our women] are out in the forest as well, but it's a different kind of play (provided by men)'. We do not wish to overplay the role of gender attributes or to stereotype men and women but the evidence supports the view that, in general, men and women provide different approaches to play and interactions with children. One Australian male Early Years teacher agrees with this. He observes that,

> Men get different reactions, responses and actions from the kids than female teachers even when doing the same activities or projects. (CareforKids 2010)

The absence of men in the Early Years workforce reduces the opportunities available to children for these different types of play and for them to have interactions with men as well as women in their day-to-day activities within their settings.

In selecting interviewees for our research, we deliberately chose three quite different Early Years settings to use as examples. We have considered common themes identified from our analysis of the interviews. It is also useful to consider how these contexts differ.

Two of the settings are based in England, one is in Norway

It is interesting to note the difference in traditional attitudes between England and Norway in terms of the acceptance of men's involvement with children generally; the higher status and pay of Norwegian Early Years teachers and the relative lack of suspicion around men working in Early Years settings. Both Leanna and Practitioner K comment on their need to gain trust. Leanna, for example, refers to a shift in parents' mental attitude 'from seeing men as an unknown quantity to now thinking they are an enormous asset to the nursery'. Practitioner K says that he has 'encountered some negative attitudes from other female Early Years staff' but 'my wife experiences a different, more positive response'. He says that it has taken time to build relationships and acceptance. For Anders and his team, they have not experienced 'initial trepidation from parents' (Latifi 2017).

Two of the interviewees are male, one female

In terms of creating a culture in which mixed gender teams can succeed, it is evident from these interviews that the gender of the leader is irrelevant. What matters is the commitment and support provided and modelled by the leader.

The settings vary in terms of the number of children cared for, the number of people employed and the location and number of sites

Two of the settings would refer to themselves as 'Forest Schools'. Practitioner K works in a domestic premises in an urban setting. There are differences in terms of the activities on offer and the environments in which these happen but the relationships and interactions between practitioners and children are common across all three settings.

The age of the settings varies, as does the length of service of the interviewees

Anders has been doing his job a long time, serving in his current role for 29 years. Little Forest Folk has only been in existence for just over three years and Practitioner K has been in his current role for nearly four years. Whilst the breadth of their experience differs widely, it is heartening that the responses from our interviewees show commonality in their understanding of the challenges, benefits and the actions needed to maintain a mixed gender Early Years team.

We bring this chapter to a close by considering some of the main ideas which have been discussed in it. Our examination of these examples of mixed gender Early Years teams demonstrates that it is possible to create and sustain more gender-balanced teams. The extent to which this is successful relies on supportive leadership and a commitment to a strong culture of practice where the professional identity of educators is established, giving them personal confidence and status regardless of gender.

The licence educators are given to be themselves in their teaching environment correlates with their job satisfaction and sense of fulfilment. The development of relationships builds trust that dispels the 'widespread fear of men in early education' (Alphonse, McGuckin and Nelson 2014) and makes it easier for more men to join the workforce. The examples of men and women working together provide models of good practice that inspire and encourage us to believe that not only is the mixed gender team attainable but it is also beneficial for all concerned. The evidence from our interviews attests to opportunities and experiences for children. In interview 1, Leanna observes that children 'learn how to interact with men and women' in her Early Years settings which 'reflect society' and provide 'all-round balance'.

It is evident from the examples in this chapter, that successful models of mixed gender Early Years teams are achieved and sustained through explicit intention, support and perseverance. This requires strong leadership, policy and commitment to the establishment of a common professional identity for all practitioners and the building of trust within the community. In the next chapter we explore some of these areas further as we present strategies and suggestions for building and sustaining mixed gender teams.

References

Alphonse, L., McGuckin, R. and Nelson, B. (2014) 'Fear of men in early childhood education.' BAMradio. Accessed 12 March 2018 at www.bamradionetwork.com/parents-channel/306-fear-of-men-in-early-childhood-education

Brock, A. (2006) 'Dimensions of Early Years professionalism – attitudes versus competences?' London: TACTYC. Accessed 12 March 2018 at https://tactyc.org.uk/pdfs/Reflection-brock.pdf

CareforKids.com.au (2010) 'Attracting more men to child care.' Accessed 12 March 2018 at www.careforkids.com.au/childcarenews/2010/september/men-in-child-care.html

Carrington, B and Skelton, C. (2003) 'Re-thinking "role models": equal opportunities in teacher recruitment in England and Wales.' *Journal of Education Policy*, 18(3,) 253–265.

Cushman, P. (2008) 'So what exactly do they want? What principals mean when they say "male role model".' *Gender and Education*, 20(2), p.123–136.

Drange, N. and Rønning, M. (2017) 'Child care center staff composition and early child development.' Discussion Papers No. 870. Oslo: Statistics Norway. Accessed 19 March 2018 at www.ssb.no/en/forskning/discussion-papers/_attachment/332823?_ts=1604982ebc8

Fisher, J. (2016) *Interacting or Interfering? Improving Interactions in the Early Years*. London: Open University Press.

Huber, J. and Traxl, B. (2017) 'Pedagogical differences and similarities between male and female educators, and their impact on boys' and girls' behaviour in early childhood education and care institutions in Austria.' Research Papers in Education. Accessed 13 March 2018 at www.tandfonline.com/doi/pdf/10.1080/02671522.2017.1353674

Lahelma, E. (2000) 'Lack of male teachers: a problem for students or teachers?' *Pedagogy, Culture and Society*, 8(2), 173–186.

Latifi, A. (2017) 'Australian childcare worker changing attitudes about male educators.' MenTeach. Accessed 13 March 2018 at http://menteach.org/node/3274

Lindsey, E. W, Mize, J. and Pettit G. S. (1997) 'Differential play patterns of mothers and fathers of sons and daughters: Implications for children's gender role development.' *Sex Roles*, Vol. 37, Nos. 9/10. Auburn University. Accessed 19 March 2018 at www.researchgate.net/profile/Eric_Lindsey3/publication/226222397_Differential_play_patterns_of_mothers_and_fathers_of_sons_and_daughters_Implications_for_children%27s_gender_role_development/links/0f31753a8c1f31714d000000/Differential-play-patterns-of-mothers-and-fathers-of-sons-and-daughters-Implications-for-childrens-gender-role-development.pdf

Ringsmose, C. and Kragh-Muller, G. (2017) 'Nordic social pedagogical approach to Early Years.' *International Perspective on Early Childhood Education and Development*. Switzerland: Springer.

Schein, E. H. (2004) *Organisational Culture and Leadership*. 3rd edn. Hoboken, New Jersey: John Wiley & Sons Inc.

Skelton, C. (2001) *Schooling the Boys: Masculinities and Primary Education*. Buckingham: Open University Press.

Sumsion, J. (2000) 'Rewards, risks and tensions: Perceptions of males enrolled in an early childhood teacher education programme.' *Asia-Pacific Journal of Teacher Education*, 28, 1.

CHAPTER 7

A Call to Action!

SIMON BROWNHILL

Overview

In this penultimate chapter we focus our attention on considering various ways to attract, recruit, retain and develop (ARRD) men in the Early Years sector. Drawing on recent literature and new/established research findings, we highlight both the potential and realised actions of individuals and organisations to increase and retain the number of men who volunteer/train/work with young children. Given 'the desperate need for affirmative action' (Uba with Cleinman 2013, p.25), we offer readers a wealth of strategies and suggestions, being mindful of successful initiatives and campaigns whilst recognising the shortcomings of various policies and schemes. In doing so, we aim to emphasise what can be accomplished, what more could be done, and what lessons can be learned to inform future endeavours. The chapter initially considers the role of the government in helping to drive the more-men-in-Early-Years agenda forwards.

Politics as a partner: the role of the government

Burgess (in Morton 2015) asserts that '[g]overnments have been talking about wanting to improve male representation in the Early Years workforce for many years now'. Indeed, if we shine a spotlight on the British government, the table overleaf shows how men who work with young children (or who do not work with them as is unfortunately the case!) have been 'on their radar' for quite a while now.

Year	Document	Detail	Reference
1998	Meeting the Childcare Challenge (Green Paper)	'2.25. Working with children tends to be seen as a predominantly female occupation. Yet male carers have much to offer, including acting as positive role models for boys – especially from families where there is no father present.'	DfEE, DSS and Ministers for Women
2001	EYDCP Planning Guidance 2001–2002	'There is an official commitment to increasing the number of male childcare workers, as shown by the target for Early Years Development and Childcare Partnerships [EYDCP] of 6 per cent male childcare workers by 2004' (Owen 2003, p.1).	DfES
2005	Children's Workforce Strategy	'Some sectors do not have a very diverse workforce with certain groups being under-represented' (p.12). 'Recognising the importance of positive male role models during a child's early development' (p.13) was acknowledged as part of a case study of good practice.	DfES
2011	Supporting Families in the Foundation Years	'153. We also want to tackle…the gender imbalance in the sector and make early education and childcare a viable career choice for all' (p.65).	DfE and DoH
2017	Early Years Workforce Strategy	'We want children in Early Years provision to have both male and female role models to guide them in their Early Years, and we want more men to choose to work in the Early Years sector' (p.24).	DfE

Whilst some readers might question whether 'education should be separate from politics' (Individual Interviewee [II] 1), we feel that this official commitment should, in part, be celebrated as it represents a continued strategic pledge to improve the number of men who are present in the Early Years workforce. However, Bartlett (2015, p.3) is quick to remind us that 'government targets and initiatives have come and gone without making significant inroads into the gender imbalance in the childcare workforce…while the political will may be there in the background, up to now this has not been translated into real, tangible improvements'. The impetus for this chapter is thus to consider ways in which 'real, tangible improvements' can be realised to aid the more-men-in-Early-Years agenda. We begin by thinking about what needs to be done by the central government.

We believe it is important for England to have a national strategy with clear targets as this helps the central government to identify specific priorities that work towards the fundamental aim of increasing the number of men who work with young children. This is very much supported by David (lead author of this book) whose views resonate with many who work in and are associated with the Early Years sector:

> We are calling on our Government to recognise the challenge we face in recruiting more men, to implement a policy that defines an explicit target for the proportion of men in the workforce and to work with us to achieve it. (Wright 2016)

Before we continue we would like to make our collaborative position clear: Our fundamental aim is not just about attracting, recruiting, retaining and developing a greater *quantity* of men in the Early Years sector; it is also about raising the *quality* of those who are attracted, recruited, retained and developed. The idea that 'any bloke will do' is simply unacceptable – we believe that young children will not flourish and succeed in their formative years if they are not supported by the best practitioners performing the best practice.

We assert that for national policies to have any kind of impact it is necessary for them to be specific in content and extensive in their considerations. By this we mean that sufficient detail is offered and recognition of the different organisations needed to realise the strategy are clearly identified. This mirrors the thinking of Owen (2003, p.7) who suggests a small suite of policy and action plan content which we have adapted and presented below in the form of a Quality checklist:

QUALITY CHECKLIST

Requirements of a **policy** must:

- ☐ Express commitment.
- ☐ Specify objectives.
- ☐ Identify criteria.
- ☐ Define priorities.
- ☐ Set a timetable/timeline.

There also needs to be an action plan that:

☐ Sets targets for training and recruitment.

☐ Identifies measures to achieve these targets.

☐ Specifies who has responsibility for which measures.

☐ Ensures an effective framework for co-ordination.

☐ Defines the resources to be applied in implementing the measures.

☐ Monitors progress.

(adapted from Owen 2003, p.7)

We see this checklist as being of particular value for all professionals in the sector as the content can be used to guide or Quality Assure the information contained in important documentation developed by Early Years settings to shape best practice, e.g. policies and SEFs/SIPs. When reflecting on the checklist above, we unfortunately see that whilst the Strategy is 'full of good intentions' (II 3) much of the quality content is seemingly *not present* in the Early Years Workforce Strategy (DfE 2017), with notable omissions in terms of timelines and specific targets (sorry David!).

ACTIVITY

Another gap that is noticeable in the Early Years Workforce Strategy (DfE 2017) is the identification of people who are needed to help realise it.

1. Challenge a colleague/peer to make a separate list of as many individuals, groups, settings and institutions, organisations, societies and associations that you/they think could help 'more men to choose to work in the Early Years sector' (DfE 2017, p.24).

2. Compare your responses with your colleague/peer – who has created the longer list?

Consider how your collective responses fare with those proposed by Owen (2003, p.7 – presented in *italicised* text) and our own suggestions (presented in normal text) below:

The careers service	Parents/carers, especially step/fathers	*Individual childcare centres*
Central government	*The training system*	Academics and researchers
People in the public eye, e.g. celebrities	*Job centres*	Men already working in the Early Years sector
Local authorities	Men in Early Years networks	The youth sector
Education institutions (Early Years, Primary, Secondary, Tertiary)	*Voluntary and private organisations*	The mass media, e.g. newspapers, magazines, radio, television, and the internet
The local community	Professional Early Years bodies	The sports and culture sector

We fully acknowledge that knowing *who* can contribute to the success of a national strategy is not enough; we need to consider *how* 'real impact' can be attained. Practical suggestions to achieve this include:

- Large scale 'longitudinal research' should be commissioned to explore the 'long term' impact of men in the Early Years sector at a 'broad' [national] level (II 1). We believe that the research findings need to be disseminated to a wide audience using a range of accessible and 'digestible' strategies for 'awareness purposes' (see Harmsworth and Turpin 2000). The research findings should also be used to 'join up with the policy' (II 1) and 'shop-floor practice' in Early Years settings.

- The 'issue of money' should be addressed through a careful review of pay and conditions in the sector to recognise the 'seriousness of the job' (II 2) and the tremendous work of all Early Years practitioners, irrespective of their gender. We believe the minimum wage for working in the Early Years is simply not good enough!

- A national Men-in-Early-Years advocate who is rooted in both policy and practice should be identified as a dedicated 'Early Years Education Minister' (II 1 and II 3) to represent the sector and work closely with the central government on policies, campaigns and strategy development.

- A promise should be made to raise the 'low status' and profile/'prestige' of the Early Years by collaborating with professionals across the full sector to 'identify, raise awareness to, and develop a shared understanding of the rewards and benefits' (II 2) of a career in the Early Years.

- Compulsory national 'gender training' (II 3) to help raise awareness to the very real difficulties men (and women) face in the Early Years sector.

- 'Advertising or good PR' should be utilised to 'make the Early Years cool/attractive' (II 3) and ensure that the more-men-in-Early-Years agenda is 'not forgotten' (II 1) in the cornucopia of education challenges that Britain continues to face (see https://tinyurl.com/y8v58zts). This advertising is also important as 'most members of the public are not aware of the effort that goes into the Early Years by professionals who work in the sector' (II 1).

We recognise that Jones' (2009, p.30) suggestion of 'Introducing a target for men in ECE' can be rather problematic given the 'random target of 6 per cent male childcare workers by 2004' which was set by the DfES in 2001 (Robert-Holmes 2013, p.348). Difficulties in recruitment and retention meant that this target was 'promptly dropped when [it was] not reached' (p.348). This highlights the importance of the work of the government being challenging yet realistic in what can be accomplished. This is true of governments in other countries who also struggle to increase the number of men in the Early Years sector. Peeters, Rohrmann and Emilsen (2015, p.302) acknowledge that '[t]he proportion of male workers remains low in most European countries. Only in Norway, Denmark and recently Turkey, more than five per cent of the Early Years work force is male'. This suggests that there are things which can be learned from the international community to improve the percentage of men working in the Early Years workforce. We offer some of this learning in a 'Lessons Learned' table below for readers to reflect on and discuss with their colleagues/peers:

Country/ countries	Detail	Lesson learned
Denmark Norway Sweden	Campaigns to recruit men into training and the workforce seemingly do help to raise the number of men choosing childcare as a career. However, it is recognised that 'campaigning needs to be continuous; if not, the number of men entering the profession drops and in some cases decreases right back to original numbers, as was found in Belgium' (Johnson 2010, p.105).	The importance of long-term, continuous campaigning.
Australia	In its Strategy, the Department of Education and Early Childhood Development in the State of Victoria (2009, p.18) outlined how it planned to '[u]ndertake a targeted campaign to promote the range of careers available in early childhood and the rewards of working with young children. The campaign will focus on school leavers and career changers.'	The importance of having targeted audiences for planned campaigns.
Scotland	Government funding was used to roll out training offered by the successful Men in Childcare project who introduced a male-only introductory course, with 'much of the recruitment coming via word of mouth and adverts in local newspapers' (Spence, n.d.).	The importance of government funding and the use of simple recruitment strategies.
New Zealand	The country recognises prior learning – defined as 'professional development or any skills and knowledge acquired through informal and non[-]formal learning' (Taguma, Litjens and Makowiecki 2012, p.61) – in order to recruit ECEC staff. This can be particularly beneficial in recruiting 'second career' men into the profession.	The importance of recognising the prior learning of individuals.
Belgium	In collaboration with umbrella organisations and the University of Ghent, '[t]he Flemish Government launched a campaign to get more men into childcare … At the request of the umbrella organisations, the government [chose] a more gender neutral name for the care profession. The reference to care in the name of the worker was replaced by a more pedagogic word. As such, 'kinderverzorger' or 'childcarer' became 'kinderbegeleider' or 'companion of children' (Peeters 2007, p.6).	The importance of gender-neutral job titles and terminology.

We recognise that whilst the importance of the government cannot be underestimated in terms of providing strategy and policy at a local/central level, we believe that training providers play a notable role in helping to attract and recruit men in the Early Years sector. It is to these providers that our discussion now turns.

Providers as a partner: the role of training providers

We begin by acknowledging that our reference to training providers is not just limited to FEIs, e.g. colleges, or HEIs, e.g. universities; we appreciate the wealth of face-to-face and online training that is provided by local aauthorities, education charities and private companies to support the IPD and CPD of students and practitioners in the Early Years sector. With this in mind, and in light of the fact that five colleges in Scotland offer 'men-only' Early Years training courses free of charge through MiC,[1] we consider practical ways that training providers should utilise their 'positive influence' in attracting and recruiting men into the Early Years workforce:

- Training providers should consider offering a suite of vocational training that works around the many demands on men's time, e.g. full-time/part-time/short one-two day courses/half day courses (AM/PM)/twilight training/early evening sessions/ weekend classes/half-term programmes/Summer Schools/ online provision. All training should be credit-bearing or at least certificated to give the training 'real worth'.

- Training providers should consider being involved in the planning and delivery of local and regional recruitment events that are specifically designed to encourage men to consider a career in the Early Years. At these events men need to 'hear how different people get into the Early Years by sharing stories' (II 2).

- Training providers should consider working closely with institution recruitment co-ordinators to set reasonable 'number goals' [our words] for education and childcare courses, developing a comprehensive and realistic strategy to achieve men targets.

---

1   Men in Childcare – funded by the Scottish Government and City of Edinburgh Council. See https://tinyurl.com/y92cttnn

- Training providers should consider developing specific marketing materials that 'communicate the benefits [of working in the Early Years to men] without sounding desperate', adopting catchy slogans such as 'All Men Can Care' (II 2). The emphasis should not necessarily be on 'being a male [practitioner], more [on] what you can offer children' (II 2).

- Training providers should consider pairing male students with male faculty members as their Personal Tutor to support their academic and professional development.

- Placement Co-ordinators should consider placing male student practitioners in settings that have a male practitioner: 'They do not necessarily have to be a male mentor for them but it should be someone who they might be able to talk to at lunchtime' (II 1). EC-MENz (the New Zealand based national network for men in early childhood education) asserts that if there is another man working in the setting male trainees/ employees are more likely to stay (see www.ecmenz.org/).

- Training providers should consider recruiting male students/ graduates to act as Student Ambassadors to support Open Days/events, talking to prospective male students and their parents/carers/families, and contributing to local media recruitment campaigns.

We believe that there is a wealth of good practice being utilised by training providers across the country to support the more-men-in-Early-Years agenda. But what lessons can we learn from their various efforts? We offer some of these in the form of a 'Lessons Learned' case study for readers to reflect on and discuss with their colleagues/peers:

'LESSONS LEARNED' CASE STUDY

Geographically located in a central county in England, 'X' College has gained a reputation for excellence in its recruitment and retention of male students on its Early Childhood and Care programmes that lead to them entering and remaining in the profession. Strategies that the course team have found particularly effective in recruitment that they were willing to share with us include:

- Developing a range of paper-based and electronic online advertising materials which contain static and moving images of a diverse range of men (in terms of age and ethnicity) in a diverse range of roles (e.g. practitioner, manager) who are working with a diverse range of young children (e.g. babies, toddlers and those of a nursery age) performing a range of activities.

- Visiting local secondary providers to talk to male students prior to them making decisions about their Work Placement choices (at Year 10) and encouraging male students (at the start of Year 11) to think about undertaking a career in the Early Years.

- Sending prospective male students personalised emails/ SMS with links to online videos about working in the Early Years that are voiced by/show male practitioners 'in action' who have successfully completed one of the courses available.

- Investing some of the programme budget on course banner adverts that are shared on social media websites, e.g. Facebook, Twitter, Instagram and YouTube.

In terms of retention, 'X' College has a 96 per cent retention of men who undertake their ECC courses. Strategies used to assure this include:

- Establishing supportive mentor/mentee ('buddy') relationships by pairing first year male students with male students in the second or third year of their programme.

- Ensuring that teaching/seminar groups have at least two male students so that men do not feel isolated or alone during taught sessions.

- Setting up a male-only support group (see Warwick, Warwick and Hopper 2012) and holding regular meetings, timetabling these after they have been on block placements as this is the time when they are 'most likely to wobble' [think about leaving the course/ profession]. ('Chloe')

- Offering a drop-in clinic once a week (day time and evening) for all students (especially men) to use for personalised academic writing support.

- Inviting male students to present their undergraduate research at the annual Student Conference to boost confidence and raise the profile of Early Childhood Education in the College research community. Opportunities to publish their research in the internal College newsletter have been accepted by three students, two of these being male.

ACTIVITY

Visit https://tinyurl.com/yd5dw9cb, considering the wealth of advice offered by the National College for Teaching and Leadership (2017). Even though the focus is on the marketing and recruitment for 'the best trainee teachers to your ITT programme', reflect on how these suggestions could be utilised and adapted by you/your setting/local training providers to aid the attraction and recruitment of men to the Early Years profession.

We particularly favour the positive connections that 'X' College have built with the local secondary provision as we believe that school-college-university partnerships (see Higher Education Funding Council for England 2010) are of real value in the ARRD of men in the Early Years sector. It is to these schools and settings that we now turn in an effort to explore what education settings could do to support the more-men-in-Early-Years agenda.

Schools and settings as partners: the role of education settings

Cunningham and Watson (2002, p.13) assert that 'counsel[l]ors and teachers in middle and high schools can do much to introduce young males to careers working with young children'. Select practical suggestions that they advocate include:

- Steering young men to Early Years 'sites [settings] when they need to fulfil…a service learning, community service, [or] career exploration' requirement as part of their studies (p.13).

- Encouraging young men to volunteer with young children as this 'can complement a future résumé by demonstrating experience and skills that few other young men can list' (p.13).

The idea of 'career exploration' is noteworthy for it is the careers guidance that is offered to students by schools and organisations which is considered to be a significant way of presenting the Early Years as a valid career option for young men. Burgess (2014, p.2) enthusiastically argues that:

> Requiring [head teachers/managers] and careers advice services …[to] examine their own prejudices and knowledge gaps, equip themselves to acknowledge, support and promote the interests of boys and men in pursuing childcare and other caring work, and to monitor outcomes, would be of huge value in improving the gender balance in employment in this sector.

We also see this as helping to eradicate the worrying practice in some schools that was experienced by a committed male practitioner we interviewed: 'Only the people who failed their exams were given childcare leaflets about vocational career pathways' (II 2). We, along with II 3, strongly oppose this practice, arguing that the profession should not be for the less academically able: if we want quality Early Years education and childcare for our young children we need the best people with the best (relevant) qualifications (see Hillman and Williams 2015).

We believe that education settings need to make their students (especially young men) aware of the many job options that are linked to working with young children – 'it's not just limited to "teacher"!' (FGP 2). The essential work of careers advisers/counsellors is recognised by Sarran, a male BEd ECCE student who believes that 'one strategy for attracting men into the profession can be accomplished by organizing career days for secondary school students as well as members of the public' (Joseph and Wright 2016, p.216). We build on this suggestion by proposing that male practitioners who actively work in the Early Years sector should be invited to these events so that they can make guest speeches, 'man' recruitment stalls, run practical workshops, and share their experiences as 'living advocates' of the profession. By doing this they can help young men to see that it is not 'weird' to want to work with young children, nor is it 'just for women' (FGP 4). Strategies we believe that should be embraced by education settings across the Early Years and Primary sectors to introduce boys to the Early Years workforce include:

Early Years	• Providing young boys with reading material (fiction and non-fiction) which show men as fathers, nurturers and teachers (Heller 1994). • Offering young boys learning resources (e.g. dressing up costumes), practical activities (e.g. talking and mark making), and rich teacher/practitioner interactions that can support them in investigating a wide variety of careers as part of the curriculum (II 3). • 'We need to encourage boys to play with dolls, to babysit, to be creative. We need to nurture them to be emotional beings so that when they grow up, they can see the endless possibilities for careers that nurture the spirit.' ('Danny', online special interest group post 2017). • Creating displays (When I am older I want to be a...) made up of the children's paintings that show men and women in non-traditional working roles.
Primary	• Using the curriculum to offer a variety of opportunities for boys to explore the roles of fathers and other men, and expand their understanding of what men can do, e.g. through PHSCE learning tasks. • Thinking carefully about the language that is used to avoid gender bias when talking about work roles and responsibilities, e.g. fire fighter rather than fireman; flight attendant rather than stewardess. • Inviting people who engage in non-traditional working roles to come and talk to children in assemblies and during class time (do ensure that they can talk at the children's level though). • Getting UKS2 boys to 'help do sports activities with the infant school children. Maybe a similar scheme for secondary?' for them to gain practical experience of working with younger children ('Marylyn', online special interest group post 2017). • Using the Early Years in core subjects, e.g. as a real context for mathematical problems or as a topic to read and write about in English lessons.

We feel that education settings should not just see their role as trying to promote the Early Years sector to their current students but also to those that have completed their studies and are now either in paid work or continued study. In 2009, Asthana reported how schools were to become *event sites* [our words] 'where heads, deputies and teachers [would] try to persuade [men] to join the profession'. Whilst the focus was to recruit men into primary teaching, we believe that this approach could have a positive impact on male recruitment if settings in the Early Years sector were willing to co-ordinate a series of local/regional 'open-door' opportunities to stimulate young men's interest by allowing them to see/gain practical experience. Further strategies that could be utilised by education settings are offered in the Activity box below for reflection and review with colleagues/peers:

ACTIVITY

Reflect on the strategies presented in the grid below, considering whether these are strategies that a) you/your setting already uses, b) you/your setting could adopt, or c) you/your setting chooses not to use. Use the suggested key to indicate your response: a) ☺, b) ☺, or c) ☹.

Strategy	Response
Openly welcome men into the setting, be they parents/carers, volunteers, student practitioners or employees (new/established).	
Be prepared to release male practitioners from their professional duties (half day/day) to attend Men's Group meetings or support more-men-in-Early-Years campaigns led by training providers, local authorities and/or education settings.	
Recruit male applicants for paid positions in the setting IF they meet the essential and desirable criteria set.	
Provide male trainees with supportive mentoring and coaching opportunities led by male practitioners where possible/appropriate.	
Provide physical space for Men's Groups to be held in the education setting during/outside the working day.	
Ensure that in-house training events consider the professional needs of both male and female practitioners, e.g. child protection.	
Use different networks (parent/carer, professional, community) to identify and actively encourage men to be volunteers/practitioners in the Early Years sector.	
Invite men and women as guest speakers to the setting to talk to staff/the children, especially those who have occupations that cross traditional gender lines, e.g. a female builder or a male nurse.	
Use role play opportunities to 'model' male educators working in the learning environment to show that they can do what female practitioners do, e.g. change the toy baby's nappy.	
'[S]peak to parents from all backgrounds about the benefits of employing male practitioners' ('Wendy', online special interest group post 2017) to change mind-sets and encourage young men/fathers to consider a career in the Early Years.	

Share your responses with others – how do they perceive your responses in light of their own thoughts?

There is no doubt in our minds that the Early Years sector is full of dedicated practitioners who strive to provide the very best for the young children that they have the good fortune of working with. The importance of this 'passion and enthusiasm...for the job' ('Jackie', online special interest group post 2017) cannot be underestimated when we reflect on the role of Men's Groups in assisting the ARRD of men in the Early Years workforce.

Men's Groups as partners: the role of...Men's Groups!

When thinking about ways to address the issue of retention in the Early Years, Zhang (2017, p.22) suggests 'establishing a network for male teachers to communicate, support, and protect each other'. Whilst we recognise the growth of online support communities, we focus our discussion on networks that allow male practitioners to 'meet up' face-to-face and 'help you to see that you are not alone' (II 2). In the infancy of our careers in ECEC, we were both introduced to the idea of networks for male educators following the reporting of Thornton's (1999, p.41) Men's Club which was designed to 'reduce the high wastage rates' among male student teachers on an ITE primary course. In recent years, a number of Men's Groups have been formed in locations across the UK including London, Bristol, Southampton and Scotland, all committed to encouraging and supporting men who work/train/volunteer in the Early Years workforce.

ACTIVITY

Select one of the three Men's Groups below by clicking on the relevant web link:

1. Bristol Men in Early Years (BMIEY) Network: www.bmiey. co.uk

2. Men in Childcare (Scotland): www.meninchildcare.co.uk/ index.htm

3. Southampton Area Men in Early Years (SAMEY): www.samey. uk

Navigate your way through the website, reflecting on the content and the key messages that are presented. What can you learn that could help you/your colleagues/peers in setting up a Men's Group in your local area?

When considering the ways that Men's Groups can assist in the recruitment and retention of male practitioners in the Early Years sector, we believe the following to be of real value:

- Members of the Men's Group could visit and give talks/ presentations at local education settings (at all levels) as representatives of the Group and of the Early Years profession – these could be given at school gatherings, career fayres, 'Dads and Lads' learning sessions, or citizenship subject teaching.

- Men's Group meetings and events could be organised throughout the year at different times (during the day, in the evening, at the weekend) so that all men are included and have a choice of when to come so that it fits around their other commitments.

- Men's Group members could 'link up with the Local Authority' (II 3) by creating a website to promote the Group and emphasise its role in encouraging men to consider the Early Years as a career choice and supporting them in times of professional need ('You often think: "I am the only one facing these issues", but a Men's Group can support your wellbeing and offer you solutions' (II 2)).

- Men's Group members could pair up prospective members of the Group with established members/practitioners, offering them 'taster sessions' that allow them to visit an Early Years setting and see what it is really like working with young children.

- Men's Groups could invite guest speakers to come and talk with (not *at*) Group meetings about ways to effectively ARRD men in the Early Years based on research and practice (these events should be 'marketed as CPD' (II 1)). This could be combined with activities that allow men to 'talk to others in small groups, developing a shared understanding and shared learning through questions and answers' (II 2).

- Men's Group members could facilitate recruitment events in the form of interactive workshops, Q&A sessions and Job Evenings (a bit like the format of Parents Evening at secondary school).

- Men's Groups could tailor planned meetings to positively respond to the wants, needs and ideas of those who attend them – 'hopefully this will help to expand and extend practice' (II 2). They could promote or 'raise awareness' (II 2) to these meetings, the Group as a whole, and the importance of men in the Early Years through interviews with the local press/radio.

- Men's Groups could signpost men to interesting podcasts about men in childcare that allow them to learn and reflect on the thinking and experiences of men across the international Early Years sector, e.g. the excellent Men In Childcare Podcast with Kathy Brodie series (visit tinyurl.com/yd8u8zuk).

- Men's Groups could support equitable practices in the sector by 'checking standards' (II 3) so that men in the Early Years are not discriminated against.

As an enthusiastic advocate of the Early Years, David (lead author of this book) is an active member of the Southampton Area Men in Early Years group and was the joint organiser of the first national Men in Early Years conference in 2016. We draw attention to David's work, not through intentional favouritism but because we feel that there are many lessons that can be learned from his efforts to benefit male practitioners in the sector and aid the more-men-in-Early-Years agenda.

ACTIVITY

Take a look at the transcript of part of a telephone interview involving the two authors of this book (Simon as the interviewer, David as the interviewee). Using a highlighter, identify any lessons learned which you feel are of value to you, your colleagues/peers, your setting and/or the local Early Years workforce in the active ARRD of male practitioners in the sector.

Simon: So, David, what do you do in the Southampton Area Men in Early Years (SAMEY) group, and how do you think the actions of the Group help to attract, recruit, retain and develop men in the sector?

David: SAMEY arose out of informal discussions between like-minded individuals who had developed a professional relationship over several years. We are all men who work in the Early Years in the Southampton area. We recognised the need for mutual support, awareness raising, advocacy and publicity. SAMEY's objectives, as listed on our website, are to [pause]:

- Promote the benefits of a career in Early Years to men/boys.

- Support male practitioners through a local network.

- Encourage and support individuals and settings through mentoring.

- Positively influence general opinions on the benefits of men working in Early Years.

Through its meetings and website, SAMEY reaches out to interested individuals of both genders with an ongoing invitation to join us either in person at our meetings or to be added to our mailing list. SAMEY works closely with the Southampton LA both in terms of publicising activities and campaigns, and also through the facilitation of activities. We are involved in mentoring and the support of individual male practitioners. We regularly support careers events in primary and secondary schools and colleges, manning a stand, engaging with students and parents to raise awareness of our need for the best people to pursue Early Years careers, and informing them that these are open to both women and men.

As you know, in 2016 SAMEY was responsible for the first ever national men in Early Years conference in Great Britain, hosted in Southampton. Later that year, it also organised a national summit in London, bringing together representatives from across the country to discuss the national agenda and to agree a set of proposals for the government. [coughs] I subsequently presented these to the Early Years Minister with the gender diversity section of the Early Years Workforce Strategy published in March 2017 resulting from this discussion, albeit with its shortcomings! SAMEY has sent representatives to participate in conferences in Poland, Norway and New Zealand. SAMEY members have spoken at events across the United Kingdom, raising awareness and building connections, including in Bristol, York, Burnley, Oxford, London and Birmingham. Mentoring and support activities include phone and email support, matching men with job vacancies and finding them successful roles [coughs]. We have supported individual male practitioners in person, as well as managers and owners of settings. We also respond to media requests for comment, articles and interviews. We have plans for networking events with continuous professional development elements.

Our overall aim is to continue to influence culture – from individual practitioners, managers and settings through to national policy. To answer your question, we believe that each interaction we engage in makes a difference, be it directly or indirectly, and is thus valid in terms of its effect on attracting, recruiting, retaining and developing men in the sector.

One of the impressive outcomes of the first national Men in Early Years conference in 2016 was the development of the National Men in Early Years Charter. II 1 considers this to be a visual way for Early Years settings to demonstrate their 'loud and proud' commitment to men in the Early Years. We present the Charter here for your perusal.[2]

NATIONAL MEN IN EARLY YEARS CHARTER

Male carers, workers and volunteers are welcome.

It is normal for boys and girls of all ages to be cared for by men and women.

We recognise that children benefit from interactions with men and women and that both genders have complementary roles in caring for and developing them.

We are seeking a balanced workforce composed of both men and women.

We promote and support Early Years teaching as a career for both genders.

---

2   A PDF is available at http://tinyurl.com/y76hsqud

We encourage and welcome job applications from men as well as women.

Signed: _____

Date: _____

When asked about the Charter, David said:

> The idea for the Charter is to raise awareness of the issue of men in the Early Years workforce in a simple and cost effective manner. By hosting it online for download and printing, it is available for anyone to access and use. The statements themselves were proposed and agreed on by the national conference attendees. The intention is for teams to discuss the content and agree to sign the Charter. By displaying a signed and dated copy of it, each individual setting makes visible its shared commitment to the set of values contained within it. It makes an explicit declaration of intent and support for action towards a balanced gender team. If this is displayed in a prominent position, it informs and reminds team members, parents and visitors of an intention to change culture at the micro level.

We recognise that much of this chapter has primarily focused on the ways in which we can attract and recruit men into the Early Years workforce. It is important that our discussion now turns more to considering ways that we can retain and develop men who actively work in the sector. Our thinking resonates with that of Bartlett (2015, p.8) who asserts that 'it's vital to remember that recruitment is only part of the story. You need to make sure you avoid a revolving door syndrome, where male Early Years workers and trainees end up dropping out because of the isolation, pressures and prejudices they can face'. Indeed, the following is of real concern, not only to us but also to the international Early Years community:

- 'Three fifths of Early Years graduates [in the United Kingdom] have considered leaving the profession in the past six months, according to a new survey' (Crown 2015).

- The average annual turnover of the early childhood workforce in the United States is very high: the rate is more than 30 per cent for all teaching staff (Porter 2012).

- 'One in five early childhood educators [in Australia] plan to leave the profession…in the next 12 months' (Irvine, Sumsion, Lunn and Thorpe 2016).

Whilst we acknowledge that the bullet points above refer to both men and women, we are mindful of the fact that men are more likely to leave the profession than women, as highlighted by Cook (n.d.). There is clearly a need to address this issue, but before we consider practical ways that this could be achieved it is deemed necessary to first reflect on some of the reasons as to why male practitioners leave the Early Years profession so that we have an understanding of the 'why' before we explore the 'how'.

Schaefer, Long and Clandinin (2012, p.107) accept that there are 'two well-established conceptualizations' or factor types which can help to explain reasons for professional attrition, these being individual and personal factors and contextual factors. We initially highlight the factors drawn from research that focuses on male educator attrition from the Trinidad and Tobago teaching profession which have been adapted from the work of Joseph and Jackman (2014, pp.76–77):

Individual and personal factors	Contextual factors
Opportunities for upward mobility	Inadequate administrative support
Jobs offering better remuneration	Little parental support
Tired of teaching	Student complaints
Burn-out	Poor student behaviour
Over qualified	Poor student performance
	Too much testing

REFLECTION

Reflect on the content of the table above. How do you think the presented factors compare to those identified by male practitioners who leave the Early Years in the English context? Share and compare your thoughts with colleagues/peers.

We believe that the following ideas below serve as additional factors (mixed) that influence the decision of male practitioners to leave the Early Years, not only in the English context but across international contexts too:

A lack of professional development opportunities	Unrealistic expectations of the job	The fear of being accused of paedophilic activity
A lack of future prospects	Isolation/loneliness	Age (at retirement age)
Personal issues	The 'politics' of the setting	Stress
Long working hours	The fear of being accused of abuse	Family issues
Low morale	The amount of paperwork	Feeling unappreciated

Whilst an awareness of these factors is of value, what is more important is that we consider meaningful and practical ways to positively address the concerning issue of male retention in the sector. Bartlett (2015, p.8) suggests offering professionals a 'package of ongoing support' which includes:

- a male practitioner network

- mentoring

- adopting a code of conduct and safer recruitment practice for employers and colleges

- dealing with any negativity from parents and female colleagues, and

- encouraging open conversations about gender.

As most of these ideas have already been discussed in this chapter, we turn our attention to additional strategies that could be added to this figurative package. Joseph and Jackman (2014, p.82) suggest that more experienced male professionals should be offered 'appropriate and competitive remuneration packages'. However, given the 'persistent low pay' in the Early Years sector (Simon, Owen and Hollingworth 2015, p.3) and our current government's reluctance to improve the pay of teachers (Cowburn 2017), we need to be realistic in the strategies we offer. With this in mind, the following ideas are considered valuable for implementation by the government (central and local), training providers, education settings, and/or Men's Groups, and are offered for readers to 'dip and pick with a tick [✓]' from:

NOTE!

Whilst there is a clear emphasis on male practitioners in the suggestions offered below, we firmly advocate these being used to help retain and develop all professionals in the Early Years sector, irrespective of their gender.

☐ Organise local/regional award ceremonies with the help of local/regional businesses to celebrate the achievements of Early Years professionals in the sector – perhaps there could be a 'Men' category?

☐ Create and sustain a collaborative culture where male practitioners and those in positions of authority maintain healthy and productive lines of professional communication to ensure that their expectations are clear, realistic and understood by all.

☐ Engage parents/carers in a diverse range of setting-based and home-based activities to build parent–male practitioner trust and support (see Brownhill 2007b for practical ideas).

☐ When men are working with older children/young people, use School Councils, friend networks and Pow Wow-style debates to ensure that male student voices are heard.

☐ Alleviate issues with male behaviour by talking to children and young people about the rewards and sanctions that they want in the setting/school – they are more likely to follow/accept these as opposed to those that are forced on them by policies and professionals (see Brownhill, Shelton and Gratton 2006; Brownhill 2007a; and Bullock and Brownhill 2011 for further practical ideas).

☐ Work as a supportive team with male colleagues in the setting, targeting young children with interventions and input to address poor development/academic performance.

☐ Engage men by encouraging them to attend conferences 'at a city level' (II 1), symposiums, seminars, colloquiums, workshops and roundtables to support their CPD and 'highlight the imbalance in the workforce' (II 3). Ensure that they share their knowledge with the team to benefit the whole setting.

☐ Ensure that formative and summative assessments undertaken in the setting are necessary and of value to aid and inform the practice of male practitioners, parents'/carers' understanding about their child, and the learning experiences for young children.

☐ Work to build a professional community of 'back-patting' and encouragement so that all staff members regularly feel valued, especially men.

☐ Embrace the mantra 'Good is Good Enough' to help male practitioners limit the amount of time that they work outside of their contracted hours on PPA activities.

☐ Offer male practitioners support when they are faced with accusations of abuse – we believe that there is nothing more important than knowing your work colleagues are behind you.

☐ Develop clear appraisal systems that set SMARTC targets and review actions on a termly basis/half yearly basis, rewarding performance to continuously motivate male practitioners in their work.

☐ Encourage male practitioners from different education settings across the children's and young people's workforce in the local area to make contact with each other (face-to-face; online) to alleviate feelings of isolation or loneliness.

☐ Ensure that conversations and discussions in the staff/ team room include and do not exclude male practitioners.

☐ Make all paperwork manageable by allowing male practitioners to engage with necessary documentation electronically, working collaboratively with colleagues to accelerate the process of completion.

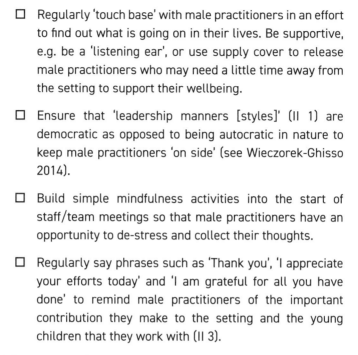

☐ Regularly 'touch base' with male practitioners in an effort to find out what is going on in their lives. Be supportive, e.g. be a 'listening ear', or use supply cover to release male practitioners who may need a little time away from the setting to support their wellbeing.

☐ Ensure that 'leadership manners [styles]' (II 1) are democratic as opposed to being autocratic in nature to keep male practitioners 'on side' (see Wieczorek-Ghisso 2014).

☐ Build simple mindfulness activities into the start of staff/team meetings so that male practitioners have an opportunity to de-stress and collect their thoughts.

☐ Regularly say phrases such as 'Thank you', 'I appreciate your efforts today' and 'I am grateful for all you have done' to remind male practitioners of the important contribution they make to the setting and the young children that they work with (II 3).

Joseph (2015, p.149) suggests that there are 'several pull factors which [actually keep men] in a profession largely dominated by women. These include:

- a passion for teaching

- making a difference by becoming a positive role model for young boys

- convenient working hours and holidays, and

- the opportunity to pursue other part-time jobs.

We believe that it is important that male practitioners are reminded of these (as and where appropriate) in an effort to help retain them in the Early Years workforce.

We bring this chapter to a close by briefly considering some of the main ideas which have been discussed in it. We have considered the important roles that the government, training providers, education settings and Men's Groups play in the ARRD of men in the Early

Years sector. The chapter has also presented readers with an abundance of strategies, approaches and suggestions which we believe have *the potential* to have 'real impact' when utilised. We stress this because we appreciate how 'different contexts, situations and expectations' (Brownhill 2015, p.210) can influence the success or failure of implemented ideas. Honig (2008, p.676) suggests that 'recruiting techniques require creativity and ingenuity to enlist men into participation in early childhood settings'. Whilst we are in support of this, we believe that there are some simple 'basics' that can help to assure the positive impact that we would all like to see in the ARRD of men in the Early Years sector. We offer these 'basics' in the form of a reflective triangle for readers to

- a) identify which qualities they currently possess (please shade in using one chosen colour), and

- b) recognise which qualities they intend to work on (please shade in using a different colour) to help them in the continuous fight for more quality men to work with young children in the Early Years sector:

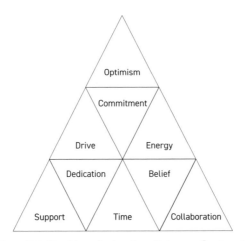

Figure 7.1: 'Basic' professional qualities: a reflective triangle

References

Asthana, A. (2009) 'Schools launch drive to recruit male teachers.' *The Guardian*, 12 July. Accessed 22 July 2017 at www.theguardian.com/education/2009/jul/12/primary-schools-male-teachers

Bartlett, D. (2015) 'Men in childcare: how can we achieve a more gender-balanced Early Years and childcare workforce?' Marlborough: Fatherhood Institute. Accessed 18 July 2017 at www.fatherhoodinstitute.org/wp-content/uploads/2015/04/Men-into-Childcare-PDF.pdf

Brownhill, S. (2007a) *Taking The Stress Out Of Bad Behaviour: Behaviour Management For 3–11 Year Olds.* London: Continuum.

Brownhill, S. (2007b) 'Working with Parents and the Local Community.' In Parker-Jenkins, M., Hewitt, D., Brownhill, S. and Sanders, T. *Aiming High: Raising Attainment of Pupils from Culturally Diverse Backgrounds.* London: Paul Chapman Publishing, pp. 78–96.

Brownhill, S. (2015) 'The "brave" man in the Early Years (0–8): The ambiguities of being a role model.' Saarbrücken, Germany: LAMBERT Academic Publishing.

Brownhill, S., Shelton, F. and Gratton, C. (2006) *100 Essential Lists for Managing Behaviour in the Early Years.* London: Continuum.

Bullock, E. and Brownhill, S. (2011) *A Quick Guide to Behaviour Management in the Early Years.* London: Sage.

Burgess, A. (2014) 'Careers guidance follow-up: Submission by the Fatherhood Institute (8 July 2014): Boys and girls, men and women, in non-traditional occupations.' Accessed 22 July 2017 at www.fatherhoodinstitute.org/wp-content/uploads/2014/07/Fatherhood-Institute-careers-guidance-followup-submission-08072014.pdf

Cook, A. F. (n.d.) *Perceptions and Beliefs Regarding Men in Elementary and Early Childhood Education.* Accessed 24 July 2017 at https://edocs.uis.edu/acook1/www/scholarly/percept.htm

Cowburn, A. (2017) 'Teachers' pay rise to stay capped at 1 per cent, Government announces.' *The Independent*, 10 July. Accessed 23 July 2017 at www.independent.co.uk/news/uk/politics/teachers-pay-cap-stay-remain-one-per-cent-government-justine-greening-education-latest-a7834246.html

Crown, H. (2015) 'Nursery workers consider leaving profession due to workload.' *Nursery World*, 23 October. Accessed 23 July 2017 at www.nurseryworld.co.uk/nursery-world/news/1154397/nursery-workers-consider-leaving-profession-due-to-workload

Cunningham, B. and Watson, L.W. (2002) 'Recruiting male teachers.' *Young Children*, 57(6), 10–15. Accessed 22 July 2017 at http://citeseerx.ist.psu.edu/viewdoc/download?doi=10.1.1.602.1860&rep=rep1&type=pdf

Department for Education and Skills (2001) *EYDCP Planning Guidance 2001–2002.* London: DfES.

DfE and DoH (2011) *Supporting Families in the Foundation Years.* DfE. Accessed 18 July 2017 at www.nwcscnsenate.nhs.uk/files/4414/7030/1374/DFE-01001-2011_supporting_families_in_the_foundation_years.pdf

DfEE, DSS and Ministers for Women (1998) *Meeting the Childcare Challenge: A Framework and Consultation Document.* London: The Stationery Office. Accessed 18 July 2017 at www.gov.uk/government/uploads/system/uploads/attachment_data/file/259817/3958.pdf

DfES (2005) 'Children's Workforce Strategy: A strategy to build a world-class workforce for children and young people.' Nottingham: DfES. Accessed 18 July 2017 at www.education.gov.uk/consultations/downloadableDocs/5958-DfES-ECM.pdf

DfE (2017) *Early Years Workforce Strategy*. Accessed 20 September 2018 at https://assets.publishing.service.gov.uk/government/uploads/system/uploads/attachment_data/file/596884/Workforce_strategy_02-03-2017.pdf

Harmsworth, S. and Turpin, S. (2000) *Creating an Effective Dissemination Strategy: An Expanded Interactive Workbook for Educational Development Projects*. Accessed 20 September 2018 at https://ajpp-online.org/resources/downloads/06-CreatingAnEffectiveDisseminationStrategy-AnExpandedWorkbook.pdf

Heller, C. (1994) 'Fathers, children, and books: Selecting picture books that portray nurturing fathers.' *Texas Child Care Quarterly (Winter)*, 14–18.

Higher Education Funding Council for England (HEFCE) (2010) 'Links between higher education institutions, schools, colleges and academies.' Accessed 24 July 2017 at www.hefce.ac.uk/pubs/rereports/year/2010/heilinks

Hillman, J. and Williams, T. (2015) *Early Years Education and Childcare: Lessons from Evidence and Future Priorities*. London: Nuffield Foundation. Accessed 24 July 2017 at www.nuffieldfoundation.org/sites/default/files/files/Early_years_education_and_childcare_Nuffield_FINAL.pdf

Honig, A. S. (2008) 'Supporting men as fathers, caregivers, and educators.' *Early Child Development and Care*, 178(7–8), 665–687.

Irvine, S. *et al.* (2016) 'One in five early childhood educators plan to leave the profession.' *The Conversation*, 22 June. Accessed 23 July 2017 at http://theconversation.com/one-in-five-early-childhood-educators-plan-to-leave-the-profession-61279

Johnson, P. (2010) 'Current Debates in Early Years Education and Provision.' In Farrelly, P. (Ed.) *Early Years Work-Based Learning*. Exeter: Learning Matters, pp.85–107.

Joseph, S. (2015) 'Surviving a feminized profession: An insight into why men choose to stay in teaching.' *Advances in Social Sciences Research Journal*, 2(6), 144–151. Accessed 23 July 2017 at http://scholarpublishing.org/index.php/ASSRJ/article/view/1238

Joseph, S. and Jackman, W.M. (2014) 'Men who teach and leave: An investigation into factors that push men out of the classroom.' *International Journal of Learning, Teaching and Educational Research*, 5(1), 72–83. Accessed 23 July 2017 at www.ijlter.org/index.php/ijlter/article/view/84

Joseph, S. and Wright, Z. (2016) 'Men as early childhood educators: Experiences and perspectives of two male prospective teachers.' *Journal of Education and Human Development*, 5(1), 213–219. Accessed 22 July 2017 at http://jehdnet.com/journals/jehd/Vol_5_No_1_March_2016/22.pdf

Morton, K. (2015) 'New drive to increase number of men in childcare.' *Nursery World*, 1 May. Accessed 17 July 2017 at www.nurseryworld.co.uk/nursery-world/news/1151122/new-drive-to-increase-number-of-men-in-childcare

Owen, C. (2003) 'Men's work? Changing the gender mix of the childcare and Early Years workforce.' *Facing the Future: Policy Papers* (6). London: Daycare Trust. Accessed 18 July 2017 at www.meninchildcare.co.uk/Mens%20Work.pdf

Peeters, J. (2007) 'Including men in early childhood education: Insights from the European experience.' *NZ Research in Early Childhood Education*, 10, 1–13. Accessed 22 July 2017 at http://stop4-7.be/files/janpeeters10.pdf

Peeters, J., Rohrmann T. and Emilsen K. (2015) 'Gender balance in ECEC: why is there so little progress?' *European Early Childhood Education Research Journal*, 23(3), 302–314.

Porter, N. (2012) 'High Turnover among Early Childhood Educators in the United States.' *Child Research Net*, 17 August. Accessed 23 July 2017 at www.childresearch.net/projects/ecec/2012_04.html

Roberts-Holmes, G. (2013) 'The English Early Years Professional Status (EYPS) and the 'split' Early Childhood Education and Care (ECEC) system.' *European Early Childhood Education Research Journal*, 21(3), 339–352.

Schaefer, L., Long, J. S. and Clandinin, D. J. (2012) 'Questioning the research on early career teacher attrition and retention.' *Alberta Journal of Educational Research*, 58(1), 106–121. Accessed 23 July 2017 at http://ajer.journalhosting.ucalgary.ca/index.php/ajer/article/download/980/863

Simon, A., Owen, C. and Hollingworth, K. (2015) 'Provision and use of preschool childcare in Britain.' London: UCL Institute of Education. Accessed 24 July 2017 at www.ucl.ac.uk/childcareinbritain/research-outputs/documents/Childcare-In-Britain-WEB.pdf

Spence, K. (n.d.) 'Experiences of Scotland and Norway in recruiting men to work in Early Years.' *DadsClub.eu.* Accessed 22 July 2017 at www.edinburghfestivalfringe.com/Dads_Club/Men_in_early_years.html

State of Victoria (Department of Education and Early Childhood Development) (2009) 'Improving Victoria's Early Childhood Workforce: Working to give Victoria's children the best start in life.' Melbourne: Early Childhood Strategy Division Department of Education and Early Childhood Development. Accessed 22 July 2017 at www.education.vic.gov.au/Documents/about/careers/ecworkforce.pdf

Taguma, M., Litjens, I. and Makowiecki, K. (2012) 'Quality Matters in Early Childhood Education and Care: Finland.' France: OECD. Accessed 22 July 2017 at www.oecd.org/education/school/49985030.pdf

Thornton, M. (1999) 'Reducing wastage among men student teachers in primary courses: A male club approach.' *Journal of Education for Teaching*, 25(1), 41–53.

Uba, G. with Cleinman, S. (2013) *Men in Early Care and Education: A Handbook or Affirmative Action.* Accessed 17 July 2017 at http://caeyc.org/main/caeyc/proposals-2014/pdfs/Uba,%20Gregory_Sat-3.pdf

Warwick, J., Warwick, P. and Hopper, B. (2012) 'Primary teacher trainee perspectives on a male-only support group: moving male trainee teachers beyond the 'freak show'.' *Teacher Development*, 16(1), 55–76.

Wieczorek-Ghisso, K. (2014) 'The adoption of leadership styles in early childhood.' *Belonging Early Years Journal*, 3(3), 29–29. Accessed 26 July 2017 at https://paisleypark.com.au/site/wp-content/uploads/Leadership-Styles-in-Early-Childhood-1.pdf

Wright, D. (2016) 'Time for action on men in childcare.' *Nursery World*, 25 January. Accessed 17 July 2017 at www.nurseryworld.co.uk/nursery-world/opinion/1155693/time-for-action-on-men-in-childcare

Zhang, W. (2017) 'Male teachers in early childhood education: Why more men? A Review of the Literature.' *Culminating Projects in Child and Family Studies*, 18. Accessed 22 July 2017 at http://repository.stcloudstate.edu/cgi/viewcontent.cgi?article=1022&context=cfs_etds

CHAPTER 8

Resources

DAVID WRIGHT

Overview

In this final chapter we bring together a collection of resources from across the world with links to supportive organisations and reference material, all of which are focused on men in the Early Years. It is our hope that these will not only provide further sources of knowledge, research and inspiration for readers, but will sustain and increase awareness to the issues and benefits of men working with young children. We also see certain resources as serving as valuable opportunities for extending personal and professional networks, allowing interested individuals to become involved in local/national/global conversations and initiatives about men in the Early Years.

As co-authors of this book we both have personal experience of ongoing collaborations and support arising from our connections with individuals and organisations represented by some of the websites, videos, social media groups and accounts presented in this chapter. In this respect, they constitute a basis for collaboration, encouragement, friendship and optimism. It is heartening to realise that there are like-minded individuals across the world who are committed to making a difference to the lives of young children through building mixed gender Early Years teams.

It is important to remember that there are wonderful examples of successful models of provision, practice and policy which are effecting positive change at a local, national and international level. We share these with the intention that readers might reflect and learn from them, planning for, applying and adapting appropriate solutions in their own context. We also offer examples of positive profiles of men who are working in the Early Years sector whose efforts should be shared, publicised and celebrated. The resources below are based on our collective knowledge. We appreciate that there may be other resources available that we are not aware of but we hope you will find these as a useful starting point for further enquiry. We invite you to join the journey of discovery!

NOTE!

At the time of writing all of these online resources were accessed to confirm that they were 'live'. However, we cannot guarantee that they will remain available or active over time. This is not an exhaustive list and there may well be additional resources that we are not aware of. As such, we encourage readers to add to this record of resources to maintain the currency of the chapter (space is made available at the end of the chapter).

Websites and web-based resources

Men in Childcare
www.meninchildcare.co.uk
Men in Childcare is a registered charity funded by The Scottish Government and City of Edinburgh Council. Since January 2001 it has been responsible for the childcare training of over 1200 men across Scotland.

The Male Practitioner
https://themalepractitioner.com
A blog sharing practice and some of the highs and lows of the state of Early Learning and Childcare by a male practitioner working in Early Learning and Childcare in Scotland for over 20 years.

DadblogUK
https://dadbloguk.com/about
Award winning UK blogger John Adams (see Chapter 2) writes about parenting, fatherhood and lifestyle issues, from his perspective as his children's main carer and what he refers to as being a 'school-run dad'.

The Male Montessorian

www.themalemontessorian.com

This website is aimed at supporting equality, inclusion and diversity in the Early Years sector. It has a blog, and resources and videos list. UK.

Kathy Brodie

www.kathybrodie.com/men-in-childcare-podcast

Kathy Brodie is a well-known and well-regarded Early Years consultant, author and trainer based in the North West of England. She is also an active advocate for men in the Early Years. Kathy started recording podcasts of 'men in childcare' in 2013. This bank of recordings now comprises over 20 enlightening interviews.

The Fatherhood Institute #MITEY (Men In The Early Years) Campaign

www.fatherhoodinstitute.org/2017/ men-in-the-early-years-mitey

#MITEY is a Fatherhood Institute campaign to help increase the diversity and gender balance of the UK Early Years workforce. Its objectives are:

- To raise awareness in the Early Years sector of why we need more men working with children and families/carers.

- To raise awareness of the opportunities and benefits in the wider population.

- To provide managers and frontline staff in the Early Years sector, including in training organisations, with resources to assist them in recruiting men.

- To promote Early Years careers to men.

- To signpost men in the Early Years sector, and those considering such work, to further support.

Surrey County Council

Surrey County Council has recorded two podcasts of interviews with male practitioners employed in Early Years settings within their Local Authority which explore the path into their current jobs, the benefits they see from their roles and their plans for their careers:

- https://tinyurl.com/y9n6j7tq – an interview with two young men describing their route into and experience in their Early Years roles.

- https://tinyurl.com/y7xjbnwr – an interview with three men who have started a career in Early Years, later in life.

York City Men into Childcare

www.men-into-childcare.org.uk

There are several interesting case studies of male practitioners to be found under the About tab: Case Studies.

Bristol Men in Early Years

www.bmiey.co.uk

The internet home of this local support group, containing details of their aims, values, events and activities. It also contains a blog, articles and links to reference items.

Southampton Area Men in Early Years (SAMEY)

www.samey.uk

The internet home of SAMEY. The site comprises information on upcoming events, past meetings, conferences and activities, as well as a blog and links page. The conference page contains several podcast interviews with male Early Years practitioners, recorded at the event in 2016.

Early Years Man

www.earlyyearsman.com

Early Years Man is a new blog from Duncan AKA Early Years Man, chronicling his experiences and observations as an Early Years practitioner in Scotland: 'I personally feel before we encourage more males in to the profession, we should first look at the quality of *all* staff, no matter their gender, sex or race.'

Menn in Barnehagen
www.mennibarnehagen.no/?page_id=208

Menn in Barnehagen (Men in Kindergartens) is a Norwegian website that was commissioned by the Ministry of Education and Research and was set up to be the recognised forum for those interested in increasing the number of men working in the Early Years sector in Norway.

The European Early Childhood Education Research Association Special Interest Group (SIG): Gender Balance
www.eecera.org/sigs/gender-balance

This group focuses on the issue of gender-balance in the ECE workforce and on the important role gender plays in adult–child relations. The SIG particularly focuses on the links between research, practice and policy, and intends to provide an academic forum for the promotion, development and dissemination of research, whilst facilitating cooperation and collaboration between researchers in the field. More information about the SIG can be found at www.siggender.eu

The World Forum Foundation
https://connect.worldforumfoundation. org/workinggroups/men-in-ece

The World Forum Foundation exists to 'connect global early childhood professionals who were working with great determination and creativity, but little support or recognition, to improve the life chances of the young children of the world'. The Men in Early Childhood Education Working Group is one of several groups supported by the World Forum Foundation. Here is an extract from its leadership statement:

> Young children continue to be cared for and educated by an almost exclusively single gender early care and education workforce. Like

shining little mirrors, children reflect back what they see in us. It is the Men in Early Care and Education Working Group's perspective that a single gender teacher and Early Years workforce serves to undermine the principles of self-determination, equal opportunity, and social justice.

ECMenz

www.ecmenz.org

ECMenz (Men in Early Childhood Education – New Zealand) was founded in 2007 as a network of men and women dedicated to highlighting the many important roles men play in the early childhood education sector in New Zealand.

Men Teach

www.menteach.org

Men Teach was started in 1979 in Minnesota, USA by Bryan Nelson with the aim of increasing the number of men working with young children. It is a non-profit clearinghouse for those seeking information and resources about men teaching in Early Childhood Education programmes, with contributions from across the world. It serves as a forum for those wishing to connect with like-minded individuals and as a resource for researchers, policy makers and media professionals.

Males in Early Childhood BlogSpot

malesinearlychildhood.blogspot.co.uk/2012/02/
more-male-ece-bloggers.html

Males in Early Childhood BlogSpot is a (slightly outdated) list of men in Early Childhood Education bloggers. Of those currently active, we highlight:

- https://abcdoes.com
  Alice Bryce-Clegg's regular writings inspiring children to reach their potential and equipping practitioners with the skills and enthusiasm to achieve this.

- http://teachertomsblog.blogspot.co.uk

Teacher Tom (Hobson) is a preschool teacher, blogger, speaker, artist who has taught pre-school for the past 15 years in Seattle, Washington. He gets up very early every morning to write a new blog post!

- https://rethinkingchildhood.com
  Tim Gill's thoughts on his interest in the changing nature of childhood. Tim's writing, independent research, consultancy and public speaking aim to have a positive impact on children's everyday lives.

- http://juliangrenier.blogspot.co.uk
  'Inside the secret garden' Julian presents his personal views on 'some of what goes on in early childhood education and care...thoughts, debates, provocations, ideas and experiences'.

- https://childcaresurfboatcrossfitdad.wordpress.com
  Australian Tony Kee's experiences as a professional childcarer and dad.

Videos
Hamburg Project More Men in Childcare
https://youtu.be/2lLhbmowcws
An EU funded project by the German government to increase the proportion of men in the Early Years workforce to 20%.

Males in Childcare
www.youtube.com/watch?v=4_GJtpp8Xfk
A 2013 film by Access Training, UK.

Men in Childcare – London Early Years Foundation (LEYF) 2014
https://vimeo.com/81021501
A promotional video, discussing the Men in Childcare network, London and profiling male practitioners who work for LEYF, UK.

Men in Montessori

https://vimeo.com/175619027

A video highlighting men working in Montessori Early Childhood Education in the UK. Montessori Centre International (MCI) is working towards making their training programme more inclusive by bringing more men into the Early Years sector (2017).

Men in Childcare

www.youtube.com/watch?v=SwNm8lkVmrU&t=13s

A 2012 film examining contemporary issues of Men in Childcare in Australia.

Men working in Early Childcare in Australia (2014)

www.youtube.com/watch?v=0E1FMq-rvoc

An Australian Broadcasting Corporation radio programme discussing male workers in childcare, specifically the lack of them and the issues surrounding it.

MENtor Program for Males in ECE

www.youtube.com/watch?v=4xJX-hSg3Lk

An introductory video to the MENtor Program for Males in ECE from the University of South Australia (2015).

Men in education (Timmy P MC)

www.youtube.com/watch?v=r4Vx4axPpms

A 2014 profile of New Zealand Early Childhood Teacher Timmy Porter AKA Timmy P MC.

A Few Good Men

www.youtube.com/watch?v=KHWrCfAlVlE

A 2015 documentary on male teachers and gender issues in the Early Childhood Education sector in New Zealand.

Top Ten Signs You're An Early Childhood Educator

www.youtube.com/watch?v=QNdeX_5XPlM

Video by Richard Cohen, United States (2010).

Male Kindergarten Teacher

www.youtube.com/watch?v=PPapgBMq5nU

A profile of a male kindergarten teacher in Memphis, United States (2013).

ECE – Men in Early Childhood Education

www.youtube.com/watch?v=xl9oe7wF0Go

A 2014 film from College of the Redwoods, California, United States.

Men & Children: The Final Frontier for Feminism

www.youtube.com/watch?v=4gmTL0xBVxA

Kindergarten teacher Jake Minton talks about why the early childhood classroom is an important front in the fight for feminism, why it matters for everyone, and what we can all do to help Dallas, United States (2015).

Getting men involved in early childhood education

www.youtube.com/watch?v=7u-5Ir4kZfo

Male staff from Educare Atlanta, United States and its parent organisation, Sheltering Arms Early Education & Family Centers, lead a discussion on the challenges and rewards of a career in early learning (2016).

Close up – Male teachers in Kindies

www.youtube.com/watch?v=k6CI0FAjLYc

A 2012 report from New Zealand.

Why There's A Shortage of Men Teachers in Early Childhood

www.youtube.com/watch?v=d2siDGHeR7w

An interview with Phil Ozanne, Early Childhood Education Lecturer at Bethlehem Tertiary Institute, New Zealand (2012).

Facebook groups

Males in Early Childhood Education, UK

www.facebook.com/Males-in-Early-Childhood-Education-234007526614527

'Males in Early Childhood is striving to spread the awareness of the need for more men educating our children during the Early Years, particularly in prior to school settings where as little as two per cent of the workforce are men.'

AMEPE: Association pour la mixité et l'égalité dans la petite enfance (Association for the promotion of gender diversity and equality in the early childhood sector)

www.facebook.com/AMEPE.asso

The purpose of the association is 'to promote gender diversity and professional equality in the early childhood sector and to combat gender stereotypes'.

Men in Child Care

www.facebook.com/groups/195109553871100

'For the men who work in early care and education… for the fathers, grandfathers, uncles, and other men that are present in the lives of young children… for the men who work on the periphery – delivering the meals, repairing things, maintaining equipment… for the women that are our steadfast allies… this is the place to share thoughts, ideas, and dreams.'

MANscaping – The Male Educator
www.facebook.com/groups/1800055820267016
Its rather wonderful description is: MANscaping – is it about being hairy, or is it about Education?

Men in Childcare
www.facebook.com/meninchildcare
The official Facebook page for the Men in Childcare European Network, administered by MIC network Ireland.

The Australian Association for Men in Early Childhood (AAMEC)
www.facebook.com/AAMECSA
The key aims of AAMEC are to provide support for men working in early childhood education and care, as well as focusing on high quality pedagogy and learning environments.

Men in Early Childhood-Colorado
www.facebook.com/Men-in-Early-Childhood-Colorado-264594143606959
Men in Early Childhood-Colorado is a professional organisation for any ECE professional in the Colorado area. The focus of the group is to retain current men who work in the ECE field and recruit additional men into the field.

Men Who Dare in Childcare – US
www.facebook.com/menwhodareinchildcare
A group who are working towards changing the image of men in the childcare world and who are hoping to attract more men to the profession for the benefit of the overall childcare community.

Twitter accounts

Men in Childcare (Ireland)

@menchildcareirl

Working to support those male pioneers presently working or training in Irish Early Years Care and Education and to encourage other men to do so.

Men in Childcare (York)

@M_I_C_York

'We are passionate about helping more men consider childcare as a career. We aim to challenge stereotypes and promote gender equality.'

Men in Early Years (Kent)

@MeninEarlyYears

'We want to raise the profile of men who work with young children by encouraging and providing opportunities to network with other men in the Early Years.'

June O'Sullivan

@JuneOSullivan

CEO of London Early Years Foundation, Founder of London Men in Childcare.

TheMaleMontessorian

@MaleMontessori

Founded in January 2015. It is about equality, diversity and inclusiveness in the Early Years.

Super Manny

@JossyCare

#Manny #EarlYearsEducator #Babysitter #BigUpTheDadsThatDo #FreeYourMind #PublicSpeaker #DomesticViolenceAdvocate Joss Cambridge-Simmons is a London based male nanny and Early Years Educator.

Neil Farmer
@neilateyfs
Early Years expert, author, trainer, coach and mentor to schools and settings.

Julian Grenier
@juliangrenier
Nursery School head teacher, NLE, Doctor in Education and author.

Tim Gill
@timrgill
Author of *No Fear*. Researcher on risk and childhood, play advocate, public speaker, dad.

Bristol Men in Early Years
@BMiEYNetwork
Supporting men in Early Years alongside promoting positive gender values.

Mr Paintpots
@Mr_Paintpots
David Wright's (lead author) Twitter account.

David Cahn
@EYBrofessional
Early Years practitioner in a Children's Centre. 'I go on about play, early childhood development and relational health.'

Jo Warin
@JoWarin1
Senior lecturer, researcher, author, Lancaster University. #MeninChildcare.

Men in Childcare (Ontario)
@MeninCC
Helping to promote men working or training to become an Early Childhood Educator.

Teacher Tom
@TheTeacherTom
Teacher Tom Hobson – teacher, blogger, speaker, artist who has taught pre-school for the past 15 years in Seattle, Washington.

MENtor4MalesInECE
@MeMales
The MENtor Program for Males in ECE aims to support men studying Early Childhood at the University of South Australia, to build professional networks, and advocate for more men in ECE.

New/additional men in Early Years websites, videos, social media accounts (reader contributions)

Concluding Comments

DAVID WRIGHT

We feel that the research, investigation, compilation and analysis of material that has contributed to this debate on men in Early Years has been informative, thought-provoking and challenging. We are sure that others would disagree with aspects of this assertion and we actively encourage them to share their own thoughts, enquiries and ideas with colleagues, at conferences and on online forums in an effort to keep the critical dialogue about men in the Early Years alive.

On the one hand it is quite disheartening to feel the sense of déjà vu in revisiting the static statistics regarding the percentage of men who are employed in the Early Years sector; the same can be said about recounting some of the entrenched attitudes towards men who want to work with our youngest children. At the same time, we have been encouraged, not only by what we have heard from others, particularly the leaders of organisations who are 'making it work' for their teams, but also what we understand in terms of the high level of support for change from parents, practitioners and politicians – *men, you are wanted!*

Our motivation in writing this book, and the timing of it, arise from our observations of a growing sense of disquiet amongst the many who recognise that there are numerous issues that need to be addressed. Our intention has been to clarify a large number of these issues, presenting a candid analysis of the various reasons for them, and considering examples of best practice in an effort to propose possible actions that can effect change. We leave it to the readers and reviewers of this book to decide whether our intention has been achieved.

So, 'where are we at?'

We began the exposition of our subject in Chapter 1 with a critical look at the current situation with regard to the number of men working in the Early Years sector in England, comparing this to both the UK and the wider international picture. We noted that whilst there was some variability in percentages across countries and over time in response to initiatives, the long established level of 2 per cent of the Early Years workforce being male persists. In examining the main reasons for this, we cannot escape the general challenge to the Early Years workforce brought about by the continuing 'low status of and insufficient regard for our Early Years practitioners' (An and Bonetti 2017). If we want the best men and women to help develop our youngest children, then we feel that both status and pay must be addressed.

Whilst our own survey of parents in Chapter 4 showed overwhelming support for a mixed gender Early Years workforce, a selection of the accompanying comments from the 14 per cent of respondents who expressed concerns about men working in Early Years contain the following troublesome words and phrases:

terrifying	suspicious	wary
lack of trust	greater risk	nervousness
men as being predatory	men having sexual urges relating to children	

We have to somehow address these concerns and perceptions if we are ever going to enable more men to work with our youngest children.

So, what is it like for men working in the Early Years?

Looking back, we have explored the notion of gender roles, ideologies and stereotypes, and agree with Williams' (2013) assertion that 'Society continues to frame ECE as a woman's domain and is seen as something stereotypically associated with women – not men'. In Chapter 3 we considered the continued 'isolation, suspicion and discrimination that male practitioners may face when working in the Early Years sector' (Farquhar et al. 2006). For many men, their position as a minority figure by virtue of their biological sex marks them out for unwanted attention. Moreover, they can be conflicted with respect to their expression of their masculinity as a marginal presence in a predominantly female workforce. As such, Warin (2016, p.99) describes how men may be 'tramlined into forms of gendered behaviour and conform to the gendered expectations of others'.

The examples of mixed gender teams presented in Chapter 6 underline the importance of building a common professional identity for the Early Years workforce across both sexes. This 'new face' for the profession, as Anders Farstad aptly describes it, helps to provide status and recognition that Early Years teaching is indeed something that men and women do together. We have noted the key role of the leaders whom we interviewed in their individual settings. Through their commitment, they have established and are able to maintain a culture of trust, respect, professional autonomy and agency that provides a supportive and encouraging environment in which both male and female Early Years professionals thrive. These are places where attitudes have changed and where men are recognised, valued and trusted alongside their female colleagues. The licence that men and women are given to be themselves and to practise pedagogy that allows for the full expression of their character is a powerful motivator. This is evident in the interviews we have conducted with leaders of settings who are seemingly aware of this and who have created the context within which positive things happen. More importantly, the support of these leaders helps to overcome initial parental suspicions about the motives of men who want to work in Early Years settings and allows time for trust to be built up. Indeed, in her interview, Leanna Barrett refers to 'an interesting shift in their [parents'] mental attitude … from seeing men as an unknown quantity to now thinking they are an enormous asset to the nursery'.

So, does it matter?

One of the interesting aspects of our research is the extent to which attitudes are a powerful force in shaping and reshaping our society. We have examined cultural attitudes at some length because it is these above all else that determine our policies and our practices. We have shown that the role of the media affects our ideas and our perceptions. Piburn (2015) quotes the work of Cunningham and Dorsey (2004) who note that 'it is not uncommon for children to learn a large portion of what they know about men from television programs and other media sources that typically portray men as bumbling or inadequate caregivers, often as violent and angry, and rarely show men capably nurturing children'. If this is true, then we would argue that it *really* matters that nurturing, fun, wild, calm, eccentric, cerebral, artistic or empathetic men are not currently involved in children's Early Years care and education. It matters for our children, for their parents/carers, for our Early Years settings, and for our society. *But is there research out there to support this?* In Chapter 1 we noted the inconclusive results from various research projects aimed at measuring the effects on outcomes for children from interacting with men and women teachers in their Early Years settings. We strongly believe that more longitudinal studies are needed in conjunction with any initiatives that increase the number of men working in Early Years, to measure the benefits (if any) in outcomes for children, both boys and girls.

Our 'call to action'

In our search for what we refer to in Chapter 7 as 'real, tangible improvements', we have adopted both a top-down and bottom-up approach! We have considered the role of individuals, organisations and policy makers in thinking practically about how to attract, recruit, retain and develop (ARRD) men in the Early Years sector. We have looked back along the path of good intentions to review former proposals, failed initiatives and missed targets in England and other countries, and have asked ourselves what can be learned from them and what can we do differently this time. We highlight and pay heed to Brownhill's (2015, p.210) guidance that 'different contexts, situations and expectations' affect the outcomes of such endeavours. In recognition of the challenges that still lie ahead, we have offered readers a 'reflective triangle' of the qualities needed to achieve the aim of establishing a mixed gender Early Years workforce. For those of us who have been involved in this campaign for some time, it is a call for us 'to go again'. For those who have maybe come across this issue for the first time, it serves as a useful summary of the internal/external resources that will need to be called upon.

In Chapter 7, we offered our proposals relating to the practical steps that could be undertaken by various stakeholders who are focused on individual components of ARRD men in the Early Years. We have suggested how training providers can successfully adapt their service offerings to attract and recruit men onto their courses. We have looked at the role of schools in raising an awareness to and supporting and encouraging boys to undertake their work experience in Early Years settings. We remain mindful of the need to 'avoid a revolving door syndrome, where male Early Years workers and trainees end up dropping out' (Bartlett 2015, p.8).

It has always been our intention, in writing this book, that our suggestions provide ideas with practical application, irrespective of whether our readers are students, professionals, training providers, senior management members or politicians. We believe there are actions that we can all take to make a change in our sphere of influence. Our call to action is thus inclusive.

As commentators on gender diversity in the Early Years workforce, we acknowledge that we are pragmatists. We recognise the very low percentage of men we are starting from and the enormity of the task that lies before us in attempting to change culture. However, we remain optimistic. *Why so?* Because the UK government acknowledges the need for a mixed gender Early Years workforce! As such, the DfE's commissioned Early Years Workforce Gender Diversity Task and Finish group reported to the Minister of Education in late Spring 2018. A response from the Government is anticipated. In March 2018, the BBC featured the issue for the first time on a national broadcast (Hemmings 2018) with a sympathetic and supportive focus on the injustice of the current exclusion of and suspicion around men working with our youngest children. A committed group of advocates continue to develop a growing Men in Early Years support network across the UK as a whole. This is linked to a worldwide network of support, connecting groups from many nations. Also, 2018 will see the third UK National Men in Early Years conference, drawing together practitioners, academics, professionals and supporters to further promote and raise the profile of the need for a mixed gender Early Years workforce.

We believe there is a real appetite for change. We hope that you, the reader, are persuaded that there is a case for a mixed gender Early Years workforce; that we have provided ideas that you can implement, and that having digested what we have written, you are motivated to find out more and to take action. We would welcome your ongoing support. It is our contention that together we can make a real difference and that we really are doing so.

References

An, R. and Bonetti, S. (2017) 'Analysis – Developing the Early Years Workforce: What does the evidence tell us?' Education Policy Institute, 8 November. Accessed 10 December 2017 at https://epi.org.uk/analysis/early-years-workforce

Bartlett, D. (2015) 'Men in childcare: How can we achieve a more gender-balanced Early Years and childcare workforce?' Marlborough: Fatherhood Institute. Accessed 18 July 2017 at www.fatherhoodinstitute.org/wp-content/uploads/2015/04/Men-into-Childcare-PDF.pdf

Brownhill, S. (2015) *The 'Brave' Man in The Early Years (0–8): The Ambiguities of Being a Role Model.* Saarbrücken, Germany: LAMBERT Academic Publishing.

Brownhill, S., Warin, J. and Wernersson, I. (Eds) (2016) *Men, Masculinities and Teaching in Early Childhood Education: International Perspectives on Gender and Care.* London: Routledge.

Farquhar, S. *et al.* (2006) *Men at Work: Sexism in Early Childhood Education.* New Zealand: Childforum Research Network. Accessed 28 June 2017 at www.childforum.com/images/stories/men.at.work.book.pdf

Hemmings, C. (2018) 'Men can be nursery teachers too.' BBC News, 14 March. Accessed 21 March 2018 at www.bbc.co.uk/news/education-43386250

Piburn, D. (2015) 'Don's Column: The Velcro Child.' *MenTeach*, 19 January. Accessed 14 March 2018 at http://menteach.org/news/dons_column_the_velcro_child

Williams, A. (2013) *Encouraging men into the ECE Sector* UNITEC, 20 April. Accessed 13 September 2017 at https://unitec.researchbank.ac.nz/handle/10652/2816

About the Authors

David Wright studied economics at University College London following which he pursued a 25-year career in IT as a computer systems programmer for multinational companies. In 1993, David's wife, Anna, established a pre-school in their home which has subsequently grown to become ten separate Early Years settings across the Southampton area, caring for nearly 1000 young children each week. In 2004 David joined Anna in running Paint Pots Nurseries. He retrained as an Early Years teacher, achieving Early Years Professional Status. As well as his day-to-day involvement with the practice, management and strategic running of an Early Years delivery organisation, David is an advocate for men in Early Years. In this capacity, he is active in the promotion of and support for a more balanced-gender Early Years workforce. David is one of the founders of the local support group Southampton Area Men in Early Years (SAMEY) who organised the first ever UK national men in Early Years conference in 2016. He has contributed to British government advisory groups on gender-balance in the Early Years workforce. David is an international speaker on Men in Early Years, a regular contributor to Early Years publications and online media, and is the UK representative to the leadership team of the World Forum working group on Men in Early Childhood Education.

Dr. Simon Brownhill is Lecturer in Education (Teaching and Learning) in the School of Education, University of Bristol where he predominantly teaches Masters students. He was previously a Senior Teaching Associate in the Faculty of Education at the University of Cambridge, working as a trainer and a researcher as part of the Education Reform and Innovation team. A former Senior Lecturer at the University of Derby, Simon taught on a range of undergraduate and postgraduate education-based courses, setting up and co-co-ordinating the PGCE 3–7 teaching route for a number of years. Prior to working in Higher Education, he was employed as a qualified class teacher, gaining experience of the full 3–11 age range in a variety of contexts and roles including Assistant Head Teacher for the Early Years (3–6) in a large, culturally diverse, inner-city primary school. His research and writing interests include supporting adult learners, children's writing, their physical development and effective behaviour management, reflection, education in Australasia, and the male role model in the Early Years (the focus of his doctoral thesis). He has been invited to present his research at local, national and international conferences including Ireland, Portugal and Indonesia (all as a Keynote Speaker). He is the co-author of Becoming a Brilliant Trainer: A Teacher's Guide to Running Sessions and Engaging Learners which was published by Routledge in 2018.

Subject Index

Author Index